If A Sermon Falls In The Forest ...

Preaching Resurrection Texts

William H. Shepherd, Jr.

CSS Publishing Company, Inc., Lima, Ohio

Library of Congress Cataloging-in-Publication Data

Shepherd, William H. (William Henry), 1957-
    If a sermon falls in the forest— : preaching Resurrection texts / William H. Shepherd.
       p. cm.
Includes bibliographical references.
    ISBN 0-7880-1937-6 (pbk. : alk. paper)
    1. Bible—Homiletical use. 2. Jesus Christ—Resurrection—Biblical teaching. 3. Bible. N.T. Gospels—Criticism, interpretation, etc. 4. Bible. N.T. Acts—Criticism, interpretation, etc. I. Title.
    BS534.5 .S54 2003
    251—dc21

                                                                    2002151953

For more information about CSS Publishing Company resources, visit our website at www.csspub.com or e-mail us at custserv@csspub.com or call (800) 241-4056.

ISBN 0-7880-1937-6   PRINTED IN U.S.A.

To
Norm
and
Geoffrey

Table Of Contents

Preface

This book springs from my ongoing quest to encourage the Church in a form of biblical interpretation that is seriously engaged with contemporary scholarship, yet theologically transparent to the average worshiping community. My previous book, *No Deed Greater Than A Word*, set forth my beliefs about the interaction of the Bible and the congregation in the sermon: that words have power to change people's lives, and that the words of a sermon in particular create a new reality called the Church; that the preacher reads the Bible within a certain interpretive community, with a congregation reading over the shoulder; that the Bible itself, read critically in all its historical, literary, theological, sociological, and anthropological diversity, is composed of words that have a peculiar power to shape our lives; that the sermon is a reading of biblical texts for the contemporary congregation, which attempts through vivid language to bring text and congregation together to a new understanding of God's work in our lives; and that the ultimate goal of preaching is to proclaim God's grace in Jesus Christ to each and every interpretive community.

Some of my readers have asked for specific examples of what this kind of preaching might look like. I could not be true to my thesis if I merely reprinted sermon manuscripts; if all that I have said is true, a manuscript or set of notes is merely the written detritus left over from what was a fresh proclamation of God's word to a particular interpretive community in a particular place and time. There is some value, however, in publishing sermons in written form, as long as their limitations are clear — the written remains contain none of the dynamics of the original, lacking the context of worship, the personalities of the preacher and congregation, the physical presence and even the voice of the preacher. But they have value both as teaching tools and spiritual reading; one can benefit from them even without being able to imagine their original setting.

But my purpose here is broader than just providing homiletical examples. This is a study of a pivotal New Testament theme — the resurrection of Jesus — and how these writings on this subject may be read in various interpretive communities. Thus the example sermons are placed in a certain context: first of all, within the context of the particular New Testament writings on which they are based, and secondly, within the context of their original liturgical presentation. I hope that this "sermon collection plus" format will benefit those interested in learning more about the New Testament teaching about the resurrection, those who must feed their congregations from the pulpit each Easter season, and those who are simply looking for reading that will further their spiritual journey.

Since this is in part intended as a teaching tool for preachers, I have left my sermons in their original manuscript form, which may make for an unusual reading experience. I do not write sermons in paragraphs, since they are not meant to be looked at, but rather in thought-units that are similar to, but do not look like, paragraphs. This looks like a simplified outline format. I find that this style helps me group my ideas in a memorable and easy-to-speak manner. While I usually do not use notes when I preach, this style, rendered in a large font, also lends itself to easy oral reading when the occasion calls for it. Since they are geared for hearing rather than reading, you may want to read them aloud to experience the full effect.

The sermons and introductions are oriented toward liturgical preaching and reflect the practices of my own tradition, the Episcopal Church. Since this is a book about how interpretation and communication are embedded in community, I make no apologies for this bias. I hope that those coming from other traditions and other ways of using the Bible in the sermon will take what they find helpful and translate it creatively into their own situations.

The readings of the New Testament found here are synthesized from a variety of thinkers I have engaged over the years. Since this is a book for general readers, I have omitted the footnotes that would indicate my debt to those scholars, but this does not lessen my indebtedness (which is indicated in part by the concluding bibliographic note). Those who are unfamiliar with the conventions of biblical scholarship should note that in describing the Gospel authors as Matthew, Mark, Luke, and John, I am merely following convention and not making a judgment on actual authorship, an issue which is beyond the scope of this work but is readily accessible in any New Testament introduction; the knotty issue of Pauline authorship is taken up briefly in the section on Paul.

I am also indebted to the congregations who looked over my shoulder as I composed these sermons, and later smiled, frowned, or looked at their shoes as they patiently listened to them; they are noted, and a bit said about each of them, in the sermon introductions.

This book is dedicated to Geoffrey Hoare and Norman Runnion, two working preachers and faithful friends who have read and commented on my work, ever keeping me grounded in the realities of parish and pulpit.

1. Reading In Community

"I read the text the same way whether I'm preparing a sermon or a Sunday school class."

My preaching student was reacting to the notion that his purpose might influence his interpretation of a biblical text. "It doesn't make any difference why I am reading it," he said, "there is one and only one correct way of reading it."

Behind this statement is the common, and common-sense, assumption that any text has one and only one meaning. Reading is the process of arriving at the correct meaning, which is what the author intended the text to mean. To twist a text into some other meaning would be to dishonor the author, and make the act of communication meaningless. To allow any text to mean anything, or even more than one thing, is to loose the girders that hold our common life together — how could we possibly communicate with one another if our words could mean just any old thing? If I send you an invitation to have dinner at my house on Sunday, I will be surprised when you show up for lunch on Saturday, and even more surprised when you tell me that I had invited you. Therefore, as a friend once put it to me, "What I write means nothing more or less than what I intended it to mean."

But life quickly throws a few curves to the common-sense view, and it's not at all clear that this common assumption will knock the ball out of the park, or even make solid contact. For one thing, as I asked my friend, if meaning is nothing more than what you intend to mean, how can we account for the common experience of not saying what you mean, or meaning what you say? I may have thought I wrote "Sunday for dinner" on the invitation, but if

I actually wrote "Saturday for lunch," the fault of communication is mine, not yours. We've all had the embarrassing experience of hearing something pop out of our mouths that we had no conceivable intention to say; how many household squabbles get started this way? Our words can fail us, and we can form them quite easily without any relation to external reality — how could there be things like hypocrisy, irony, satire, and misunderstanding if our words meant exactly and only what we intended them to mean? Sometimes we use words without really knowing what they mean — in my younger days, I got the idea that "prolific" meant "having a striking profile" rather than "highly fruitful"; when I made a comment about a "prolific nose" my friends laughed and suggested I get new glasses — I must be seeing lots of little noses trailing behind.

The Peasants Are Revolting

And how will we account for words that mean more than one thing? I once wrote a book on "character" and discovered that this word had about fourteen different meanings, ranging from a literary personage (my subject) to a mark on a page or a letter in the alphabet to one's personal style or moral fiber. If I speak of a "cycle," I could be referring to a recurring pattern, a collection of musical compositions, or a two-wheeled conveyance. "Play" can refer to children's activities, a professional sports event, musical performance, theatrical performance, or the degree of looseness between a nut and a bolt. If I am "playing on their passions," it has nothing whatsoever to do with a "Passion Play." The archaic word "shrive" (from which we get "Shrove Tuesday") can mean two almost opposite things — to assign penance or to give absolution. The words "their" and "there" are pronounced the same yet mean entirely different things, and when you use them aloud in a sentence, nobody can see how you spelled them, so how can anyone know which you meant?

The answer, of course, is that the meaning of words usually becomes clear once you put them into a sentence. The words "Polish shoes" will probably strike you as something you can purchase in a store in Krakow. However, the meaning changes entirely when I change the punctuation and make it a command: "Polish shoes!"

Speaking these words, my meaning will become clear with the pronunciation. On a strictly written basis, however, the words make sense only when put into a sentence.

Yet even sentences can mean different things in different contexts. Even with the exclamation point, the sign saying "Polish shoes!" will have a different meaning depending on whether it is hung in the window of an enthusiastic shoe repairer or an import/export dealer. If I say, "Look at that cat!" what do you picture? Depending on where we are standing, you might picture the neighborhood tomcat, the lion behind bars at the zoo, or a certain kind of sailboat at the beach. When the Wizard of Id tells the king, "The peasants are revolting!" the king replies lackadaisically, "They certainly are," and we can only conclude that the king has not seen the angry crowds outside the moat.

Is There A Text In This Sermon?

It's obvious that a lot of our humor comes from the capacity of language to mean several things at once. But there are also serious consequences of the inherent elasticity of language. The primary consequence is that all language is communal — or we might say the reverse, that language is elastic because it is communal. Only when we agree together on the meaning of words in sentences do those words actually convey meaning. I cannot communicate with you unless we have some agreement on what we are communicating. Language is a playful circle: I must use words to talk to you, but I cannot use those words unless they speak to you. Only when I talk and you listen does communication happen.

A famous demonstration of the communal nature of language comes from the literary critic Stanley Fish, in his book, *Is There a Text in This Class?* Professor Fish wrote an assignment on the board for his class, a simple list of names:

Jacobs-Rosenbaum
Levin
Thorne
Hayes
Ohman (?)

13

The last name ended in a question mark because Fish was not sure of the spelling. When a new class filed into the classroom, the deviously playful professor told them that the writing on the board was a seventeenth-century religious poem. The class dutifully proceeded to interpret the assignment list as a poem — it was shaped in the form of a cross, it contained allusions to Jacob's ladder, the Virgin Mary, the crown of thorns, the tribe of Levi, and the Exodus. Even the question mark at the end of "Ohman" (taken as "Oh man" or "Amen") was given significance — it must mark the ambiguity between the Jewish and Christian symbols in the poem, the class said. No one in the class had any trouble interpreting this academic laundry list as a poem.

The point is not that words can mean anything that we want them to mean, but that meaning always takes place in context. Those who are looking for poetry can find poetry in a mundane list; they will see what they are expecting to see, given half a chance. In essence, they make a poem, because they are looking for a poem. Professor Fish thus spoke of his class as an "interpretive community." They had, together, exercised their collective social, cultural, and linguistic programming, and had come up with a poem where no poem had existed before.

Congregations, too, are interpretive communities. They come looking for something from the preacher. They are not expecting a laundry list, a poetry reading, or a movie review. They are not even hoping for a learned biblical exegesis or history lesson, though some have perhaps grown to expect such. They actually have come looking for a word from God. Not an abstract word, either, but something that will make a difference to them in the coming week, something that will help them get out of bed in the morning, get dressed, get the kids to school, get to the office, and plod on through the week as if it all were meaningful in the grand scheme of things. Make no mistake about it: people come to churches to hear something momentous about themselves and the world they live in.

Congregations as interpretive communities have histories. They are not blank pages. They have been conditioned by many sermons heard over many Sundays. Many preachers get in trouble when they fail to take into account the history of what people have heard from the pulpit; to some extent, that history has conditioned what they are able to hear. If the new pastor comes in with storybook sermons that wander in Garrison Keilloresque style but never come to a conclusion, the congregation who spent thirty years listening to outline-style sermons with three alliterative points may greet that preacher with, "Whatever happened to the sermon?"

To complicate the matter, congregations as interpretive communities are composed of individuals, who themselves are part of multiple interpretive communities. The lawyer speaks legal language, but may not know what to say to the auto mechanic beyond, "The thingamajig is noisier than usual." The doctor can communicate clearly and precisely with the nurse in medical language, but most of us can't follow all the dialogue on *ER* without an interpreter. I've served congregations that included Ph.D. professors and illiterate homemakers; what has Regis to do with Schopenhauer?

Individuals as well as communities have histories. Some folk never get beyond the faith they learned in Sunday school; the elaborate theology spun out by the preacher may seem needlessly complex to one who believes, "The Bible said it; I believe it; that settles it." Sometimes the subtleties of a preacher's work may be totally lost, because the audience lacks the interpretive framework the preacher brings to the sermon. I once used an image of God as a mother gathering up her children despite their misbehavior. I was surprised to hear a woman identifying herself not with the children but with the mother — she had missed my point in the sermon, because she could never think of God as a mother, but easily thought of herself as the mother. In effect, she created her own sermon out of the raw materials I had offered in a very different vein.

If A Sermon Falls In The Forest
So words can be ambiguous, if not downright deceptive. Sentences can slip away just when we think we've grasped them. Audiences can twist and turn and go sailing down alleys that the preacher never knew the sermon opened up. Should we toss our hands in despair and admit that we'll never really be able to talk to

one another, that ambiguity pervades the simplest request, let alone talk about God?

I think rather that we should rejoice. The very ambiguity that makes communication so difficult is what allows preaching to happen in the first place. If a biblical text were accessible only to Israelites gathered around a smoking mountain, or to Corinthians huddled outside a pagan meat market wondering whether to buy, then we of all people would be most to be pitied. It is precisely because language is so flexible that the Bible can speak to us across the ages.

If Christians were constrained by the original contexts of biblical texts, they would be a sorry lot indeed. How would we follow Paul's instructions about eating meat offered to idols, once the pagan sacrificial system had been put to rest? If our Christianity were predicated on keeping his commandments literally, we would be forced to open our own idol temples simply to be faithful to his word! Doctrinally and theologically, we would be impoverished, since doctrines such as the Trinity are implied but never actually stated as such in the Bible. If we were limited to the world views of biblical folk, I would be writing this on a scroll rather than a wordprocessor, because the modern science that created the microprocessor would never have been possible.

Language, once written, becomes open to reinterpretation by new communities. This is the heart of the sermon. Biblical texts that were written for a certain community in a certain place and time become open to new communities in different places and times. The texts stay the same, but their meaning shifts according to new and different circumstances. In effect, biblical texts become new texts each time they are preached, because they have now been interpreted for a particular community.

Thus my answer to the question raised at the beginning of the chapter: Is the biblical text the same for a Sunday school class as for a sermon? The answer is yes and no. The words of the Bible are surely the same. The tools we use to read and understand the text are the same, but the audiences are different; a Sunday school class is expecting something other than a sermon. Since the interpreter knows from the beginning that the audience is a class rather than a worship service, the reading is indeed different. If I am reading in order to produce a sermon, I am looking for something that is preachable. If I am preparing for a Sunday school class, I am looking for something else.

The crucial difference between the sermon and other forms of biblical interpretation is the audience. The audience for the sermon is the amorphous group of folk who have by habit or accident gathered to hear a word from God. Some come together week by week; others have wandered in only for this morning. They are looking for something in particular from the preacher. The whole context — pews, candles, music, lighting, stained-glass windows, and the other accouterments of worship — tell of a very particular context. A different situation would call for a different sort of discourse; the church is a one-of-a-kind interpretive community. It bears little or no resemblance to, say, the lecture room, where the biblical interpreter speaks to a roomful of scholars who know Greek, Hebrew, and the collected works of Rudolf Bultmann. Try telling them that you prepared for the lecture exactly the way you prepared for your weekly sermon.

The audience is also the key to the particular movement of the sermon from text to congregation. I spent some years trying to figure out the "missing link" of the sermon: what magic step takes me from biblical interpretation to sermon composition? Sure, I knew how to do what scholars call "exegesis," or the close reading of a biblical text; I could parse the text, put it into historical, literary, and theological context, determine the setting in life for the passage and where it fit into the overall scheme of Christian thought. And I also knew how to preach — how to weave the text in and out of modern life, how to use imagery and story and example to pull the Bible into the news headlines, and vice versa. What I didn't know was how I was moving from one to another. I was doing it instinctively. Oh, I knew I was doing brainstorming as I was going along, letting the text seep into my imagination, looking at life for the entire week through the lens of a text I would have to preach on Sunday. But there still seemed to me to be a black box between the last line of my notes on the biblical text and the first line of my

17

sermon. One day it hit me: there was not a gap there, but a transition. It was simply the movement from one audience to the next. How I came up with the content of my sermon was completely different from how I delivered that content, because the audience was different. In studying the text, I was working within the framework of the biblical scholar; I spoke the language of the commentaries, and I was part of an audience that knew the ins and outs of technical biblical interpretation. When I turned to the sermon itself, I was simply switching audiences; I was now oriented toward the congregation, trying to take what I knew about the text in that other context and make it meaningful to Joe in the third pew right, who had lost a leg in the war; to Jan two rows back, whose daughter-in-law was dying of cancer; and to Jill in the back row, whose child was in drug rehab. My focus shifted from the world of the first century, seen through the eyes of a seminary graduate, to the people who live with varying degrees of confusion in the present century.

The difference between the sermon and other forms of biblical interpretation is simply the audience — the sermon is the Bible for those who come to worship and experience God for themselves. Thus the sermon is not a history lesson, thought it may include history. It is not a discourse on Greek and Hebrew vocabulary, though linguistic study may be part of the background for the message. The sermon is not a series of propositions, or stories, or examples, or comments on the State of Things in This World. The sermon is a reading of the biblical text for a people who do not necessarily live and breathe that text, but look to it for some guidance as to God's presence in their own lives. In effect, the sermon reads the Bible and modern life, and finds a point where the two can meet.

Join Our Audience
This is a book about the way the intended audience determines how we approach and interpret a biblical text. It is governed by two beliefs: first, the diversity of scripture, and second, the diversity of interpretive communities.

First, the overwhelming consensus of modern biblical scholarship points to the diversity of the biblical witness, but it does not take an advanced degree to know this — any careful reader of the Bible knows it already. The word "Bible" means not "book" but "books," and these books were compiled and edited over centuries and across borders. Even within the relatively narrow confines of the New Testament, or the Gospels in particular, there is a good deal of diversity — Matthew is not Mark, nor is Luke John. If they were all saying exactly the same thing, there would be no need to have all of them. We could, for example, ditch Mark and read only Matthew. But then we would be missing the distinctive witness that Mark provides.

There is a theological reason for holding to a diverse biblical canon. Simply put, God speaks in more than one way. God has been revealed to more than one interpretive community. If there really are significant differences among the various writings of the Bible, we had best find out what the significance is. We believe that God speaks most truly in these texts, so we owe it to ourselves to understand them as clearly as possible. Part of that understanding includes understanding the differences between them. In many and various ways God has spoken, and continues to speak to us through a diverse biblical witness.

The second principle behind this book is the diversity of interpretive communities. If every congregation were the same, there would be no reason for a preacher not to write up one sermon for each Sunday of the year (or for lectionary churches, one for each Sunday in the three-year cycle), and preach them over and over again, no matter where the pulpit. But each congregation is a different interpretive community, with different histories, social and economic situations, liturgical traditions, spiritual leanings, and a whole host of factors brought to it by society and the individuals that make it up. This is why a sermon moves with such difficulty from Sunday morning to the printed page. The Sunday morning crowd exists in that time and place, with the preacher present, with interaction among those present. You can't take that experience and write it down; the words on the page may be the same words spoken that morning, but the sermon will not be the same — it has been transplanted to a new interpretive community, that consisting of readers, not hearers, and who knows but that the same words even a week later may come to mean something new?

The diversity of the biblical text and its interpretive communities has shaped this book in a practical way. My conviction throughout is that each New Testament author is best understood in a literary as well as historical, theological, sociological, and anthropological context — these are, after all, *writings* we are dealing with, and particularly in the case of the Gospels, these writings work in a particular symbolic literary fashion. The teachings and stories concerning the resurrection consist of some of the most diverse material in the New Testament. Thus I have dealt with the various Gospels, Acts, and the writings of Paul in separate chapters; in each, I try to place the resurrection of Jesus within the context of my own reading of each separate author's work as a whole. Each chapter begins with a study of the particular way the resurrection of Jesus can be understood in the context of that particular piece of literature. It goes without saying that these are the readings of one individual who stands within a certain interpretive community, and that there are many other possible readings; I claim only that my construal is one plausible way of understanding these documents in the context of the Christian faith, and you may or may not find them useful. These sections are written for a general reading audience; they do not assume any particular expertise in technical biblical studies, but can be read with profit by anyone interested in learning more about the New Testament, as well as pastors and teachers looking for new ways to interpret familiar passages. While they were not written for the context of worship, as were the sermons that follow, they do reflect my own theological and spiritual understanding.

Each of these sections is in turn followed by a number of individual readings for particular interpretive contexts — that is, each chapter contains one or more sermons. Since I am convinced that each sermon involves a particular shaping of a biblical text for a particular congregation, I have included introductions to each of the sermons, detailing where and when they were preached, and discussing some of the homiletical and interpretive issues I had to

20

deal with as I composed and preached the sermons. These sections will be of greatest interest to preachers, but they can along with the sermons be read by anyone hoping to find a devotional or educational gem. I hope that the introductions will set each of the sermons into a context, so that those who read them will be able to listen in on what one interpretive community received in hopes of hearing a word from God that particular Sunday. The sermons themselves stand or fall on their own merit, whether as models for preachers or as fodder for your own spiritual journey. Just remember: they weren't really written for you.

2. Preaching Resurrection In Matthew

"What would you do if you knew you had only one more week to live?" It was one of those questions the camp speaker loved to rattle teenagers with. At age sixteen, I had plenty of things undone. But the speaker immediately supplied the one correct answer for us: "Not a thing." If we were disciples of Jesus, there was nothing to do but keep being disciples. "Not one thing."

Matthew presents the resurrection of Jesus as the beginning of the end of the world. The last days are begun, but they are not to be spent in the fruitless pursuit of unfulfilled dreams. Rather, disciples are to bear fruit — they are to make new disciples in all the world, with Jesus at their side.

Angels And Earthquakes

Matthew describes the discovery of Jesus' empty tomb in vivid terms, using imagery that would be familiar to an audience of Hebrew Bible readers — imagery that evoked the very God of that same Bible. Two witnesses to Jesus' burial, Mary Magdalene and "the other Mary" (identified as "the mother of James and Joseph" in 27:56), approach his tomb out of curiosity (28:1). What they find is cataclysm: a "great earthquake" occurs, like that which accompanied Jesus' death (27:51). Before their eyes, "an angel of the Lord descending from heaven" rolls back the great stone that sealed the tomb and sits upon it (28:2). He is described in the stereotypical biblical language of angelic beings, his form as bright as lightning and clothing white as snow (28:3); in the Old Testament, the "angel of the Lord" is often used interchangeably with "God," so what we see here is actually the presence of divine glory.

Some scholars believe that when Matthew says "the first day of the week was dawning," he is using the Jewish reckoning where the day begins at sunset (Luke 23:54 uses the same verb *epiphosko*, "to dawn," to describe the "beginning" of the Sabbath Friday evening); the flashing angelic being would be even more striking in the dark. One normally cannot face the divine light and live, so the soldiers guarding the tomb drop as dead men. The women, however, are told not to fear, and are invited to see that Jesus is no longer in the tomb, and to tell his disciples that he has been raised from the dead and will meet them in Galilee (28:5-7). Nevertheless, the women leave with fear, mixed with great joy (28:8).

Matthew, who sees Jesus as the fulfillment of the Jewish Law (5:17), here speaks Old Testament fluently. Earthquakes are traditional signs of the coming of God (Exodus 19:18; 1 Kings 19:11-12; Psalm 114:7). The "angel of the Lord" is described in terms reminiscent of the "Ancient of Days" who appears in Daniel 7:9 and 10:5-6. The reaction of the guards echoes that of Daniel to his heavenly visitation: he dropped like a dead man (Daniel 10:8-9, 15-17). In drawing on Daniel in particular (which was written in a genre scholars call "apocalyptic"), Matthew hints that what is happening here is the fulfillment of what the prophets have said about the last days. Jesus' resurrection is the beginning of the end (cf. 24:34, "This generation will not pass away until all these things have taken place").

The rest of the chapter makes it clear what the disciples are to be about in these last days. Foremost, it is worship. As the women run from the tomb, Jesus himself meets them. They fall at his feet and worship him (*proskyneo,* 28:9). So too, Jesus meets the eleven in Galilee: "When they saw him, they worshiped him (*proskyneo*); but some doubted" (28:17). That worship is the correct response to the risen Jesus is proved by what he says next: "All authority in heaven and on earth has been given to me" (28:18). One to whom all authority is given is indeed worthy of worship. And everyone can do it: Jesus tells them to make disciples of "all nations" (28:19), which we might translate, "all the Gentiles," i.e., not just the Jews. A glance through the rest of Matthew shows that such worship is not misplaced. No other Gospel places such an emphasis on the worship of Jesus. At the beginning of Matthew, worship by the Gentiles is foreshadowed by the wise men, who knelt before Jesus and "paid him homage" (*proskyneo*, 2:11); the word Matthew uses means literally "to fall on one's knees," and thus can be used for the worship of God or the honor of a ruler. Others who fall before Jesus include a leper who seeks healing (8:2), a ruler who seeks the life of his daughter (9:18), the disciples who see Jesus walking on the water (14:33), and a Canaanite woman whose daughter is tormented by demons (15:25). By the time we get to the women at the tomb, there is clearly more than just homage to a king involved here.

Jesus is in fact, to his disciples, more than just a teacher, he is "Lord." Matthew's Gospel does emphasize the teaching of Jesus; Matthew arranges the various sayings into five large blocks, often said to be a new Law of God, in imitation and fulfillment of the five books of Moses in the Old Testament. Yet Jesus' disciples never call him "Teacher" or even "Rabbi." It is the outsiders, even the enemies of Jesus, who use these terms: scribes (8:19; 12:38), Pharisees (12:38; 22:16, 36), Sadducees (22:24), unbelievers (19:16). Disciples and those who come to Jesus in faith address him as "Lord." Again, there is some ambiguity that Matthew plays with here; the word "Lord" (*kyrios*) can be simply a polite form of address, "Sir." Yet *kyrios* is the same word used of God throughout the Greek translation of the Hebrew Bible; the divine overtone is always present in this address used, and used only, by disciples. The one exception proves the rule: when Jesus at the Last Supper predicts that one of them will betray him, the disciples ask, "Surely not I, Lord?" all except for Judas, who says, "Surely not I, Rabbi?" (26:20-25). The only disciple to call Jesus "Rabbi" is Judas, who does so at the moment of betrayal (26:49).

Believers call Jesus "Lord" and appropriately worship him because he is "Emmanuel," "God with us" (1:23). This is the promise Jesus makes to his disciples at the close of Matthew's story: "And remember, I am with you always, to the end of the age" (28:20). Matthew's portrayal of Jesus as worthy of worship is remarkable, since Jesus himself says that the Lord alone is to be worshiped (4:8-10). Jesus is worshiped because he is indeed the

"Lord," "God with us," and his resurrection, amid the fanfare of language dealing with the last things, proves his credentials.

So when the women fall before him, they are right to take hold of his feet in praise. These women had accompanied him all the way from Galilee and had provided for him all along (27:55-56). Now they "see" (27:55; 28:1) all that has happened. He sends them off with a message directed to his "brothers" (28:10), that is, the male disciples who ran away when he was arrested (26:56); now the men too will "see" Jesus in Galilee (28:10). These women are true disciples who have been with him all the way; they become the first of many witnesses to his death and resurrection. He keeps his promise even as he makes it; Matthew says that "Jesus met them" as they ran to tell the others (28:9), but we might translate that as Jesus "fell in with" or "accompanied" them (*hypantao*). Jesus is indeed "with" his disciples at the beginning of the end of the age.

Dead Men And Not So Dead Men

"When you have eliminated the impossible, whatever remains, however improbable, must be the truth." The adage that Sherlock Holmes lived by is applied in different ways by Matthew the storyteller, and by those characters in the story who see Jesus as perhaps Teacher but not Lord. For the chief priests, the obvious impossibility of resurrection points to an alternative that with a little financial help will meet with some success. For Matthew, the priests' story is itself impossible, leaving resurrection as the only truth.

Ironically, the guards at the tomb become "like dead men" when the dead man is raised (28:4). Matthew subtly uses these soldiers to weave together his passion and resurrection accounts. At the cross, Matthew pictures not just a centurion but a troop of soldiers "guarding" (*terountes*) Jesus (27:54). When Jesus dies, the earth shakes (*seio*) and the tombs of the saintly dead are opened; Matthew tells us that the resurrected saints will be seen by many (27:51-53). The guards who see the earthquake and what took place respond with fear (*phobeo*) and confess the truth, however inadvertently: "Truly this man was God's son" (27:54). So too at the

26

tomb, the guards (*terountes,* 28:4) see the earthquake (*seismos,* 28:2), they themselves shake (*seio*) with fear (*phobos,* 28:4); here, however, they are the ones who become like the dead, and it is Jesus who is raised and appears to the women. Rather than responding in faith, the guards report "everything that had happened" (28:11) to the chief priests, who had asked for the guards in the first place.

The priests, for their part, stick to their original story. Matthew tells us that they had gone to Pilate, requesting a guard, precisely because Jesus had said, "After three days I will rise again" (27:62-63). That being in their view impossible, the guard was necessary lest "his disciples go and steal him away, and tell the people, 'He has been raised from the dead,' and the last deception would be worse than the first" (27:64). When the priests hear what has really happened, they tell the guards to claim that the disciples came by night to take the body while they were sleeping (28:12-13). Matthew tells us that the guards did what they were "taught" (*didasko,* 28:15); as often before in this Gospel, Matthew portrays the Jewish leaders as false teachers (cf. chapter 23). The effects of their false teaching linger, and the narrator gives us a rare direct glimpse into Matthew's own day: "This story is still told among the Jews to this day" (28:15).

The false teaching of the Jewish leaders is accompanied by false and improper use of possessions. Wealth is the medium through which their teaching is heard. The soldiers are given "a large sum of money (*arguria*)" to propagate their story (28:12). The soldiers take the money and "do as they were taught" (28:15). Matthew has previously warned us of the hypocrisy of false use of possessions (6:2-4), and indicted the Jewish leaders in particular for hypocrisy when it comes to giving (23:23). Their improper use of their money is shown clearly in the famous episode with Judas, who betrays Jesus for thirty pieces of silver (*arguria*). When he returns it, the leaders have trouble finding a religiously acceptable way of disposing of it (26:14-16; 27:3-10). The chief priests' use of possessions throughout the story of Jesus' death and resurrection stands in stark contrast to that of Joseph of Arimathea, who in the time of need gives freely a fine, newly-hewn tomb (27:57-60).

Matthew shows how money can enslave those who fall prey to its power (cf. the story of the rich young man, 19:16-22); the Jewish leaders take on all the characteristics of the wicked tenants who try to wrest the vineyard from its true owner (21:33-45), or the wicked servants who do not take proper care of the masters' property (24:48-51). Disciples like Joseph, by contrast, are stewards who make proper use of the master's possessions (24:45-47); they are slaves who recognize that they are entrusted with possessions in order to make the kingdom prosper (25:14-30). The consequences of proper or improper use of possessions are ultimate, because human beings are dependent upon God for all things and can never repay the debt. Entrusted with the care of God's domain, we are stewards who can serve only one master, and must prove ourselves worthy of God's trust by the proper disposition of our possessions. Matthew makes a clear contrast between the two options: serve God or wealth (6:24). The Jewish leaders fail the test, with long-term consequences. The harm of their false teaching is compounded and intensified by the poor stewardship that buttresses it.

Last but not least, Matthew proves their teaching to be false even as they promulgate it. It is false because it is impossible. The guards' story is to be, "His disciples came by night and stole him away while we were asleep" (28:13). The Jewish leaders certainly lie when they claim that this story will keep them out of hot water with the governor (28:14). Sleeping on watch was no less a serious lapse of military discipline in that day than it is now. Further, the story is contradictory: if the guards were sleeping, how do they know what happened? Even if someone stole the body, how could they know that Jesus' disciples did the stealing? Not only do the Jewish leaders provide false teaching, but it's not very good false teaching. Their witness would never stand up in a court of law.

Matthew presents the Jewish leaders as highly culpable for their false teaching and witness. It is little wonder that Matthew has come under fire in recent years for seeming anti-Semitic, and that preachers have been warned to avoid or even disavow his more problematic and polemic statements. The preacher should not take this problem lightly: what are modern congregations to make, for example, of the response of the people to Pilate's symbolic hand-washing, "His blood be on us and on our children" (27:25)? The Jewish biblical scholar Samuel Sandmel tells the story of a Christian who attacks his Jewish neighbor on Palm Sunday:

"Why are you beating me? We've been neighbors for years without a problem," says the Jew.

"You Jews killed Jesus," replies the Christian.

"But that was 2,000 years ago!"

"I just found out about it today!"

The careful reader will observe that Matthew's story is more nuanced than a simple condemnation of Jews for the death of Jesus. For one thing, Matthew's hard words are for the most part directed against the Jewish leaders — not Jews as a body. They are particularly aimed toward those leaders as false teachers. Matthew's harshest words are directed toward those whom he considers to have led the masses astray.

For another, Matthew's words should be read in the context of ancient polemical practice, which could be surprisingly nasty, particularly between rival but related groups, as the church and synagogue no doubt were in Matthew's day. In ancient arguments, it was standard practice to employ *ad hominem* attacks: your opponents were always unworthy, usually liars, cheats, hypocrites, and bad guys all around. You didn't just make your case; you insulted your opponent. Then, as now, arguments were all the more heated among those groups who held much in common — sometimes so much that outsiders could hardly tell them apart. It is doubtful that the broad majority of people in the Roman empire of Matthew's day would have understood the debate between Jew and Christian, if they even knew about it (and since the number of Jews in the empire was small, and the number of Christians even less, it is unlikely that the average outsider would have been familiar with this debate). Matthew clearly presents Jesus and his disciples as Jews themselves (this point is amazingly still lost on some modern Christians), in a debate with other Jews. Matthew was engaged in internal politics at a time when Christianity was just beginning to emerge from Judaism, and he used standard rhetorical methods

29

to show that in his view, Christians were the true heirs of the Jewish tradition. Matthew was a Jew arguing for his particular brand of messianic Judaism, and he employed all the rhetorical effects available to him to make his case. Today in Western society we are more careful to teach our children to make more substantive arguments, and hope that they will escape the name-calling phase somewhere in their school years. Extreme polemic is considered to be in bad taste outside of the political op-ed pages, where we assume it to be inflated for partisanship's sake.

Further, Matthew's story should be read as a whole, not in pieces. If we begin reading the story of Jesus in Jerusalem at the beginning, we emerge with a different picture of the hand-washing scene, one that reinforces Matthew's argument against the false teaching of the leaders. Jesus enters Jerusalem in fulfillment of prophecy and the crowds proclaim him "Son of David" (21:1-11). "Hosanna to the Son of David! Blessed is the one who comes in the name of the Lord! Hosanna in the highest heaven!" (21:9). When asked whom they are talking about, the crowds reply, "This is the prophet Jesus from Nazareth in Galilee" (21:10). Later, in the temple, *children* cry out, "Hosanna to the Son of David," invoking the wrath of the chief priests and scribes (21:15). The implication is that the people have led their children into worship; the children are imitating the parents. Unfortunately, the crowds are not themselves sufficiently instructed: they think Jesus is merely a "prophet," not "Lord." Not being so instructed, they later stand before Pilate unprepared to confess their faith. Unfortunately, in Matthew's view, they take responsibility for teaching their children falsely as well, and allow their children to share blood responsibility before Pilate (27:24-25). Matthew makes it quite clear where the ultimate blame for this incident lies: in the false teaching of the chief priests and elders, who have "persuaded" the crowds to ask for Jesus' death (27:20). When read as a whole, the story emerges as a warning on two counts. First, as with the story of the guards at the tomb (28:15), false teaching carries bitter fruits to successive generations. False teaching is passed on from the teachers to their followers and tragically to their children. Second, worship without sound instruction is empty. One may hope that Christians will apply these warnings to their own assemblies rather than pointing fingers elsewhere. We cannot snip from our Bibles Matthew's harsh language; we can only counter with sound instruction its false use and manipulation for the purposes of strife and hatred.

King Of The Hill

The closing section of Matthew's Gospel picks up the narrative thread left from the story of the women disciples at the tomb: true to Jesus' word (28:10) and the prediction of the angel of the Lord (28:7), the eleven male disciples ("brothers," 28:10) go to the mountain in Galilee (28:16). They join in worship of the resurrected Lord, though some doubt (28:17). Jesus acknowledges that their worship is well-placed: "All authority in heaven and on earth has been given to me" (28:18). The scene binds together two of Matthew's main images of Jesus: Lord and Teacher. The two cannot be separated; Jesus cannot be Teacher without being Lord. On the mountain, Jesus is the all-powerful resurrected Lord, and the Teacher who speaks his final words on the mountain of revelation. This is climax as well as end of Gospel: the royal Messiah, Son of David, Son of God, Teacher of the Law, is now enthroned as King. The disciples in turn are commissioned to continue Jesus' ministry, to mirror his actions in their mission of bearing the fruits of discipleship.

The Great Commission is the final step in the disciples' training and preparation for their future mission. They are to become mirror images of Jesus in their own disciple-making: "Go therefore and make disciples of all nations, baptizing them in the name of the Father and of the Son and of the Holy Spirit, and teaching them to obey everything that I have commanded you" (28:19-20). English translations often obscure the force of the exhortation, which lands squarely on the main imperative, "make disciples" (*matheteuo*). The other verbs in the sentence ("go," "baptize," "teach") are not Greek imperatives but participles, used either as subsidiary imperatives, or more likely as instrumental, stressing the means by which disciples are to be made: "Make disciples, by

31

going and baptizing and teaching...." Their main job is to replicate themselves; like their Lord, they are to gather around themselves students of his teaching. The time until the end of the age (28:20) is to be spent making more disciples. They are to bear fruit (cf. the Parable of the Sower, 13:23).

The mission includes community-formation and teaching. Baptism is the formation of a community "where two or three are gathered together" to be with the resurrected Jesus (18:19-20). The continued worship of these small communities is a crucial part of disciple-making. Matthew has not included baptism as a part of Jesus' teaching until now, apart from his own example of being baptized by John the Baptist. When Jesus was baptized, he told John it was to "fulfill all righteousness" (3:15); that is, to be baptized is thus a part of following the way of righteousness that Jesus teaches (5:6, 10; 6:33). Matthew assumes the practice of his own community in reporting this command, baptism being done in the name of the Trinity: Father, Son, and Holy Spirit.

Teaching is a necessary part of the worship gatherings. Again, the idea is to replicate the work of Jesus. The subject of the teaching is "everything I have commanded you." The goal is obedience (28:20). Throughout Matthew's story, the disciples are presented as students of the Lord. They are good students for the most part; unlike the disciples in Mark, they seem to understand most of what Jesus has to say. At the end of his parable discourse, he asks if they have understood his teaching; they answer, "Yes" (13:51). When Jesus walks on the water, the disciples are not astounded (as in Mark 6:51-52), but they confess, "Truly you are the Son of God" (Matthew 14:33). Yet there is one stumbling block Matthew's disciples cannot quite overcome: they do not understand his death (16:22-24; 17:23). The disciples are unprepared to stand by Jesus at the cross (26:56), being ill-prepared to understand his death, despite his predictions (16:21; 17:9, 22-23; 20:17-18). By the end of the story, however, most of the cobwebs have been cleared away (though some still doubt, 28:17). In becoming witnesses to his resurrection they are now finished with their training, and are fully ready to take their places in the teaching mission. They are truly scribes of the kingdom of heaven (13:52).

In the picture of the resurrected Lord standing on the mountain of revelation to teach, there is an unmistakable allusion to Moses, who brought the Law of God down from Mount Sinai (cf. 5:1). Matthew thus expands and elaborates his picture of Jesus as the authoritative teacher and interpreter of the Mosaic Law (*Torah* in Hebrew). Jesus, contrary to popular opinion, explicitly denies that he came to change or abolish the Law; in fact, he says that "until heaven and earth pass away, not one letter, not one stroke of a letter, will pass from the law until all is accomplished" (5:17-18). "I have come not to abolish but to fulfill," he says (5:17). But what does Matthew mean when he describes Jesus as one who fulfills Torah? At the least, he means that Jesus is both teacher of Torah, and that he is himself the fulfillment of Torah.

Jesus' function as Teacher of Torah is seen throughout Matthew; I have already mentioned that some scholars see Matthew has containing five blocks of teaching, corresponding to the five books of Moses (chapters 5-7, 10, 13, 18, 24-25). His role as interpreter of Torah is stressed most vividly in the six antitheses of the Sermon on the Mount: "You have heard it said ... but I say ..." (5:21, 27, 31, 33, 38, 43). Jesus offers his own authoritative interpretation of the commands of Torah. He teaches Torah as a radical demand on one's life. In the cases of murder and adultery, he demands an inner disposition that goes beyond mere adherence to the external commands: the disciple is to forswear not only angry actions, but anger itself (5:21-26), not only adultery but the intention to commit adultery (5:27-30). In the cases of divorce and oaths, Jesus demands absolute obedience to the intent of Torah; marriage is not to be dismissed lightly (5:31-32), nor is one's word held casually (5:33-37). Finally, in the case of retribution and love, Jesus demands a response that goes beyond the letter of the Law, giving in the face of evil (5:38-42), and love and prayer in the face of hatred (5:43-47). Jesus sums up his teaching on the ethical dimensions of Torah when he commends the imitation of God: "Be perfect, therefore, as your heavenly Father is perfect." Only absolute obedience will do. Matthew makes it clear that the obedience in question is obedience to Torah *as Jesus teaches it and passes it along to be taught to others:* "Therefore, whoever breaks one of the least of these commandments, and teaches others to do the same, will be called least in the kingdom of heaven; but whoever does them and teaches them will be called great in the kingdom of heaven" (5:19).

Clearly, the reference to those "in the kingdom of heaven" refers to Jesus' disciples, since Jesus' message is the "kingdom of heaven has come near" (4:17; cf. 11:11). Jesus gives the authoritative interpretation of Torah (7:28-29), and the disciples are in turn delegated that authority; Jesus gives them the power to "bind and loose" (16:9; 18:18), terms used in the Jewish Rabbinic tradition to signify the determination of what Torah allows and forbids. In other words, the disciples are given authority to interpret Torah in the tradition of Jesus. The disciples are to be "scribes trained for the kingdom of heaven," who are "like the master of a household who brings out of his treasure what is new and what is old" (13:52). What is old is the Mosaic tradition; what is new is the authoritative interpretation of it given by Jesus. That old/new teaching is to be handed on to further generations by the disciples. Obedience to this tradition thus becomes a mark of community membership: to do the will of God as revealed in Jesus' teaching of Torah is to become part of his family (12:46-50).

Jesus is also himself the fulfillment of Torah. "Torah" was often used in an extended sense to mean not just the five books of Moses, but the entire collection of the Hebrew Bible that Christians would come to call the Old Testament. Matthew cites the Old Testament more than any other Gospel. He juxtaposes specific texts with events in Jesus' life, so that text and life interpret each other (e.g., 1:23; 13:14-17). Throughout Jesus' life, what he says and does and everything that happens to him proves the words of Torah true. For Matthew, this is divine confirmation that Jesus is Lord and Messiah. Further, what Jesus says about Torah, he later says about his own words: They will never pass away (5:18; 24:35). His own words stand as the authoritative teaching of Torah, because he himself is the fulfillment of the words of Torah. So too his disciples are expected to do the will of God, as Jesus teaches it to them, and to interpret it for new disciples.

It is worth noting that Matthew designates the entire community as holders of the teaching office. Not just Peter, but all the disciples are called to "bind and loose" (18:18). Hierarchy is discouraged, and the measurement for leadership in the community is service: "You are not to be called rabbi, for you have one teacher, and you are all students ... Nor are you to be called instructors, for you have one instructor, the Messiah. The greatest among you will be your servant" (23:8, 10-11). Thus no disciple takes on the role of Jesus; rather, all together imitate him as Teacher. There is in the community no one fount of wisdom who pours knowledge into the heads of fellow disciples, but a round table of scribes who exercise the teaching office together — God's will is discerned in groups. The ongoing presence of Jesus as Teacher is to be found in the small community of two or three that has gathered around him, the family that does the will of God as he taught it.

The mission of bearing fruit is to be universal: the disciples are specifically sent to "all nations," or "all the Gentiles" (*panta ta ethne*, 28:19). Here Matthew draws out the implications of the various hints laid down throughout the story: Wise Gentiles worship him (2:11) since he is the light to the Gentiles (4:15-16; 12:18-21); Gentiles have faith in him when Israelites do not (8:10); a Canaanite woman takes the crumbs from his table (15:21-28), and many will come from east and west to sit at that table (8:11-12). Ironically, even the Roman soldiers responsible for his death speak words that recognize Jesus as the Son of God (27:54). Jesus' prophecy to the Jewish leaders will prove true: "The Kingdom of God will be taken away from you and given to a nation (*ethnos*) producing the fruits of it" (21:43, author's translation). At the end of his earthly life, and at the beginning of his resurrected life, Jesus' mission is extended beyond "the lost sheep of the house of Israel" (15:24; 10:5-6; cf. 9:36; 10:23; 19:28). These hints laid throughout the book are now given explicit fulfillment in the command of the resurrected Lord.

Ironically, Matthew's community has completely absorbed this prophesied mission to all nations, so much so that the meaning of the word "nation/Gentile" has in some cases shifted to designate those outside the community. "Gentiles" has become in Matthew's community not so much an ethnic designation but the condition from which they have been saved (5:47; 6:7, 32; 18:17; 20:25). The universal reach of Jesus' teaching and its total identification with the tradition of Moses have resulted by Matthew's time in a complete shift of identity. Christians are no longer outsiders but brothers and sisters of a new community.

The Gospel ends with the promise given at its beginning: Jesus is "God with us" (1:23). "Remember, I am with you always, to the end of the age" (28:20). The NRSV translation of *idou* (an imperative of the verb "to see," normally translated "behold, look") as "remember" is perhaps idiosyncratic, as *idou* was generally used as a sort of exclamation point, drawing attention to what follows. But both "remember" and "look" point to the function of the disciple, preacher, and teacher as the Gospel closes. The ongoing job of disciples is to produce fruit — to make more disciples, to teach us to remember the teachings of the Master, yes — but also to point out the ways that the resurrected Lord is still at work in the community, still with us. The preacher points to Jesus' teaching, as embodied in the Gospel of Matthew, and says, "Remember." The preacher also points to the living Lord among the congregation, at work in the teaching and the worship of the community, and says, "Look."

The Morning After

Easter Vigil — Matthew 28:1-10
March 29, 1997

Easter Vigil is one of my favorite liturgies, and one of the hidden treasures of *The Book of Common Prayer.* It is essentially the Christian Passover; it begins in the darkness with the striking of a new fire, continues by candlelight through the recitation of God's great acts for the people Israel, and then bursts into full light with the first Eucharist of Easter. However, I am always disappointed when I come to church on Easter Eve and get the same Easter sermon everyone is going to get the next morning. Easter Eve is the only opportunity the lectionary provides to read Matthew's empty tomb account (unless we choose it as the alternate reading for Easter Day Year A, in which case we will miss John's version), and the final commissioning of the disciples by the risen Jesus at the end of the chapter is read only on Trinity Sunday in Year A, where the focus may well be on the Godhead, not resurrection. So we may lose Matthew's distinct resurrection emphasis entirely if we let Easter morning's Mark, Luke, or John color Matthew on Easter Eve. To the harried preacher who has already produced enough sermons this Holy Week, I note that the Easter Vigil texts, like those of Maundy Thursday and Good Friday, are the same every year; notes on the text made this year will save much research next year. Also, since Easter Vigil is a long service, the proclamation of the gospel on this night is best kept brief; in the sermon that follows, I felt no need to be wordy.

This sermon was preached at St. Luke's Episcopal Church in Katonah, New York, a diverse congregation in a small town in one of the more affluent areas surrounding New York City, that drew its congregation from a number of small surrounding towns. It begins by drawing on the general human experience of letdown after excitement to highlight Matthew's promise that discipleship brings no letdown; Jesus will be with them always. In the end, Matthew's challenge to make disciples everywhere is brought home to this particular parish, where the church staff list in the weekly

37

bulletin took a cue from Matthew's vision of an egalitarian community of scribes teaching each other the ways of the Lord, by citing the entire congregation as "ministers."

———————

There is a question that has been bothering me for some time.
> I have to admit that it is of no earth-shattering importance.
> Maybe even kind of trivial.
> But still, I wonder.
> This is my question: What does Superman do after he saves the world?
> How do you follow up on that?
> Lex Luthor has been vanquished and Metropolis is safe.
> So what do you do after that, if you're Clark Kent, a.k.a. Superman?
> Go back to your office and type up the story?
> Do you stop by at the pub on the first floor for a quick drink with Jimmy Olsen and Perry White?
> Or do you just go home and pop the tops off a few beers, turn on Letterman, and dream of Lois Lane?
> I imagine a scruffy superhero waking up the next morning at 10:30 with a hangover and a bad case of Day-after-Christmas syndrome.

It's got to be a disappointment, that next day.
> And I imagine it's the same no matter what kind of superhero you are.
> What does Michael Jordan do after he wins the last game of the playoff?
> We know about inaugural balls, but what happens next in the White House?
> And what happens if you're Bruce Springsteen or Snoop Doggy Dogg and you've just sold your quadrillionth record album?

It would be very interesting to be a fly on the wall in Beverly
Hills, in the house of one of the movie stars that took home
a little statue the other night.

All that excitement, and the next day, all you have to show
for it is this funny-looking faceless little guy called
Oscar.

Well, we all know December 26.

I can't help but think that's exactly how the disciples felt when
they heard the news.

The women come in with the believe-it-or-not story.

Mary Magdalene and the other Mary tell of the tomb, the stone,
the earthquake, the angel of the Lord, with face like lightning and clothes as white as snow.

Mary and Mary tell of guards like dead men, the empty tomb,
and the words of the angel: "He is not here; he is risen."

And they are shaking, because it's not just the strange events
and the voice of the angel.

The women have actually seen Jesus, they've held his feet in
their hands as they threw themselves on the ground before
him.

They've heard his voice.

And for Peter and the other disciples, it's like Christmas —
well, it's really like Easter — but it's like Christmas and
the Superbowl and Oscar night all rolled into one.

It's a wild, natural high.

And then they come down to the ground.

As soon as they hear what the angel and what Jesus actually
said.

"He is going ahead of you to Galilee," said the angel.

Jesus tells the two women, "Tell my brothers to go to Galilee."

Galilee!

Surely there must be some mistake.

The Lord is risen indeed, and you want to go where?

39

We've just gotten to the show, and you want to go back to the
minor leagues?

That's where we started from, we've been there, done that, we
worked hard to get *here*.

Why not put Jesus on our shoulders and march into the city,
into Jerusalem, to the temple? I'm sure we can get those
folk we had last week shouting "Hosanna"; there must be
plenty of leftover palm branches.

Why not put him on the boat straight to Rome — the emperor
should see this for himself.

But you, Jesus, risen triumphant from the dead — you just
want us to go home?

But, of course, these disciples can't see into their future.

They don't know what's going to happen next.

They are not superheroes, not Air Jordans, not movie stars
living in the last five minutes of their allotted fifteen.

Nor are they some kind of lesser hero, the ex-high-school football player who scored the big touchdown his senior year
and hasn't stopped talking about it for the last thirty.

No. Galilee will not be an anticlimax, but only a beginning.

Matthew gives a hint as he tells the story, though the translation we just read doesn't quite get it across.

When Jesus appeared to the women, he didn't "meet" them,
as we read tonight.

Rather he "accompanied" them, he walked along with them
on the road.

Jesus goes with them as they go to tell the others the good
news.

He walks with them as they carry out their orders.

Just as he will soon tell all of them, "I am with you always,
even to the end of the age."

They are just at the beginning of a mission that will change
the face of the world and the course of history.

It's not over yet.
They have yet to reach the climax.

Their mission is our mission.
It's just as we say in our bulletin: "The Parish Family, Ministers."
We continue the work of those two women, those first disciples.
And we do it in the same place they were sent: back home.
Back in Bedford, Katonah, Bedford Hills, South Salem, wherever we're from.
Jesus meets us here and goes with us back there so we can spread the story.
He is risen, he is alive, he lives here among us, and will be with us always.
Now, go home.
Go back where you came from, and tell the news.

3. Preaching Resurrection In Mark

The first time I heard Mark's Gospel preached at Easter, the preacher told us that in seminary they had called Mark "the Gospel with no ending," because it closed with the enigmatic double negative, "They said nothing to no one, for they were afraid." I thought it a strange statement, since I knew full well that my Bible at home had eleven verses after this no-ending ending. And that's all I remember about the sermon.

There is no escaping, even on the most basic level, the problem of the ending of Mark's Gospel, and it is a problem that will color our whole understanding of resurrection in Mark. A quick glance at most Bible translations reveals the confusion. Older translations such as the King James Version simply print twenty verses in Mark 16. More recent translations, such as the New Revised Standard Version, often set off sections of the final chapter under separate headings: "The Shorter Ending of Mark," and "The Longer Ending of Mark." In neither case is it clear to anyone who doesn't read the fine print that these endings were not actually written by the original author of Mark. The oldest and best manuscripts of the Greek New Testament — all hand-copied, of course, long before the printing press — end Mark at verse 8. Verses 9 through 20 ("The Longer Ending") are obviously a pastiche of resurrection stories cobbled together from the other Gospels, and no doubt were added by some scribe who could not stand the apparently unfinished story. That this was not the original ending of Mark is shown by the presence of "The Shorter Ending," an eloquent mouthful composed by yet another scribe who had no inkling about how to imitate the literary style of the real Mark (who could never have

43

spat out anything like "the sacred and imperishable proclamation of eternal salvation"). The real ending of Mark is neither of these additions, which should be printed with the fine print and the footnotes of our modern translations.

It was once fashionable to believe that scribe who wrote the "Longer Ending" had the right instinct — Mark must have written something like this conclusion to his story, but in the dark recesses of early Christian history the page was torn and the ending lost (an alternate thesis was that Mark took sick, died, was imprisoned, or otherwise prevented from finishing his work at this precise point when he had almost but not quite finished the story). Certainly, scholars pontificated, the story could not have ended with the women doubly silent (a double negative is emphatic in Greek) — Matthew, Luke, and John make it clear that the women did speak of what they saw at the tomb. The ending is all the more jarring when read in Greek, since the sentence ends with a preposition (yes, you can do that in Greek) — and no self-respecting Greek writer, it was claimed, would end a chapter with a preposition, let alone an entire book. Yet over the years no one has ever turned up a manuscript that contains any continuation of Mark's story past this final statement, while we have found examples of Greek writers using a preposition to end a chapter, and yes, even a book. Even the most ardent holdouts among scholars have had to admit that there is no evidence that Mark ever intended or provided an ending other than, "They said nothing to no one, for they were afraid" (16:8, author's translation).

Solving a scholarly textual problem hardly addresses the emotional issue of presenting a congregation with a Gospel that seems to end on a note of fear, faithlessness, and downright disobedience. It is tempting to minimize the problem of the women's silence, to move too quickly to "But of course they talked...." One might even attempt to justify the practice of putting the textual additions to Mark in the same typeface as the original text in modern translations, on the basis that Mark should be read in light of the stories it sits among, the stories of Matthew, Luke, and John. Or one could just ignore the problem as being above the heads of the average congregation, or for that matter, average clergy. I once taught at a seminary that had displayed on a grand arch in its chapel the version of the Great Commission found in the Longer Ending of Mark, "Go into all the world and proclaim the gospel to the whole creation"; though it seemed to me highly ironic to have a non-Bible verse plastered in front of us at every worship service, no one ever went up there with a can of whitewash.

If we allow Mark to speak for himself, we will have to come to terms with his ending (and it may be a little more than condescending to think that church folk cannot understand why someone would have tacked on an easier ending). A closer reading of Mark shows that the end of the writing is not necessarily the end of the story, that there is more to resurrection than an empty tomb and some frightened women. If it seems mysterious that Mark would leave us with a picture of these trembling women in a state of fear and uncertainty, it is perhaps because one of Mark's favorite categories is "mystery."

Elementary, My Dear Mark

I like to read Mark as a mystery story. The subject of the mystery turns out to be Jesus himself, and is best expressed by the disciples: "Who then is this, that even the wind and the sea obey him?" (4:41; cf. 1:27). By the end of the story, we the readers can answer their question — or can we?

The story begins with certainty enough: "The beginning of the good news of Jesus Christ, the Son of God" (1:1). Jesus is said to be the "Christ" or "Messiah," the Anointed One and promised leader of Israel. Nothing could be plainer. But even here, there is ambiguity amid the certainty. "Beginning" is ambiguous: it can refer to the beginning of the Gospel of Mark, but also the beginning of the "good news" itself; that is, the story of faith, belief, and discipleship. This "good news" is both a message and a genre of literature. Even "of" is ambiguous, because Jesus is both the subject and the object of the message — it is Jesus' own message, but also a message about Jesus. We might seem on more solid ground with "the Son of God," but due to the perverse turnings of fate, the evidence that these words were actually penned by Mark is thin. (The manuscript evidence leans slightly toward including these words as part of Mark's original text, but there is enough doubt that most editions of the Greek New Testament put them in brackets). Assuming we accept the words as Mark's, to say that Jesus is "Son of God" is to give him a title of kingship, both in the Hebrew and Greco-Roman traditions of the first century.

Thus Mark begins with some room for interpretive play, but no apparent mystery at all. We know exactly who and exactly what we are going to deal with: the good news of a royal Messiah. But when we peer closely enough, we notice cracks in the wall, which will widen as we read on.

Mark gives us none of the traditional stories about the young Jesus. There is no manger, no inn, no shepherds, no child wrapped in swaddling cloths who grows up to be a precocious adolescent among the Temple scholars (all part of Luke's Gospel), as well as no census, no star, and no wise men (Matthew's version). In other words, Jesus' earthly origins, as far as Mark tells the story, are a mystery.

What we do learn is that a "messenger" brings "good news" (a play on words in Greek, where the *angelos* brings *euangelia*). His name is John, and he is described as a "baptizer" (1:4). He comes from the "wilderness," (*eremos,* 1:3) which implies that he is an *outsider* in relation to the establishment. He dresses like an outsider — actually, he dresses like Elijah, one of the Old Testament prophets, who was said to be a forerunner of the Messiah (Malachi 4:5) — in "camel's hair, with a leather belt," eating locusts and wild honey (1:6). He brings a message of repentance, and Mark claims that "people from the whole Judean countryside and all the people of Jerusalem" responded (1:5) — some see this as exaggeration, but Mark may allude to the notion that the Messiah's appearance would be hailed by mass worldwide repentance. Sure enough, John says that he is merely a forerunner, that a "stronger one" will follow him (1:7).

Can we be surprised then that Jesus himself appears next? If we had any doubts, they are dispelled when the divine actors take over. The heavens are ripped open, a dove (symbolizing the Spirit) descends, the voice of God speaks. Jesus is driven into the wilderness to be tempted by Satan and tended by angels (1:9-13).

However, except for the divine characters, it is only we the readers who know all this. "*You* are my Son, the Beloved," says God, "with *you* I am well pleased" (1:11). The heavenly voice is along the lines of a mystical experience, heard only by Jesus, not by John or the crowd; we the readers overhear. No one else sees Jesus tempted in the wilderness and waited on by angels. It might be tempting to think of ourselves as *insiders* — unlike the human characters in the story, we know what they don't. We were tipped off by the opening verse, and now, we can say with some satisfaction, we have inside information. It is merely a minor irritation to remember that when John was pictured as coming from the wilderness, he was indirectly characterized as an outsider, and that Jesus himself has gone into the wilderness (*eremos*, 1:12).

Jesus comes out of the wilderness to confirm John's message: "The time is fulfilled, and the kingdom of God has come near; repent, and believe in the good news" (1:14-15). Like John, Jesus starts his work away from the centers of power — in Galilee, definitely back seat to Jerusalem — one might even say, the boondocks. Jesus continues there the message that John preached, of repentance. He even suggests all our expectations will be fulfilled, because the Kingdom has come near (but is not yet "here").

Yet he does not define what he means by "Kingdom of God." His contemporaries would probably hear in that expression a promise of a renewed Davidic monarchy, the restoration of the royal line of Israel in the face of Roman occupation. Some, however, would have heard something more otherworldly: direct divine rule of the earth. Which is it? It is a question that we must take with us through the story. Jesus will not commit himself until nearly the end.

Certainly Jesus doesn't do anything right off the bat to make us think he is going to stage a coup in Jerusalem. Indeed, the following stories about him are a little odd. Walking by the sea, he spots some fishermen, and invites them to join him in a fishing expedition of his own (1:16-17). A little further on, he does it again (1:19-20). Why do Simon and Andrew and James and John go? A traditional suggestion is that they already knew Jesus, but Mark does not even hint at this. The disciples seem to know something

47

— or are they just mysteriously compelled? We the readers know why they go; we read the first verse, we know that Jesus is the Messiah. But how do they know? Mark does not spell it out. He simply presents them as *insiders*.

The reaction of the crowd is different (1:21-28). The crowd is "astonished" at his teaching (1:22, 27) — they do not believe, but are flustered. Their mistake is to compare him to other human teachers, "for he taught as one having authority, and not as the scribes" (1:22), a mistake the supernatural characters in the story, as well as we the readers, do not make. Though Jesus' fame spreads, it is not entirely clear that the multitudes understand what they see and hear.

The demons, however, are clear about who Jesus is, "the Holy One of God" (1:24). Jesus strangely does not affirm this identification. Rather, he issues a strong order of silence, commanding the demon to "muzzle" himself in the manner of an animal, as if Jesus did not want anyone to know who he was (1:25). The crowd, indeed, does not catch on, but responds with more amazement (1:27). They ask the key question, "What is this?" To them it is a mystery. To further compound the mystery, when Jesus performs subsequent exorcisms, he specifically commands the demons not to speak, "because they knew him" (1:34). It is as if Jesus does not want to be known!

Indeed, when morning dawns the next day, Jesus has again gone into the wilderness (*eremos*), the place of temptation, to pray (1:35). When Simon and the rest suggest that the crowd is looking for him, Jesus announces his intention to move on to the next town. Again, it is almost as if Jesus does not want to indulge in fame. The effect is heightened in the Greek text of Mark, which suggests that Simon's "pursuit" to find Jesus borders on "persecution" (*katadioko*, 1:36). Do these disciples really understand whom they are dealing with?

Their confusion was no doubt compounded by the appearance of a leper who asked to be made clean (1:40-45). Jesus "sternly orders" him to disappear, to strict observance of the Old Testament rituals concerning this kind of healing, and to absolute silence. The healed man, of course, ignores Jesus completely, and tells his tale through the town, so that Jesus is forced into open country to accommodate the crowds. Again, he retreats to the wilderness.

By now, we the readers may well ask with the crowd, "What is this?" There is a tension between the Jesus of the narration and the Jesus of the story. The narrator speaks to us of a Messiah, the Son of God. However, the story is one of a reluctant miracle worker, one who would rather not have the publicity, thank you very much. He doesn't seem to fulfill anyone's expectation of the Kingdom. Some people follow him for no apparent reason. Yet the people who see his miracles have the least understanding of who he is, and absolutely no desire to follow his orders. And why does he want to keep all of this a secret? Even his disciples, the insiders, don't seem to know. Neither do we.

To get ahead of the story, this tension between knowledge and ignorance, between faith and doubt, between insider and outsider, is in the nature of things for Mark. At the same time that Mark assures us of the certainties of the universe, he undermines our overconfidence in our own perceptions. He tells us that Jesus is Messiah, yet he shows us a Messiah that we can't quite figure out. His portrait of Jesus is at once firm and vague, solid and vaporous. It's like grasping a piece of water. The word he will later use is in fact "mystery" (4:11). It is something that you can never quite grasp, even if you are an insider. It is a mystery not in the sense of a puzzle that can be solved, but in the sense of the grand question of human existence, the great ineffable uncertainty of living by faith in a world of doubt. Who is Jesus? How do we know for sure? Do we really understand what we mean when we call him Messiah, Son of God?

One device Mark uses to communicate his mystery is to sharpen, then blur, the lines between insiders and outsiders. The string of controversy stories in 2:1—3:6 clearly draws the lines of opposition to Jesus, culminating in a plot to take his life (3:6). Having established that the Pharisees and scribes are his enemies, Jesus then appoints twelve disciples to be "apostles" or missionaries (3:13-19). Yet even here, one named Judas will turn out to be an outsider after all (3:19). Even these disciples are not permitted to hear the demons proclaiming Jesus' true identity (3:12).

49

The true nature of the insider/outsider distinction is shown in a story that uses one of Mark's favorite literary techniques, the sandwich structure: he begins one story, moves elsewhere to tell another story, and then returns to finish the original story. Jesus' family appears to restrain him from speaking to the crowds, saying that "he has gone out of his mind" (3:21). The scribes draw out the implication of this statement: he is in fact (as mentally-ill persons were considered in that society) possessed by demons (3:22). In reply Jesus establishes that he is actually the "stronger one" proclaimed by John, who has entered the strong man's house and tied him up (3:27). Jesus is possessed of a greater Spirit. The scribes show their true colors by opposing the work of this Spirit (3:28-30). Ironically, he makes reference to a "house divided" when he refers to Satan's kingdom (3:24-25), while his own family sides with his enemies! But it is also clear that Jesus has a different definition of family: when Mark returns to the original story, the crowd tells Jesus that his family waits for him outside (3:31-32). Jesus replies that those gathered around him are in fact his family: "Whoever does the will of God is my brother and mother and sister" (3:34-35). The lines are clearly drawn: the outsiders are hard-hearted, resistant, and even demonic. The insiders are familial and obedient.

Yet it soon becomes apparent that there is a glitch in the system for insiders. There is enough mystery in Jesus to make being an insider precarious (and an insider will be Jesus' ultimate downfall!). This is brought home to the disciples almost as a slap in the face. Jesus sits to teach a large crowd, and tells them a parable (4:1-9). The disciples corner him alone for an interpretation, which turns out to be more than they bargained for (4:10). Jesus tells them, "To you has been given the mystery (*mysterion*) of the Kingdom of God" (4:11). Mark's language could mean either that the subject of the mystery is the Kingdom, or that the Kingdom is itself the mystery, or both. For the disciples, the latter sense predominates. The *mysterion* is not so much a "secret" in the sense of a puzzle about the Kingdom that needs an answer, but the actual "mystery" that is itself the Kingdom of God — not the mystery "about" the Kingdom but the mystery "of" the Kingdom. As we have already seen, the Kingdom is near, but it tends to slip through our grasp. The disciples have been given and made part of this mysterious, slippery Kingdom.

But for the outsiders, says Jesus, everything is in code, in parables to be exact (4:11), for the surprising reason that the code keeps the outsiders out! "For those outside, everything comes in parables, *in order that* they may indeed look, but not perceive, and may indeed listen, but not understand; so that they may not turn again and be forgiven" (4:11-12). The purpose of the speaking in parables is not to enhance understanding but prevent it! For the outsiders, the mystery is indeed "about" the Kingdom — a puzzle to which they lack the solution. While the notion that the parables are intended to obscure meaning and prevent repentance may offend our modern liberal sensibilities, keep in mind that Mark is telling a story here, and a kind of mystery story at that. Jesus' parables themselves point toward an end to the story that reveals all: lamps that are put on lamp stands (4:21), seeds that grow secretly yet sprout hugely (4:26-29). "There is nothing hidden except to be disclosed; nor is anything secret, except to come to light" (4:22). The mystery will be revealed in the end. At this point in the story, it remains in secret code.

The disciples, being insiders, receive the key to the code, that is, Jesus' interpretation. What is simply a puzzle to the outsiders is in fact true mystery for them, because they have to figure out the larger implications of his teaching. They are the ultimate insiders in that they hear both the code and the key, both the puzzle and its solution. Yet it is clear that the solutions prove to be yet more mysterious: despite the disciples' insider status, they apparently understand less and less as time goes on.

They leave his parable teaching session to cross the lake (4:35-41). They fret in the wake of a storm while Jesus sleeps, and wake him: "Teacher, do you not care that we are perishing?" But they are dumbfounded when he rebukes the winds and calms the waves. They ask one another, "Who then is this, that even the wind and the sea obey him?" While they have a privileged position, clearly they have not grasped the nature of the privilege, or really understood whom they have in the boat with them. Jesus diagnoses their

51

problem succinctly: "Why are you afraid? Have you no faith?" Though the mystery of the Kingdom is explained to them, they are not immune to misunderstanding, since it is the very nature of such a mystery to remain mysterious. One cannot totally grasp the presence of God in one's midst.

Mark makes his point so often and so pointedly that the disciples end up looking like the Keystone Kops of faith. Jesus walks on water, and, like the unbelieving crowds, they are astounded (6:47-52). Jesus feeds 5,000 with five loaves and two fish (6:30-44), yet the disciples seem not to remember this when they find themselves with 4,000 hungry folk and only seven loaves on hand (8:1-10). When Jesus confronts them with the details of what they have not understood, they end up even more confused (8:14-21). It is tempting to read the stories of the healing of the deaf man (7:31-37), the blind man (8:22-26), and blind Bartimaeus (10:46-52) as allegories of the disciples' progress in faith (or lack thereof), especially when sandwiched in the middle is Peter's half-witted confession: Jesus is, as the reader has known all along, "The Messiah," (8:29), yet when Jesus specifies that being Messiah involves suffering, betrayal, and death, Peter has the temerity to rebuke him (8:31-33). These disciples can see, but only trees, walking (8:24). Jesus pointedly invokes the same language used to describe the outsiders: "Do you still not perceive or understand? Are your hearts hardened? Do you have eyes, and fail to see? Do you have ears, and fail to hear?" (8:17-18).

Mark gives us an incredibly skillful portrait of disciples in training. Sandwiched in with these three healing stories is a trice-repeated pattern of storytelling: Jesus predicts that he will suffer, die, and be raised by God (8:31; 9:31; 10:33); the disciples in some way misunderstand him (8:32-33; 9:33-34; 10:35-37); Jesus uses the opportunity to deliver even more teaching on the nature of his Messiahship. The disciples are invited again and again to receive their hearing and sight. Yet they clearly do not want the kind of suffering Messiah Jesus speaks of, and they do not understand what he means by "raised from the dead" (9:32). Though they are given insider status, though they have in their possession the key to the code, it remains a mystery to them. Such is the nature of the beast.

The question for the reader, looking at the end of Mark's Gospel, is whether the disciples ever in fact figure it out. Do they in the end crack the code? Or does it remain a mystery? For that matter, what is the reader to make of all this, particularly since Mark ends the entire story on a note of mystery and silence? Fortunately, Mark leaves some clues about how to crack what can be cracked of the code.

Foreshadowing, The Sign Of Quality Literature

The cartoon strip *Bloom County* once offered a facetious assertion of its place in the literary canon by working in comic bits that hinted at the next plot development, since "foreshadowing," Opus the Penguin assured us, "is the sign of quality literature," something you weren't going to get from Dagwood Bumstead or Beetle Bailey. Foreshadowing is also an attribute of ancient literature, and you'll find it in Mark. Mark foreshadows the resurrection of Jesus.

Such foreshadowing in the first half of Mark's story is subtle. The crowds speculate that Jesus manifests the power of resurrection: "John the baptizer has been raised from the dead; and for this reason these powers are at work in him" (6:14). Others see in him Elijah or one of the prophets (6:15). Herod, when informed of Jesus' deeds, agrees that "John, whom I beheaded, has been raised" (6:16). Soon after, Jesus takes a mysterious walk on the lake, where he appears to be a ghost (6:47-52); some scholars believe that this story was originally a resurrection appearance that Mark "misplaced"! That resurrection is possible Jesus demonstrates to the Sadducees from scripture later in the story (12:18-27).

Jesus becomes explicit about his own resurrection in the second half of Mark's story. At Caesarea Philippi, Jesus asks his disciples, "Who do people say that I am?" (8:27-33). They repeat the rumors the crowd has bandied about, that he is the resurrected presence of John, Elijah, or one of the prophets. When Jesus asks them, "Who do *you* say that I am?" Peter answers for the others in the words the reader has known from the beginning: "You are the Messiah." Jesus responds with the first of three explicit predictions of his death and resurrection: "Then he began to teach them that the Son of Man must undergo great suffering, and be rejected by the elders, the chief priests, and the scribes, and be killed, and after three days rise again" (8:31; cf. 9:31; 10:33-34). Even here, Jesus is slightly coy, referring to himself by the ambiguous title "Son of Man," an expression which means simply "human being," but also alludes to the mysterious heavenly figure appearing in the Book of Daniel. Only when he stands before the high priest at trial does he apply the words of Daniel to himself and explicitly admit to being the Messiah: "Again the high priest asked him, 'Are you the Messiah, the Son of the Blessed One?' Jesus said, 'I am; and "you will see the Son of Man seated at the right hand of the Power," and "coming with the clouds of heaven" ' " (14:61-62, quoting Daniel 7:13-14; Psalm 110:1). For now, Jesus keeps the foreshadowing shadowy.

The disciples, of course, are not present for Jesus' confession before the high priest. Indeed, as we have seen, they do not entirely understand Jesus' predictions of his resurrection, and they scatter when he is arrested (14:30; cf. 14:27). However, Jesus offers them (and us) hints that they will regroup around a resurrected Messiah. "After I am raised up," he tells them, "I will go before you to Galilee" (14:28). That the disciples will indeed meet Jesus in Galilee is confirmed by the young man at the tomb, when he tells the women, "But go, tell his disciples and Peter that he is going ahead of you to Galilee; there you will see him, just as he told you." Mark uses this twofold narrative prophecy to point beyond the end of his narrative; the writing ends, but the story does not. Foreshadowing extends Mark's story beyond its own confines. Though the text ends shortly after, with the silence of the women, the story carries on subtly in these words of Jesus (whom we have no reason to doubt) and in those of the young man (who is also a reliable witness). In fact, the reliability of the young man's witness is essential to the true ending of Mark's story. Without him, Jesus' future would die on the closed lips of the women.

I've Got You Covered

The women who visit the tomb are not in fact the first witnesses of the resurrection in Mark. That honor belongs to this young man in the white robe. But who, exactly, is he?

54

Conventional wisdom has it that, being dressed in white, he is an angel. Matthew's version makes it explicit: "An angel of the Lord, descending from heaven ... His appearance was like lightning, and his clothing white as snow" (Matthew 28:2-3). Luke speaks of "two men in dazzling clothes" (Luke 24:4). Mark's version is by comparison restrained; sitting in the tomb on the right side is simply "a young man (*neaniskos*), dressed in a white robe" (Mark 16:5). Do the clothes make the angel? Or is there some other reason this young man is dressed in white?

We might ask whether there are any other "young men" in Mark's story, and the answer would take us back to one of the most mysterious passages in the Gospel (so much so that the story was dropped from the other Gospels). When Jesus was arrested, all his disciples fled (14:50). Mark adds, "A certain young man (*neaniskos*) was following him, wearing nothing but a linen cloth. They caught hold of him, but he left the linen cloth and ran off naked" (14:51-52). Traditionally, this young man has often been identified as young John Mark, adding a touching bit of anonymous autobiographical reportage to the account passed down to him by Peter. Later scholarship, more dubious about the connection between this Gospel and Peter, has had even less convincing things to say about the young man; at best, he is seen as symbolic of the flight of the disciples, who must have felt stripped of all cover.

There is a bit of truth in both suggestions, if the young man in chapter 14 and the young man at the tomb are one and the same (and there is no other reference to a "young man" in Mark). The young man who flees naked could symbolize the community of disciples, Mark's own community, who did in fact despair and flee when Jesus' words about his arrest, suffering, and torture proved to be true. Later, the young man speaks for the whole community when he confesses, "He has been raised" (16:6), with special references to Peter and the rest of the Eleven (16:7). What has happened to him in the meantime? The experience of the resurrected Jesus. The young man foreshadows the experience of the disciples, who despite the fumbling doubt that plagues them throughout the story, and the final failure to stand with Jesus in his suffering, nevertheless, according to Jesus' own testimony, come to believe in One risen from the dead. No doubt the young man speaks for Mark and his audience as well.

The young man symbolizes the Markan community. This impression is reinforced by yet another Markan story, connected by subtle literary clues to the end of the Gospel. In chapter 5, Jesus comes across a demoniac in the country of the Gerasenes. Here is one naked among the tombs, seized by the enemy — in this case, a Legion of demons. When the people of that region hear that Jesus has transformed him, they find him sitting, clothed and in his right mind, and they become afraid, begging Jesus to leave them. He wishes to follow Jesus (i.e., to be a disciple), but Jesus tells him to go and tell what the Lord has done — the only healed person in the first half of the Gospel who is not told to keep quiet. The man does in fact proclaim his experience in the Decapolis — Gentile country (5:1-20). The parallels with the story of the young man are quite astounding; here too is one who was naked but now clothed and in his right mind, proclaiming his experience of the risen Lord — and if the young man is indeed symbolic of the (largely Gentile, traditionally Roman) Markan community, this proclamation will take place in Gentile country. The demoniac too becomes a model disciple for Mark's audience; they can indeed see Jesus again in Galilee (16:7), every time they read this story. They also see themselves.

So Mark's story pushes beyond itself. On its face, it ends with fearful silence. But those who crack the parabolic code and see beyond the story to the interpretation that Jesus himself provides (4:11, 34) know that the real ending is "Go, tell." That the disciples, even the women at the tomb, learned this lesson is not only foreshadowed, but implicit; else, there would have been no Gospel at all.

Fear And Trembling In Mark

So why does Mark leave us with fear, trembling, and amazement? More importantly, why does Mark leave us to puzzle out the real ending of the story on our own? I believe that for Mark, it's simply in the nature of the beast.

By leaving his story open-ended, Mark leaves us to fill in the blanks, not just about how the story ends, but how it carries on. How will we the readers respond to this story? With fearful silence, like the women? By fleeing, like the men? Or will we respond with the young man at the tomb and his Gerasene counterpart, and go, tell what we have seen, and what the Lord has done for us? The stark ending leaves the choice strictly to us.

For Mark, this is the only way the story can end. We're dealing with a mystery. Fear, trembling, puzzlement are inherent to the encounter, as his portrait of the disciples shows. Even those closest to Jesus do not fully understand what he is about. The disciples' example shows that humility before the mystery is prudent. Those who stood bravely before impending danger when it was only hypothetical proved spineless before the reality.

Lest we place too much emphasis on the transforming nature of the resurrection experience, remember that the young man was the only one who responded to the empty tomb with faith. The women see the same sight, hear the proclamation of the young man, are reminded of Jesus' own words on the subject, and are still overwhelmed by fear. Again, this is the nature of the beast. The presence of the divine is overwhelming. To come face to face with the fact of the empty tomb ought to humble us, if not silence us.

Though silence is the last word, the last command is "Go, tell." The warning of the ending is as strong as the promise, and opens the abyss as well as heaven. The final irony is tragic, a failure at the moment of success. The women cling to the strategy of concealment long past its time, long past the time Jesus himself had already opened the mystery to all comers with the words, "I am" (14:62). Despite the command to talk, the text ends with a blank.

Still, the promise of Galilee beckons. Will we go there to meet him? Will we join the one who was naked and terrorized by evil, yet is now clothed and in his right mind, proclaiming the risen Lord? Mark leaves the answer to us, and we shiver.

The Blank Last Page

Easter Day — March 30, 1997
Mark 16:1-8

The problem of preaching on Easter Day is that the congregation is filled with strange faces. Friends and family of regular members appear along with occasional visitors and those folk who come only on Christmas and Easter. The net effect is often that the preacher feels like the guest — what happened to the usual crowd in their usual places? Preachers use various strategies to address this mass of strangers. One old fundamentalist told me that this (along with Mother's Day) was when he gave them hellfire and brimstone, hoping to scare a few converts into the kingdom (the weak version of this tactic is to "welcome" the twice-a-year visitors with the unsubtle implication that they should show up more often). Another preacher once suggested that on these occasions, content was superfluous, and all that was called for was "a toast." I aim for somewhere in the middle — a sermon that does in fact proclaim the Good News of God but is fairly accessible. The reader can judge how well I have done the job. In this case, I took for a starting place not just a well-known movie, but a bit of then-recent and controversial scientific news. Note that the text-critical problem of the abrupt Markan ending is dealt with as a step in the argument of the sermon; it is in fact crucial to the overall development of the sermon's theme, not a quaint scholarly footnote. This sermon was preached at St. Luke's Episcopal Church in Katonah, New York.

———

Somewhere back in a civilization "Gone with the Wind," Miss Scarlett was having a baby.

Captain Butler about dropped his drink when they finally let him in to see his daughter.

And Miss Melanie said to Mamie, "Oh, the happiest days are when babies are born."

And so it's been through the ages.

New life brings a smile.

The baby may be crying but everyone else is laughing.

Only the old curmudgeon frowns on a spring day when the daffodils first peek out of the ground.

Winter is over and the grass is green and the trees begin to leaf, and it's hard to be sad.

The happiest days have always been the days of new life.

But well into the civilization of the "Brave New World," maybe we're not so sure anymore.

In the days of Dolly the Sheep, new life has grown a scary side.

We're not so happy until we know exactly where the baby comes from.

Test tube babies and *in vitro* fertilization may have given us pause.

But cloning has really opened up a can ...

One little ewe lamb has stirred up a whole nest of legal and ethical sheepdogs, not to mention a slew of bad jokes and comic strips.

All it took was one cloned sheep for us to see the dark side of new life, where you can't see what's coming, and you're not sure you're going to like it.

Of course, anyone who's seen the end of the movie knows that there's always been a dark side to the baby business.

Miss Melie doesn't make it when she tries for the second son, and she leaves Ashley and Rhett and Scarlett and all the others in tears.

Anyone who's had a troubled pregnancy, or given birth to a sick child, or had a miscarriage, knows that there's always been a dark side to new life.

It's something the women in Mark's Gospel knew —
Mary Magdalene, and Mary the mother of James, and Salome,
learned it the hard way, though not in childbirth, but on
the other side.
They were the women who according to Mark took the spices
to anoint the body of Jesus in a funeral ritual.
They had intended to follow the old customs all along, so they
made sure they followed when Jesus was taken down off
the cross and put in a tomb cut into the rock and given by
a shadowy benefactor named Joseph of Arimathea. They
watched as Joseph and his men put Jesus in the cave and
rolled the large stone in front of the opening.
In fact, they wondered on the way whether they would have
the strength among themselves to move that stone out of
the way.
But when they got there, according to Mark, the stone had
already been moved.
Inside the tomb they found not Jesus, but a mysterious young
man with a strange message, and a charge for these women:
"Go, tell Peter and the others."
It was too much for them.
If this was resurrection, if this was new life, God could keep
it.
The women ran out of the tomb in fear and terror and pure
disbelief.
Mark tells us that they did exactly the opposite of what they
were told to do.
They didn't say a word.
Mark uses an emphatic double negative to get point across:
"They said nothing to no one," he says, "for they were
afraid."

Which wouldn't be such a problem, except that *that* is the last line
in the Gospel of Mark.

Oh, I know that in your family Bible back home you've got a dozen or so more verses at the end of Mark.

But the ending you'll find in the King James Version and some other translations was written long after Mark was dead.

There are actually several different versions of an ending that different people at different times tried to tack on to Mark.

But the earliest manuscripts of the Gospel of Mark end here, at chapter 16, verse 8, and we now know that's pretty much where Mark wanted to end it.

Mark's Gospel ends in silence and fear, an enigma with no resolution, women who say nothing, who have been given the message of new life, but can see only its dark side.

Which of course is why we have all these other add-on endings to Mark.

No one wants to end on a sour note.

You don't want to remember the spring day that's rainy and cold and windy and blew all the flowers out of the garden.

The happiest days are when babies are born, Miss Scarlett, and if it wasn't that way we can at least tell the story that way, or at the very least, tell everyone that tomorrow is another day.

You can't leave those women silent and afraid, anymore than you can leave Jesus in the grave.

And there are reasons not to leave those women with their lips zipped.

For one thing, there's just plain logic.

They couldn't have been silent forever.

They must have told somebody, sometime.

Otherwise Mark would not have had a story to write.

It's just plain logic.

But there are also little hints that Mark has left behind in his story — subtle flecks in the narrative paint that tell us that

61

Mark wasn't all gloom and doom, that he was able to see something besides the fear and the terror and the silence, something other than the dark side of new life.

I'll point out one of the strangest and most subtle hints Mark left behind: The young man at the tomb.

Note that Mark never calls him an "angel." Everyone wants to make him an angel, but Mark never says that. Mark just has a young man clothed in a white robe sitting at the tomb with the message of new life: "He is not here; he is risen."

Who then is this mysterious young man?

Well, there's only one other "young man" in Mark's story. When Jesus was arrested at Gethsemane, Mark tells us, and only Mark of all the Gospels, there was a young man following him, dressed only in a linen cloth, and they tried to seize him, but the cloth came away in their hands, and he streaked away.

Like all the disciples, he fled, embarrassed and ashamed, and in this case, literally naked.

So what if the young man at the tomb is the same young man, once naked and confused and now clothed and in his right mind, once embarrassed like all the others but now the first to tell the good news?

If I'm right, this nameless young man is simply the original disciple, the first true convert, a representative of and a symbol for all the disciples, who though they have forsaken Jesus and fled, will soon meet him in Galilee and become his witnesses —

Members of a community of forgiveness, not perfection.

The mysterious young man is Every Disciple.

He's the message of Mark in a nutshell.

Why then does Mark leave us on such a downer?

Why no stories of Peter and the others in Galilee, no hint that the three women finally came out of hiding to tell their story?

Why does Mark leave us in the dark, with women in fear and terror saying nothing to no one?

Well, maybe he doesn't want us to get cocky.

There's nothing worse than believers that are too sure of themselves.

Mark could have left us sort of a warning.

But I'd like to suggest another reason.

Maybe Mark just means to leave the story open-ended.

And Mark leaves the story open-ended, because he doesn't know what *you* are going to do with it.

When you hear the story, when you walk into the empty tomb, what happens next?

Will you be like the young man and repeat the message you have been given?

Or will you run away in silence?

You see, Mark didn't know, couldn't know, what brought you to his story.

Mark didn't know you were going to be here today.

And Mark couldn't know and wouldn't care why you came today.

It doesn't make any difference, whether it's custom or pressure or simply tradition.

You could be the most devout person in the whole world who never misses a chance to go to church, or you could sit here squirming the whole time.

You could be one of those persons who dresses up on Easter to take Mom to church before the big meal, or someone who just wandered in off the street by accident.

Mark doesn't care.

Because Mark knows you're about to meet Jesus.

For Mark the resurrection isn't about empty tombs and parlor tricks. It's about responding to the living Jesus in faith.

We know that Christ is alive because Christ is alive with us,
we see Jesus in the faces sitting next to us, we live with
him in the stories we tell one another, in the bread and
wine we share. We have faith that Jesus is here with us.
If we believe in the new life, it's because we believe there's
someone once dead, now living with us.

And so Mark left the ending of his story up in the air, because the
ending is up to us to write.
The story is now ours to finish.
And Mark wants to know how you're going to fill in the blank.
The ending's up to you.
What happens next?

4. Preaching Resurrection In Luke

One Easter Season I sat down with an adult Bible class and a page copied out of Burton Throckmorton's *Gospel Parallels,* which arranges Matthew, Mark, and Luke in parallel columns for easy comparison. This day we looked at the empty tomb narratives. Step by step, I led them through the differences: the names and number of the women, the absence of Matthew's earthquake in either Mark or Luke, God's various personnel stationed at the tomb (an angel in Matthew, a young man in Mark, two men in dazzling clothes in Luke), the various responses of the women (silence in Mark, fear and joy in Matthew, remembrance in Luke). Most of all, I concentrated on the differences in the message delivered to the women: Mark's young man tells the women not to be amazed: "You seek Jesus of Nazareth, who was crucified. He has risen, he is not here; see the place where they laid him. But go, tell his disciples and Peter that he is going before you to Galilee; there you will see him, as he told you" (Mark 16:6-7). Matthew's angel says almost exactly the same thing, changing the word order a bit, exhorting the women not to be "afraid" (instead of "amazed"), and adding Jesus' resurrection to the message they are to deliver to the disciples. But Luke's two men speak quite differently, using few of the words in Matthew or Mark: "Why do you seek the living among the dead? Remember how he told you while he was still in Galilee, that the Son of Man must be delivered into the hands of sinful men, and be crucified, and on the third day rise" (Luke 24:5-7). I concluded the comparison of the three resurrection stories by saying that they were similar, but with significant differences.

One of the class members began to argue with me. "The differences are not significant," he said, and launched into an analogy with a traffic accident: a loud crash turns your head, there are two cars askew in the intersection, smoke rising from the dented hoods. When the cop comes to take the report, there are as many versions of the accident as there are witnesses: the light was green, the light was red, the first car hit the second, or vice-versa. "The fact remains that the accident happened. The wrecked cars are sitting right there. The differences between the witnesses are insignificant."

It's a common but unfortunate analogy. When the car accident case goes to court, the differences between the witnesses will be quite significant to someone's bank account — it will make a big difference whether the light was green or red, whether one car hit another. The judge will have to weigh conflicting testimony, in order to come to a decision. If there is no way to resolve the conflicting witness, the lawsuit may end in a draw. Applying a legal standard of evidence to the Gospel accounts would not be very satisfactory in the long run — the witnesses are no longer living, for one thing, and there is no way to cross-examine them.

The real question, when it comes to the differing Gospel accounts of the empty tomb, is "What *is* the significance?" We may indeed conclude that as far as the historical fact of an empty tomb, the differences are not particularly significant — all three accounts agree that women found the tomb empty and received a message that he had been raised from the dead. Those of more skeptical bent will try to make the case that the differences among the witnesses show that their testimony is inconsistent and cannot be trusted. Either way, a judgment cannot be made solely on the word of these three witnesses. The decision to believe in a risen Jesus cannot be decided on the empty tomb narratives alone. The risen Jesus is by definition still alive, and will encounter us outside the words of scripture — in prayer, in the community of his disciples, in the bread and wine that is his body and blood.

The significance of the various Gospel accounts of Jesus' resurrection is not the significance of historical fact, but of faith. The Gospels are not *history* but *story*. Each has shaped the traditions about Jesus in its own way. Luke in particular is not so much interested in disputing Matthew or Mark's facts as he is in expressing his own views on the significance of what has happened. Luke gives a different charge to the women at the tomb because of the way he understands Jesus' place in the whole scheme of God. Luke tells them to remember what they already know — what has already been revealed to them in the scriptures as taught by Jesus: that a prophet has been among them, and is about to come among them the second time.

Remember

I find a striking difference between the story of the empty tomb in Luke and that found in the other Synoptic Gospels (Matthew and Mark, who together with Luke are called "synoptic" because they are so similar and thus "see together," in contrast with John). The difference is found in the opening word of Luke's two men: "Remember" (Luke 24:6). Not, "Go, tell," as in Matthew and Mark, but "Remember." It's an easy point of entry for the preacher and teacher, because for most of us, a command to "remember" is a relief, compared with "go, tell." I'd much rather sit in my chair and remember, rather than go out into the wind and the cold and start telling. But Luke doesn't want to make it comfy for us — far from it. To "remember" is crucial to becoming what Luke expects disciples to be: witnesses to and ministers of the Word.

Luke's command is to "remember" because Luke writes the continuation of the biblical narrative. His narrative begins in Old Testament fashion, recounting the revelation to a barren old couple that they will receive the gift of miraculous birth. The priest Zechariah is serving faithfully in the temple when an angel of the Lord appears to him to announce the birth of a prophet (Luke 1:5-25). John is described in terms of the ancient Nazirites, and in terms of the prophet Elijah: "For he will be great in the sight of the Lord. He must never drink wine or strong drink; even before his birth he will be filled with the Holy Spirit. He will turn many of the people of Israel to the Lord their God. With the spirit and power of Elijah he will go before him, to turn the hearts of parents to their children, and the disobedient to the wisdom of the righteous, to make ready a people prepared for the Lord" (1:15-17). Already the story line is clear: God is about to visit the people of Israel, and Israel will soon face a choice whether to turn from disobedience to righteousness. As it turns out, John is just a preparatory prophet: the birth of Jesus is yet to be announced, and when it is, the language is far more glorious: "He will be great, and will be called the Son of the Most High, and the Lord God will give to him the throne of his ancestor David. He will reign over the house of Jacob forever, and of his kingdom there will be no end" (1:32-33). While the stories of John and Jesus run parallel, there is never any doubt that Jesus is superior.

Luke's language in these early chapters is filled with Old Testament forms and images concerning Israel and the prophets. For Luke, God has a divine plan, and the plan has been foretold. Mary speaks in Old Testament cadences when she declares that "from now on all generations will call me blessed" (1:48; her song of praise echoes that of Hannah in 1 Samuel 2:1-10). The prophets Simeon and Anna declare the future for Jesus; Simeon takes the child in his arms and says, "Master, now you are dismissing your servant in peace, according to your word; for my eyes have seen your salvation, which you have prepared in the presence of all peoples, a light for revelation to the Gentiles and for glory to your people Israel" (2:29-32). Zechariah in particular makes it clear that God's divine plan has been already made known in scripture (1:69-70).

Luke expressly refers to God's "plan" (*boule,* Luke 7:30; and often in Luke's companion volume, the Book of Acts, 2:23; 4:28; 5:38; 13:36; 20:27). More often, Luke uses the expression "it was necessary" (*dei*) in the sense of "it was ordained by God" (Luke 2:49; 4:43; 9:22; 13:33; 17:25; 21:9; 22:37; 24:7, 26, 44; Acts 1:16; 3:21; 4:12; 9:16; 14:22; 17:3; 23:11; 27:24). God's plan must be carried out; Luke is almost fatalistic in this belief. The source of his conviction is the Old Testament scriptures.

Over and over again, Luke reminds us that God's divine plan can be found in the scripture. Luke frequently refers to "what was written" (Luke 4:17; 18:31; 20:17; 21:22; 22:37; 24:44, 46) in the scriptures or "writings" (Luke 4:21; 24:27, 32, 45; Acts 1:16; 8:32,

35; 17:2, 11; 18:24, 28). He also refers explicitly to Moses, the Law, the Psalms, and the prophets (4:17; 18:31; 24:27, 44). The scriptures have foretold the suffering, death, and resurrection of the Messiah (9:22; 13:33; 17:25; 18:31-34; 22:37; 24:26-27, 44-46; Acts 2:23; 13:27-29; 17:2-3). More than that, they have laid down the overall pattern of Jesus' role in God's plan.

The plan is that of the prophet and the people. This is most clearly seen in the companion volume to the Gospel of Luke, the Book of Acts, in that long and strange speech given by Stephen just before he is pelted to death with stones by an angry crowd. Stephen, though chosen to minister to the mundane needs of the early Christian community (Acts 6:1-6), is described in stereo-typically Old Testament terms as a prophet: he is "full of grace and power" and does "great wonders and signs among the people" (6:8), since he is "full of faith and the Holy Spirit" (6:5). His preach-ing incurs the wrath of some Jews visiting from the hinterlands, who haul him before the Temple authorities and induce false wit-nesses to accuse him of blasphemy against the Temple and the Law of Moses (6:8-14). Stephen's reply, delivered with "the face of an angel" (6:15), i.e., as a messenger (*angelos*) sent from God, proves to be a long and apparently rambling reiteration of the story of the patriarchs and the Exodus from Egypt (7:2-53). Yet there is a plot and a structure to this speech that corresponds to Luke's own story (which is why he spends so much time on it). The story of the patriarchs must be told, because it is crucial to what is hap-pening to the people of Israel in the preaching of Stephen and the apostles. God gave a promise to Abraham, though the promise was not fulfilled for many years, until after Israel was sold into slavery into Egypt. God sent to captive Israel a prophet named Moses, who "was powerful in his words and in his deeds" (7:22). Moses was forced to flee Egypt after he killed an Egyptian in order to free an Israelite from oppression (7:23-24); here Stephen gives the story of Moses a crucial twist, because in his view (and Luke's), Moses was acting as a liberator (7:24-25), but he was not received as such: "He supposed that his kinsfolk would understand that God through him was rescuing them, but they did not understand" (7:25). In fact, the next day, the people reject him, saying, "Who made you a ruler and a judge over us?" (7:27), and he leaves for Midian (7:26-29). But God was not finished with Moses. He sends him to the people of Israel in Egypt a second time, now commissioned as a "ruler and liberator" (7:35) who, like Stephen and the other prophets of God, does "signs and wonders" (7:36). Moses describes himself as a "prophet," but most importantly for Luke, promises the people of Israel that "God will raise up a prophet for you from your own people, as he raised me up" (7:37) — in other words, God will raise up a prophet like Moses. Stephen gives the story of Moses a sad ending, telling the tale of the golden calf (7:38-43), which shows the propensity of a people unwilling to listen to their prophets. Then very quickly he brings the story up through Joshua and David and Solomon to the present day (7:44-48), when those standing in judgment on him have repeated the mistakes of Israel at Sinai: "You stiff-necked people, uncircumcised in heart and ears, you are forever opposing the Holy Spirit, just as your ancestors used to do. Which of the prophets did your ancestors not persecute? They killed those who foretold the coming of the Righteous One, and now you have become his betrayers and murderers" (7:51-52). Stephen's hearers respond to this word predictably, by doing exactly what he has accused them of (7:54-60).

It is clear that for Luke, God's plan is the plan set forth in the story of the prophet Moses, and in the prophet like Moses, Jesus. Like Moses, Jesus was sent twice to the people. At his first appearing, he was rejected, and in fact killed, but God called him out of the grave, and sent him again, this time through the agency of the new prophets of God, the Christian community (Acts 2:43; 5:12). The question is, will the people respond? Luke's answer is that the people are divided; in particular, the leaders of the people continue to reject the prophet Jesus and his disciple-prophets, but a good many of the people of Israel do respond to the message (e.g., Acts 2:41, 46; 5:14; 6:7; 9:31). The people of Israel are in fact reconstituted as the new body of those who have responded to the prophet like Moses (Acts 1:15-26). Once the message has been given to the people of Israel, God can now proceed with a new work, also foretold in the scriptures: the taking of the word of the prophet like Moses beyond Israel and to the Gentiles (Acts 10-28).

The theme of the prophet and the people echoes throughout Luke-Acts. Did you ever wonder why the people get so mad at Jesus when he speaks at the synagogue at Capernaum (Luke 4:14-30)? Like any faithful Jewish male, he stands to read from the scripture. He reads from Isaiah, "The Spirit of the Lord is upon me, because he has anointed me to bring good news to the poor. He has sent me to proclaim release to the captives and recovery of sight to the blind, to let the oppressed go free, to proclaim the year of the Lord's favor" (4:18-19). When he sits to teach, he claims the role of the prophet: "Today this scripture has been fulfilled in your hearing" (4:21). The crowd is at first complimentary, even amazed at the words that come from his mouth (4:22). But what he has to say next does not please them, because it is a direct indictment of their unbelief: "No prophet is accepted in the prophet's hometown" (4:24). Worse yet are the two examples Jesus chooses: Elijah and the widow of Zarephath, and Elisha and Naaman (4:25-27; cf. 1 Kings 17:1-6; 2 Kings 5:1-14); in each case, the prophet is sent not to his hometown, but actually to outsiders — to Gentiles, in both cases. Jesus' listeners are enraged and attempt to kill him, but he slips through them unharmed, to go and preach another day. Here is the Lukan story in a nutshell.

Another story that has puzzled readers, but becomes clearer in light of the Lukan theme of the prophet and the people, is Luke's Parable of the Pounds (Luke 19:11-27), which is quite different from Matthew's Parable of the Talents (Matthew 25:14-30). Many have thought that this parable deals with the early church's concern with Jesus' prolonged absence (the so-called "delay of the parousia" or Second Coming): why, asked the early Christians, have we waited so long for Jesus to return as promised and set things right? But when Luke says that Jesus' listeners "supposed that the kingdom of God was to appear immediately," he in no way indicates that these listeners were wrong in their expectation of the coming kingdom. What they failed to understand was that "the kingdom is among you" (Luke 17:21), in the person of the King himself, Jesus. That Jesus himself is Luke's king is clear from 19:12, "a nobleman went to a distant country to get royal power for himself and then return"; the allusion is to Jesus' ascension and future return (Acts 1:9-11; cf. the Davidic imagery applied to Jesus in Acts 2:32-35). The nobleman leaves despite the opposition already built up and openly declared against him (Luke 19:14). His return with royal power brings not financial gain (as in Matthew) but power: the rewards given to the good slaves include authority over cities (19:17, 19); here again, the allusion to the apostles' assumption of authority over the people in the Book of Acts is clear. In the end, the enemies of the king will be punished (Luke 19:27). Once again, Luke demonstrates his overall plot line: the prophet is sent to the people, rejected by some while others take on the work of the prophetic ministry, until the prophet comes again, this time with judgment on those who refuse to accept him. What is emphasized in this instance is that Jesus is more than just a run-of-the-mill prophet; when he returns, it is with royal power.

Thus, to get back to Luke's resurrection account, the women at the tomb have a lot to "remember." The most important thing the women and the other disciples can do at this crisis point is to "remember." "Remember how he told you, while he was still in Galilee, that the Son of Man must be handed over to sinners, and crucified, and on the third day rise again" (24:6-7). The two men (their "dazzling clothes" probably indicates that they are angels) give the women a concise summary of God's plan, as already reported to them by Jesus. Jesus has already told the disciples exactly what will happen according to God's plan; the words here echo Jesus' own words in 9:22, "The Son of Man must undergo great suffering, and be rejected by the elders, chief priests, and scribes, and be killed, and on the third day be raised." Note that the command to "remember" assumes that the women were in fact with Jesus in Galilee to hear these words; for Luke at least, there is no question that the women were disciples in their own right (cf. 8:1-3; 23:55). In fact, the women and not the male disciples become the first believers: Luke tells us that the women did remember (24:8) and returned to tell Peter and the others — but the men refused to listen! "These words seemed to them an idle tale, and they did not believe them" (24:11). Luke includes the story of Peter going to see the empty tomb for himself, but his trip does not issue in belief but amazement: "Then he went home, amazed at what had happened" (24:12; note that this verse does not appear in all ancient manuscripts of Luke, and may be a later addition based on John 20:3-10).

The women are to remember what Jesus said, but more than that — they are to remember that what Jesus taught them was the messianic interpretation of scripture. This is a lesson that must and will be repeated.

The Greatest Bible Study In The History Of The World
The resurrected Jesus himself does the teaching. On the road to Emmaus, two disciples meet a stranger (Luke 24:13-35). One of the disciples is named Cleopas (24:18); the other is unnamed, and for years readers have assumed that this "disciple" was male. But as we have already seen, women are disciples in their own right, according to Luke's Gospel, and most of Luke's male characters have a female counterpart (like the temple prophets Simeon and Anna, Luke 2:25-38). I like to think that perhaps the second disciple may have been Cleopas' wife (who else would he be traveling with?).

The stranger is identified to the reader as Jesus, but in his resurrected state he possesses a cloaking device: "Their eyes were kept from recognizing him" (24:16). Here is an instance of dramatic irony in Luke: the reader of his story knows something the characters in the story do not know, and cannot know until they have experienced what the reader already knows, which is the true story. The reader knows that the stranger is the risen Jesus; the two disciples will not be able to see him clearly until the climactic moment of the story.

The discussion between the stranger and the two disciples begins with the back story, as the stranger asks, "What are you discussing with each other as you walk along the way?" (24:17). Luke adds a poignant pause that shows the seriousness of the disciples' predicament, and that Jesus' death was in their minds no fantasy: in response to the stranger's question, "They stood still, looking sad" (24:17). The two disciples express their surprise that the stranger does not know about recent events (24:18); this is another instance of Lukan irony, since it is the disciples themselves who do not know the whole story, and so do not know the story at all. Their summary of what they do know recapitulates key Lukan themes: Jesus of Nazareth "was a prophet mighty in deed and word before God and all the people" (24:19), but the leaders of the people handed him over to the Romans for crucifixion (24:20), thus crushing the hopes that Jesus would set the people free (24:21). They add the new turn of events on the third day: the witness of the women at the tomb (24:22-24).

The stranger responds to their account with the verbal equivalent of a rap on the ear with a ruler; the disciples have been bad students, "foolish," and "slow of heart," since they have not learned their lesson from "all that the prophets have declared" (24:25). The suffering Messiah and his subsequent glory were matters of God's plan, divine necessity (*dei*, 24:26). So also was the conclusion of the story, witnessed by the women and those who followed them to the empty tomb; if the lesson from the prophets was not enough, the witness of the women and the others should have been enough. But since these recalcitrant students have still not learned their lesson, Jesus in the guise of the stranger tries to instill it in them once again: "Then beginning with Moses and all the prophets, he interpreted to them the things about himself in all the scriptures" (24:27). Luke makes sure we know that the lesson is comprehensive: it covers the entire span of the Hebrew Bible — Moses, the Prophets, and *all* the scriptures. It was the greatest Bible study in the history of the world.

Yet study alone is not enough. When the stranger attempts to go on ahead, the two disciples in the spirit of the ancient virtue of hospitality offer to share their bread and lodgings (24:29-30). This allows Luke to portray dramatically the experience of the risen Jesus in the Christian community, in such a way that no one could mistake how his disciples experience the continuing presence of Jesus. The description of the meal echoes that of the last supper (cf. 22:19): the stranger "took bread, blessed, and broke it, and gave it to them" (24:30). At that eucharistic moment, the disciples'

74

eyes are opened, and they recognize the stranger as Jesus (24:31). Only the experience of the risen Jesus in the breaking of the bread allows them to acknowledge the truth of his teaching: "Were not our hearts burning with us while he was talking to us on the road, while he was opening the scriptures to us?" (24:32). The story depicts the Lukan resurrection experience in a nutshell: the risen Lord is known in the messianic teaching of the scripture, and in the sharing of the eucharistic meal. It is important to note that however important the experience of the resurrected may be to Luke, he shows it to be a fleeting, ephemeral encounter; Jesus vanishes from their sight as soon as they recognize him. Throughout Luke's resurrection narratives, Jesus appears only to leave again, because he is not subject to human will, nor can he be pinned down to any human agency; the risen Jesus is in fact present in the Holy Spirit, which, as John puts it, "blows where it will" (John 3:8). Luke does not give comfort to those who would claim exclusive possession of the risen Christ.

The recognition of Jesus in the breaking of the bread results in renewed witness. The two disciples return to Jerusalem despite the late hour (Luke 24:33). There they report their entire story (24:35), only to find that in their absence Jesus has appeared to Simon Peter (24:34, a story otherwise untold, but cf. 1 Corinthians 15:5). True recognition of the risen Jesus always prompts one to share the news, in Luke's view. Just to solidify their recognition and witness, Jesus then appears to the entire gathered assembly (Luke 24:36-49).

I once was telling this story as part of a sermon to a small congregation, and I invited them to make the connection between the story and the Church's eucharistic practices for themselves. "What does this story remind you of?" I asked. One person in the back row blurted out, "A fairy tale." It was the most blatant expression of disbelief I have ever experienced in a church (the person later covered up by saying, "It's a fairy tale to think that anyone invites a stranger home anymore"). But the person had a point. The story on the face of it is wildly improbable. It is indeed a fairy tale, apart from the continuing experience of eating with Jesus, which for Luke provides proof of Jesus' new life.

75

It's Fishy

Luke addresses the skeptics. He pictures Jesus showing his hands and feet — not to prove he was crucified (Luke doesn't explicitly mention a nailing to the cross; it is possible that his picture may have been of someone roped rather than nailed to the crossbar) but to prove he was corporeal (24:39-40). Similarly, his eating of a piece of fish proves that he was not, as they supposed, a ghost (24:41-43). Jesus reassures them that he is exactly what he seems to be: "See that it is I myself" (24:39).

Interestingly, Luke shows that the realistic response to all this involves a certain amount of skepticism. They "disbelieved for joy," and were "still wondering" when he ate the fish (24:41). Luke delineates a progression of emotional reactions, as the disciples become progressively assured that this is no fairy tale, and no illusion. Fear (24:37, cf. 24:5) turns to wonder (24:41, cf. 24:12), and eventually to the unadulterated joy that finds its voice in worship (24:53).

The disciples reach the final stage of worship only as they see him ascend to heaven that very day (24:50; inexplicably, Luke depicts a different sequence in Acts, where Jesus stays a full forty days teaching the disciples before leaving; in the Gospel, the ascension takes place on the day of resurrection). They worship only after they have had a full explanation of the matter. Thus Jesus repeats the teaching given to the two disciples on the road to Emmaus (24:44-49).

For Luke, the conviction of the resurrection involves the continued experience of the risen Jesus in the community. The experience is mediated by teaching; in particular, by the teaching of the Old Testament scriptures interpreted by and about the Messiah. The experience also involves a shared meal (24:30, 42-43). The experience of his own community is for Luke rooted in the experience shared by those first disciples. To believe otherwise is to be "foolish" and "slow of heart" (24:25).

Yet the rap of the ruler on the ear is light. The first disciples, too, were slow to believe, slow to learn, slow to perceive the truth standing in front of them. While Luke in the end leaves no room for skepticism, he allows that disbelief is an appropriate response along the road to faith.

Second Verse, Same As The First

The teaching of Jesus which ends Luke's Gospel provides a transition to Luke's second volume. Reiterating Luke's main themes, Jesus' final speech also points ahead to the story that is to come (24:44-49), a story which follows much the same pattern as the story which has been told so far.

Again, we hear that all of this has been told before. The messianic teaching of scripture is paramount, and here nothing new is added: "These are my words that I spoke to you while I was still with you" (24:44). The teaching is comprehensive, covers the entire scripture, and involves the fulfillment of prophetic promise: "Everything written about me in the law of Moses, the prophets, and the psalms must be fulfilled" (24:44). Jesus again teaches them the basics. Luke makes it clear that a true understanding of all this requires not just the experience of the risen Jesus but his active mediation: "He opened their minds to understand the scriptures" (24:45). True understanding of the scripture comes only through the risen Lord. Once again in Luke, faith requires not only the experience of being with Jesus, but his own interpretative Word.

Luke summarizes the teaching for the sake of the reader (24:46-49). Again, the suffering and vindication of the Messiah are emphasized (24:46). But the summary is decidedly forward-looking. In the name of the Messiah, repentance and forgiveness of sins is to be proclaimed (24:47). The disciples themselves are to be the witnesses (24:48). Luke thus indicates that their future role is of one piece with their training (cf. 9:1-2; 1:2). Yet his wording anticipates the story of the Book of Acts. "Repentance" (*metanoia*) was part of the message of John the Baptist (Luke 3:3, 8), but rarely found on Jesus' own lips (only at 5:32; 15:7; the verb form is found more often, 10:13; 11:32; 13:3, 5; 15:7, 10; 16:30; 17:3-4); the disciples, however, will often speak of *metanoia* in their preaching (Acts 5:31; 11:18; 13:24; 19:4; 20:21; 26:20; in the verb form, Acts 2:38; 3:19; 8:22; 17:30; 26:20). Forgiveness of sins (*aphesis hamartion*) likewise is found on the lips of John the Baptist (Luke 3:3), Zechariah (1:77), and from Jesus in a scriptural quotation (4:18), but it figures much more often in the preaching in Acts (Acts 2:38; 5:31; 10:43; 13:38; 26:18; the verb form *aphiemi*

77

is used in the sense "forgive" in Luke 5:20-24; 7:47-49; 11:4; 12:10; 17:3-4; 23:34; Acts 8:22).

The proclamation of repentance and forgiveness is to be carried "to all nations, beginning with Jerusalem" (Luke 24:47). The universal mission — to the Gentiles, non-Jewish peoples, as well as to Jews — has been hinted at often in Luke, and it will be only gradually implemented in Acts. Simeon sounds the theme when he looks at the infant Jesus as he says, "My eyes have seen your salvation which you have prepared in the presence of all the peoples" (note the plural), because this child is "a light for revelation to the Gentiles" as well as the glory of Israel (Luke 2:30-32). John the Baptist claims that "All flesh shall see the salvation of God" (3:6). Jesus angers his first synagogue audience, at his hometown of Nazareth, by citing with approval the ministries of Elijah and Elisha to Gentiles, and implying that he himself would find a better reception among Gentiles (4:16-30). Indeed he does find a more hospitable reception among some Gentiles (the Centurion, 7:1-10; the Gerasene Demoniac, 8:26-39) than he does from his own people (cf. the lament over Jerusalem, 13:31-35). In the Book of Acts, the disciples are commissioned to witness to Jesus "in Jerusalem, in all Judea and Samaria, and to the ends of the earth" (Acts 1:8); however, the actual spread of the mission to the Gentiles involves a long, complicated, Spirit-led process (see especially Acts 10-15).

Jesus also tells the disciples that they are soon to receive "the promise of the father," which will result in their being "clothed with power from on high" (Luke 24:49). Jesus' elliptical statement is clarified at the beginning of the Book of Acts, where the "promise of the Father" is equated with the prophecy of John the Baptist that "you will be baptized by/with the Holy Spirit not many days from now" (Acts 1:4-5). Again, the coming of the Holy Spirit to empower the disciples' witness is hinted at in Luke, and made explicit in Acts. In teaching on prayer, Jesus assures the disciples that the Father will give them the Holy Spirit (Luke 11:13), which is the same Spirit that empowers Jesus himself (3:21-22; 4:1-15, 18-19; 10:21). The Spirit, Jesus promises, will give them courage to speak under fire (Luke 12:11-12; cf. Acts 4:1-22; 5:12-42). In

Acts, Luke dramatizes the giving of the Spirit at Pentecost and makes this scene the grand opening of the disciples' new mission (Acts 2). Throughout Acts, the Spirit functions primarily as the force that enables the disciples to witness to Jesus. One can hardly turn a page in Acts without stumbling across a reference to the Spirit's empowerment of the disciples' witness. While Jesus does appear in person on occasion in the Book of Acts, (Acts 7:55-56; 9:1-9, 27), for the most part the risen Lord will be with the disciples in a new and more powerful way, in the form of the Spirit.

The Gospel's final scene leaves these disciples ready and waiting in Jerusalem. Jesus is taken from them into heaven in the middle of a blessing (Luke 24:50-51). Finally, the disciples make the correct response to what they have seen and heard: they worship him (24:52). Returning to Jerusalem, they go to the temple to continue their worship and await the next stage of their mission with and for the risen Lord (24:52-53).

Bean Bag

Easter Day, Year C — Luke 24:1-10
April 16, 1995

This sermon was preached at Emmanuel Episcopal Church, a small parish in Quakertown, Pennsylvania, a working-class town located south of Bethlehem. This particular sermon was preached at the 8:00 a.m. service only, since the main service at 10:00 a.m. that day featured a children's sermon; the 8:00 crowd was a small but faithful group that preferred their worship straight and to the point — no music, no fuss, no frills, and generally shorter sermons (this one being about eight minutes long, as opposed to the ten-to-fifteen-minute sermons I usually preached at the later service). People often mistakenly use the term "homily" for this kind of sermon, thinking the "-ly" ending denotes something smaller ("homily" is actually derived from a Greek word and means the same thing as the Latin-derived "sermon"); I resist calling it a "sermonette," in deference to the old saw, "Sermonettes make Christianettes." Call it simply, in honor of those eight o'clockers, the "no-frills sermon."

My approach to the shorter sermon in this case was to cut the words I might have used in a fuller development of the theme, since the sermon left less time for people to think things through. I limited use of examples and illustrations (and as a rule I eliminate jokes from this kind of sermon — eight o'clockers rarely laugh; it's too early in the morning, and there aren't enough of them). I did not cut examples entirely, however, so that the people would have something contemporary to hang on to. In my use of both biblical material and modern examples, I was fairly direct; here I flat out drew conclusions (such as calling the beans a "symbol") that in a longer sermon I would have led people to. Yet it was important to retain some of the allusive power of the stories, or else the congregation would have too little to occupy their minds. In shortening the sermon time, I was counting on an aspect of familiarity, the connection of the theme to the behavior of that particular congregation; these faithful people knew and lived the

80

words I was saying, so I hoped to be articulating their own week-in and week-out experience and placing it in a broader context.

My thanks to my wife Nancy for suggesting the final story.

"Remember."

That's what the two strange men said to the women.

"Remember."

That may not seem like much. A bit of string tied around the finger.

But that's all they needed. "Remember."

There is no doubt about the credentials of the women.

Anyone who says that Jesus didn't have any women disciples hasn't read the Gospel of Luke. Luke makes it very clear that a large group of women came with him from Galilee, and they supported him and the others, and made his mission possible. They were disciples.

And they were witnesses. They were there, watching from a distance, when he hung on the cross. They were there when the soldiers pulled him down, there when Joseph of Arimathea put him in the rock-hewn tomb. They were there, they saw it all with their own eyes — Mary Magdalene, Joanna, Mary the mother of James, and all the rest.

And they were there early that morning, when they looked into the open mouth of the cave to see that it was empty.

But that does not yet mean, according to Luke, that they believed.

Instead, Luke says, they were "perplexed." They didn't understand. They just didn't get it.

So the message from the two strangers bordered on scolding: "Why do you seek the living among the dead? Don't you remember?"

It was the same way with the male disciples back at the house. When the women finally came running in with the news,

81

they didn't believe it either. Luke tells us that the men thought it was a joke, or a fantasy. An idle tale, Luke tells us.

What was missing were the words of Jesus.

"Remember." "Remember how he told you, while he was still in Galilee, that the Son of Man must be handed over, and crucified, and rise again."

You see, the magic here is what a priest friend of mine calls "deep magic." It's not just a wave of the wand, abracadabra, watch me pull a rabbit out of my hat. An empty tomb is an empty tomb, who knows what happened here? Doesn't prove a thing.

The deep magic takes place over time. It must be remembered.

I sometimes hear from people who don't belong to the church, but they want me to do a baptism or a wedding. I always ask them, "Why do you want to get married, or have the baptism, or whatever?" And they usually say, "Because we want God's blessing."

I always have to say, "I can do no magic."

The blessing isn't a wave of the hand, a few words from a book.

The blessing is being here, week after week, year in and year out, letting the words wash over you and soak in.

The blessing is having something to remember.

Over the course of time, it does change you.

As it changed the women, once they remembered his words.

As it would change Peter, James, John, and all the others.

It changed one woman I know. She came to church like a lot of people. Kids in school, time to get them religion. It's not so bad just to sit for an hour. Nothing on TV Sunday morning anyway. This is a woman of no particular virtue, never done anything in her life she didn't have to do.

But the more she sat there in the church, the less she was able to just sit.

She saw a notice one day in the church bulletin that the soup kitchen needed donations. She went to the grocery store that afternoon and bought a big bag of beans. But as she was walking out to the car, the bag fell to the parking lot, and the beans poured out all over the pavement.

But she didn't mind. She saw the beans pouring out of the bag as symbols of the love that was beginning to pour out to her, the love already pouring out from her. And she knew that there was more where that came from.

She went back inside and bought another bag of beans.

There is more where that came from. Much more. The love keeps coming and coming and coming from a Lord who is not among the dead but among the living.

All we need do to get that love is to show up and let it soak in.

Take A Meeting

Easter 3, Year B — Luke 24:36-48
April 13, 1997

Here is another example of a shorter sermon, almost staccato in its approach to language and story. Words, sentences, and examples have been pared down to essentials. One might ask, then, what the joke is doing at the beginning of the sermon. It's a good question, because a sermon should never contain jokes unless there is a good reason (and no, "just for a laugh" is not a good enough reason. I once heard someone suggest that the preacher should throw a joke into a sermon every five minutes or so, "just to keep people awake." But what does that say about the rest of the sermon? By all means, keep people awake, but keep them awake throughout — with vivid language and interesting content!). The reason for this particular joke is that it sets the stage: It raises the issue of asking something of God, in order to help the readers identify with the disciples, who ask something of Jesus. Once identified with the disciples, the hearers are then prepared to identify with the mission they share with those disciples.

This sermon was preached to a handful of folk at St. Luke's in Katonah, New York, a small but diverse congregation in a small town, at the 8:00 a.m. service, where they like it short and sweet. And yes, the exception proves the rule — they did laugh at the joke.

So a man walks into church one day and starts talking to God.

"God," he says, "is it true that a million years to you is like a second?"

And God says yes, it's true, a million years is like a second.

And the man says, "So a million dollars — that would be like a penny."

And God says yes, that's right, a million dollars is like a penny.

So the man says, "God, could I have a penny?"

And God says, "Sure. Just a second."

So when the genie comes with the three wishes, what do you ask
for?
A million bucks?
World peace?
A cure for cancer?
Or do you get real smart, and ask for unlimited wishes?

In light of that sort of wisdom, the disciples in Luke's Gospel seem
a bit, well, shortsighted.
Here you've got the risen Jesus standing before you in the
flesh, and what do you ask for?
A million bucks?
World peace?
A cure for cancer?
No. You ask him to take a bite of trout.
Talk about anticlimactic!
The biggest news in the history of the world turns into an ordi-
nary lunch.
The God of the universe orders takeout.
Here you have the genie with the three wishes, and all you can
think of is your stomach.

But this lunch is more important than you might think.
The issue is whether Jesus really *is* standing before them in
the flesh.
It could be a ghost, a fantasy, a vision.
It could be a device of the devil.
Is Jesus really here, or is it a trick of the light, a phantasmal
irreality?

And so Jesus takes a bite of the fish, just as he ate it with them and
5,000 others on a green meadow in Galilee.

85

He is as concrete and tangible as a piece of fish, as real as a
bite of bread.
He is flesh and blood.

And he is the same Jesus who died on the cross.
The risen Lord is the crucified man.
His hands and his side are proof enough of that.
This is no ghost standing before them, but a resurrected, cru-
cified Messiah.
Their joy mixed with unbelief moves toward pure joy.

Jesus' next move seems a little less logical.
He doesn't do what we would do.
He doesn't call a press conference.
He doesn't stage a march on Jerusalem.
There will be no headlines, bold print, all caps, three-inch type:
"Jesus Alive."
He doesn't work like that.
Rather, he sits them down to a Bible study.
Not new material, mind you, but a review.
He has already told them in his own words how everything
written in the Law of Moses and the Prophets and the
Psalms is fulfilled in him.
The future is the past, already written — how the Messiah
must suffer and rise, and repentance and forgiveness of
sins is proclaimed to all the nations.
"And you," he says as he points around the room, "you are my
witnesses to all this."
"It's in your laps now."
All they needed was someone to explain it to them, to embody
it for them.
Jesus is the true interpreter of scripture.
And he says that the scriptures point to him.
Then he turns around and points to us.

Because in so many ways, it's so much the same for us.

It is the same for us.

No, we don't have Jesus standing before us in the flesh.

But we have the bread which is his body, the wine that is his blood.

We still meet the risen Jesus at the table.

And no, we don't have Jesus in the pulpit, interpreting all things in the scriptures concerning himself.

But we tell the same stories. We read the same Bible.

And we pay attention to what Jesus says about the scriptures.

We listen in as Jesus points the way.

The community still meets the risen Christ in the word and at the table.

We still prepare ourselves to spread the news about repentance and forgiveness of sins to all the nations.

We are still witnesses.

And it's not a big deal —

It's not a million bucks.

It's not a bid for world peace.

It's not a cure for cancer.

But nonetheless, it may well be, that this meeting — this congregation, this celebration of word and table — this may well be the most important meeting going on at this hour on the face of the earth.

Coming Around The Corner

Easter 3, Year B — Luke 24:36b-48
April 17, 1994

I admit I have mixed feelings about the preacher telling personal stories in sermons. On the one hand, I am all for stories, and the richest stories are often drawn from one's own life. They are sure-fire ways to introduce into the sermon the all-important connection between the gospel and a real person who lives a real life, lest the message seem too abstract, or the examples too artificial. Personal stories also create a great sense of intimacy between preacher and congregation: faces brighten, eyes light up, people say, "We like getting to know you."

This gets us to the other hand: it is precisely because of this kind of intimacy that I have become wary of the preacher's personal stories. All too often, the "I" story gets in the way of the gospel message; the sermon stops being a message about God, as the personality of the preacher takes over. This is particularly true where the story casts the preacher in a light either unfavorable or too favorable, if the story is about the preacher's failure or tragedy ("Oh, our poor pastor, we'll have to take care of her!") or the preacher's success, good fortune, or triumph ("Our pastor is the greatest!"). The personal story in the sermon can thus be quite manipulative, and if exposed to a steady diet of it, people may respond accordingly ("There she goes again — she needs a therapist, not a congregation." "If I hear one more story about how he saved somebody, I'm going to scream!").

One solution to this dilemma is for the preacher to be very careful about telling stories where he or she is either the hero or the goat. Stories that puff up the preacher or are in danger of becoming ploys for the hearers' sympathy are best left aside. There are lots of other personal stories. One need not be afraid of using the word "I" in a sermon, but stories should focus not on the "I" but elsewhere. However, I've found that even so, these kinds of personal stories can be a distraction; I once told a story about a family Christmas gathering that in no way centered on myself, but the only response I got afterwards was, "What city did your family live in?" Face it, people are always going to be curious about the personal lives of clergy, and there's nothing wrong with that, but you don't want it to get in the way of your proclamation. A possible way to avoid even this kind of irrelevancy is to recast the story in the third person — not "I was walking down the street one day, and I ..." but "There was a woman walking down the street one day, and she...." This way, you can tell the story without *you* getting in the way. It also gives you a good gauge on how relevant and effective the story is — if it loses *all* its power when cast in the third person, then perhaps that power came from somewhere other than God. And yes, there may be people who nod their heads, smile, and say, "Oh, we knew it was you all along!" but that's okay — it's their conclusion, not something you hit them over the head with.

All that being said, there are a few times in one's life when you can hardly ignore what has happened to you during the week, and the links between life and gospel become most obvious, most difficult, most profound. At such times the preacher can hardly stand up and preach a disembodied gospel. This sermon followed one of those weeks in my life. It was preached at St. George's Episcopal Church, Pennsville, a small congregation in rural New Jersey, who sent me quite a few sympathy cards, and also, I hope, heard God's gospel in this message.

As many of you know, my father died last Sunday.

    On Monday, my brothers, my mother, and I went to the funeral home, and picked out a nice metal box for his ashes, and an inexpensive but attractive combustible casket for his body.

    On Tuesday, we went back to see his body in the casket.

    On Wednesday, we tried to put his ashes in the ground, but it was raining, and the hole filled with muddy water. We left the metal box with the man from the cemetery, who told us he would bury it as soon as the ground was dry.

Still, after the funeral, my mother said that she expected to see him walk around the corner any time now, open up the car door, get in, and say, "Let's go home."

We all expected him to walk around the corner any time.

Something that would never happen.

But suppose it did?

A hallucination, or a ghost?

We'd be scared, confused.

Even convinced of the reality, we'd be dizzy.

Our only reaction could be joy, mixed with disbelief, mixed with wonder.

Which is precisely the reaction Luke gives the disciples.

When Jesus comes and stands among them, and says, "Peace be with you."

They do not chime in together, "And also with you."

No. They are startled and terrified. They think of ghosts and spirits.

And when he shows them his hands and his feet, they wonder and disbelieve for pure joy.

And when he puts a piece of broiled fish in his mouth, they are simply amazed.

After all, the disciples were nothing if not human.

And once you've seen the body in the casket, you don't expect to see it again.

You certainly don't expect to have it to the house for dinner.

Nor do you invite it for a lecture series.

But the risen Jesus of Luke's Gospel goes on to conduct the greatest Bible study in the history of the world.

"He opened their minds to understand the scriptures," Luke says.

Because it is oh-so-important for Luke that everything has a purpose in the mind of God.

90

"Thus it is written, that the Messiah must suffer,

"That he will rise from the dead,

"That repentance and forgiveness of sins will be proclaimed,

"That *you* are witnesses," he says.

Thus it is written, because God wants it that way.

All the pieces of this puzzle interlock somewhere deep within the Deity.

Christians believe in Resurrection.

Not resuscitation, nor reincarnation.

Jesus is not a ghost, nor a spirit.

You can't get in touch with him by consulting your crystals, not in this nor in any previous life.

He is a resurrected body, as concrete and tangible as a piece of fish.

And to be with him is as real as biting a piece of bread.

We humans need the physical, the touching.

Just as you can never really be sure that he is dead unless you see him in the casket, unless you feel the cold metal of the box about to go in the ground.

So the disciples could never really believe that he was risen, unless they had seen his hands and his feet, and watched him eat a piece of broiled fish.

And we who have never seen him, never touched him, still need the tactile.

Which is why Jesus gives us bread and wine in memory of him.

Still, bread and wine alone are not enough.

Because we need not just the event, but also the interpretation.

We need to make meaning out of events, to press the colored cardboard pieces of the puzzle together.

Because when the doctor tells us what it is, at least we know, and we can deal with knowing — it's just a little swelling in the muscle, take some Tylenol, that'll bring it down.

But not to know — could it be a sprain, or is it arthritis? Pain without interpretation is unbearable.

And so Jesus interprets his words and his scriptures to the disciples.

Jesus interprets himself through the scriptures as he sits at table with his friends.

Just as we read his words, his scriptures, every time we sit at his table.

And we say to each other, "The Body of Christ, the Bread of Heaven." "The Blood of Christ, the Cup of Salvation."

Those of us who were not there, who did not light the fire for the fish or clean up the plates — we still need the touch, we still need the meaning.

And so we break bread as he taught us, we read the scriptures that speak of him, and we remember his words.

We live surrounded by death.

The dead in their many varieties encircle us.

Some of the names make the headlines each week: this last week, the rock star Kurt Cobain, the writer Ralph Ellison, and Betty Furness, who for years and years sold us Westinghouse refrigerators.

Sometimes we just get the numbers: five in a burned Philadelphia rowhouse, 26 in downed helicopters in Iraq, hundreds, thousands, even tens of thousands over the years in a place we can barely find on the map called Rwanda.

And sometimes just one name that stands out among the others: my father's obituary amid twenty others in alphabetical order in *The Indianapolis Star*.

It doesn't take much looking to see oh-so-clearly pain and suffering and death.

But you can't avoid death, if you believe in resurrection.
He showed his hands and feet, he ate the fish, to prove that the one who died is the one who rose.
Easter is forever joined to Good Friday, and you can't have the new life of God without the cross.
The risen Christ is the same Jesus who died, and died horribly.
You are witnesses of these things, he says.
Which does not mean that all we do is talk about it.
You are witnesses, he says, and that means you witness in *your* hands and feet.
He calls us to live as he did: to live for others.
And living for others is always, inevitably painful.
But if there's anything we learn from the example of Jesus, it's that pain has a purpose.
We don't call it the Cup of Salvation for nothing.
Pain is bearable when it has meaning; if we can touch our wounds, it is only because Jesus has given them a name.

Yet just beyond our touch is the place where we live with Him.
Just beyond the combustible casket and the metal box, the muddy hole waiting to take ashes to ashes, and dust to dust.
We believe in the resurrection of the dead: which is to say, that the last word is not spoken at the funeral home. The death that surrounds us does not hold us under siege.
We believe in the resurrection of the dead, and lacking for the moment his hands and his feet and his mouth, we touch bread and wine, and we mouth his words.
And we talk of a life just beyond our reach.
A place beyond death, beyond the wounds, the shedding of blood.
A life which makes sense of that blood as the Cup of Salvation.

Disbelieved For Joy

Easter 3, Year B — Luke 24:36b-48
May 7, 2000

Christian preachers need to live in the real world. In the fake preacher's world, the congregational "we" is always faithful, always believing, always knows where we are in the church year, and remembers every Bible story and article of faith by heart (by contrast, the preacher's "you" usually embodies less desirable traits). In the real world, most people believe in God three or four days out of seven, when they think about it. I think it's important for preachers not to pretend to be any more certain of things than they really are, or at least to open the sermon up to the possibility that one could have another point of view. This is not so much a matter of defending the faith (or not) as it is a strategy for conveying the faith; humility needs to have a role in preaching, particularly where belief can be fragile ground. The subject of resurrection gives us an obvious point of entry to the mind of the skeptic. Jesus himself had to "open the minds" of certain skeptics he encountered among the disciples, according to Luke. This sermon takes Luke's notion that discipleship means witness to the death and resurrection of Jesus, and applies it to a present congregation that, on its good days, continues to experience Jesus as mysteriously alive.

This sermon is organized around a cluster of ideas and images that recur throughout. The opening stories resonate through the whole, and not just because of the recurring theme of doubt. I introduced the physicist in the second story (courtesy of the *New York Times*) in order to make use of the image of atomic particles several times later in the sermon. This "image grid" (I owe the term to David Buttrick) helps establish the main theme in the ears of the hearers. Similarly, the recurring verb "to know" in contrast with "faith" helps highlight the theme.

One of my favorite devices for ending a sermon is to tell a story. Sometimes the stories serve as parables, giving the listeners something that I hope will linger in the mind long after the actual words of the sermon have faded. The final story here introduces a new image that sums things up and leaves the hearers with a sense, literally, of motion. Thanks to Melanie Pepper for contributing this story.

This sermon was preached at Grace and St. Peter's Episcopal Church in Hamden, Connecticut, a very diverse group of people living in a small town outside of New Haven. The congregation ranged from wealthy to middle-class, black professionals to white blue collar workers, Yale professors to illiterates, all of whom share a penchant for worship and preaching. After this sermon, one self-described skeptic said, "I'm almost eighty years old, and I've been waiting almost eighty years to hear this sermon."

The little Jewish boy came home from the synagogue.

"What did you study today?" said his mother.

"Israel at the Red Sea," he said.

"And what happened to Israel at the Red Sea?" she asked.

"It was great," he said. "Moses and the people were chased by the Egyptian army and backed up against the water with no escape. So Moses got on his walkie-talkie and called in the Israeli air force, fighters and bombers flew in, and the Egyptians were routed."

"Is that *really* what they told you at the synagogue?" she said.

"No," he said, "but if I told you what they *really* said, you'd never believe me."

Robert L. Park is a professional skeptic.

By day he works as a physicist at the University of Maryland.

But what he's really known for is doubt. He exposes health scams, bad science, and bogus claims about the supernatural. He's the kind of guy who shines the light on companies that label salt water as a health supplement and sell it for $34.95 a bottle.

95

Robert Park started young. When he was twelve, he went to his minister and began to question some of the things he had heard in Sunday school. "It just seems illogical ..." he began to say.

But the minister interrupted him and said, "You know, you can go to hell just as quick for doubting as for stealing."

And on that day, a great mind was lost to the church forever.

I personally am not so scared of doubt, as I am of credulity.

I worry about the people who buy those expensive bottles of salt water for their health.

I worry more about the people who sell it.

I remember a class once where we were talking about the resurrection of Jesus.

One person said, "I *know* that God raised Jesus."

I was shocked. "You *know*?" I said. "How can you *know* something that is by definition unknowable, something that is an article of faith? The problem with the verb 'to know' is that there is no humility there. And if faith is anything, it is humble. If you simply *know,* what room is there left for faith?"

It seems to me that a lot of the problems in this world are caused by people who simply *know*.

It ought to be hard to believe.

Resurrection is like one of those impossible puzzles in physics, where the particle can be in two places at the same time, or where measuring one particle changes the properties of another.

Resurrection is at least that mind-boggling, and more.

With the resurrection of Jesus, we've moved from the realm of theorem to that of mystery.

This is the difference between a puzzle and a mystery: Puzzles can be solved. Mysteries have to be lived with.

96

Resurrection is a mystery, and it ought to be hard to believe.
We ought to be constantly on the verge of chucking it.
Otherwise, we haven't taken it seriously.

Look at the disciples in Luke's Gospel.
When they saw Jesus alive, did they say, "I know"?
They were startled and frightened. They looked for alternative
explanations: "Maybe it is a ghost," they said.
And they had proof!
They saw his hands and feet; they could reach out and touch
him.
They saw him eat a piece of fish. Ghosts do not eat.
And still, Luke tells us, "They disbelieved for joy, and wondered."

It's not until he opened their minds that they really understood.
The experience required teaching.
So he told them everything that was written about him in Moses
and the Prophets and the Psalms.
It was the greatest Bible study in the history of the world.
"Thus it is written, that the Messiah should suffer and on the
third day rise from the dead, and that repentance and for-
giveness of sins should be preached in his name to all na-
tions, beginning from Jerusalem."
And he looked straight at them and said, "You are witnesses."

Now if it were me, I don't think I would have wasted my breath.
In the first place, these are the same people in this room who
ran away from the cross.
And there are just not enough of them — just a handful of
people in this room.
If I were God, I'd tell everyone.
I'd write my name across the sky.
I'd inscribe it on the surface of every mountain, every rock,
every atomic particle.

I'd make it impossible not to believe, not to "know."
I certainly would not leave it to a handful of dubious witnesses
in dreary old Jerusalem.

Why did God give the "proof" of bodily resurrection to just this
handful?
I think it was so that Christianity would never be in danger of
becoming a theorem.
It's never going to be something you "know," something you
can learn from a book.
Faith requires people to be witnesses.
It can be spread only by witnesses — people who testify to
what they have experienced, who are humble enough to
say, "Yes, I know it's impossible," and who yet can say, "I
believe it's true" — people who cannot not say it's true.
Witnesses — if not to the original fish eating, witnesses then
at least to the continuation of the eating among those who
believe that Jesus is still with them.

Because the point is not whether once upon a time Jesus rose, it's
whether he's still alive and still with us.
This is where faith is different from a theorem; it's not a matter of simply what you "know."
To believe in the resurrection of Jesus is to believe that he is
with us here today — in bread and wine, in prayer, in the
stories and the faces of the witnesses. He is here.
If not, who cares?
If the bread and wine signify nothing, why bother?
If there is no living Messiah, don't take it personally, but Sunday mornings I'd be home in bed.
But if there is even a particle-sized chance that the resurrection of Jesus is true, that he is alive and among us still,
then it's worth more than my Sunday morning.
It's worth my whole life.

A friend of mine went to church one Easter Sunday to hear the preacher say that "believing in the resurrection is as easy as riding a bicycle."

She didn't know whether to laugh or cry.

She had spent her Saturday trying to teach her seven-year-old daughter how to ride her first two-wheeler, through scraped knees and tears and words that seven-year-olds aren't supposed to know yet.

Some of us find Easter faith more like *learning* to ride a bicycle, a wobbly journey with lots of falling, scraping, and crying.

Still, we keep getting up and back on the seat.

How else are we going to get anywhere?

5. Preaching Resurrection In John

Someone once complained that in the Gospel of John, Jesus walks two feet above the ground. After only a few pages it is clear that we are not dealing with a simple peasant who told familiar stories about seeds, yeast, and the birds of the air. Jesus is "the Word made flesh" (1:14) and that Word is no less than the source of creation, the very Divine Being (1:1-3). To decide for or against Jesus is to choose life, light, truth, indeed God — or not (1:10-14). To some, John almost seems guilty of giving us a "docetic" Jesus — one who only "seems" to be human.

This is obvious overstatement — in some ways the Jesus of John is most human, experiencing human frailty (2:4; 4:6; 12:27; 13:21) and human pleasure (2:1-11; 12:3; 13:23; 15:13-15). As every Bible trivia player knows, the shortest verse in the Bible depicts a very human Messiah: "Jesus wept" (11:35, RSV). In every over-statement there is a nugget of truth, however. In this case, the truth is that John does not radically distinguish the pre-resurrection Jesus from the risen Jesus. In fact, some scholars have suggested that the risen Jesus is so obviously present throughout the Gospel that John could have done away with the resurrection narratives entirely.

The portrait of Jesus in John is qualitatively different from those of the other Gospels. It is not just that John follows a com-pletely different narrative framework, which centers the story in Judea rather than Galilee, posits an older Jesus (about fifty, John 8:57) in a three-year rather than one-year ministry, and focuses the revelation of Jesus on the major feasts that involved the pil-grimage to Jerusalem (2:13; 5:1; 6:4; 7:2; 10:22; 12:12). And it is not just that the chronology and events of Jesus' final days are different: Jesus is crucified at the same time the paschal lamb was slaughtered (19:31), so the Last Supper is no Passover, and the appearances at the empty tomb are to Mary (20:11-19), twice to his disciples in Jerusalem (20:19-29), and in Galilee on the lake-shore, not the mountain (21:1-14). The whole feel of John is different from the others: there are no exorcisms and few healings, and these are considered not ends in themselves but "signs" that evoke. faith in a larger reality. There are no parables, but rather long abstract discourses about "light" and "truth"; the discourses are almost allegories, pointing not to the "kingdom of God," but to Jesus himself. The reader has been told from the beginning that this Jesus is the pre-incarnate "Word" of God; as the story proceeds, it keeps returning to the theme of Jesus' true identity. The focus in John is inevitably on the person of Jesus — no ordinary person at that. Scholars have long pondered the actual relationship between John and the other Gospels (most believe that they shared a common source independently), but it is clear that we have here storytelling of a rather different, and more exalted, order.

So the Jesus who walks through the Gospel of John is larger than life, already in communion with the risen Christ found at the end of the story. The Easter texts we find in lectionaries are not all "resurrection texts"(e.g., John 10; 13; 14; 15; 17); the risen Christ is assumed in advance throughout the Gospel.

As we have seen throughout, the closing chapters of the Gospels are intimately related to the rest of the story, and you can't fully understand the resurrection accounts without placing them within the larger story. Given the intimate connection in John between the earthly Jesus and the exalted Jesus, and given the laser-sharp focus on the identity of this Jesus in the Gospel of John, the need to tell the end of the story in light of what came before is all the more pressing.

The Clock Is Ticking

John's brand of theological narrative is distinctive: his revelation is in the telling of the story, as the reader puzzles out that which cannot be entirely known. John keeps twisting and turning away, so that we have to stay with the story in order to understand

Jesus — who in the end can never be fully grasped (20:17). John's method is to swirl together words and images that shift and transform and change color as the story proceeds, particularly in long discourses by Jesus and/or the narrator. What often seems to be redundant repetition proves on closer examination to be clever shaping of material. The story weaves in and out of itself. For example, two disciples hear John the Baptist proclaim Jesus "the Lamb of God," and they follow him. They ask him, "Where are you staying?" and he replies, "Come and see" (1:35-39). The reader who comes and sees will later learn the importance of "staying" (*meno,* "remaining" or "abiding") with Jesus (15:1-11). Another potential disciple, Nicodemus, tries to come and see, but is unable to grasp what he hears, because Jesus demands that he think two things at once: "No one can see the kingdom of God without being born *anothen*" — a word which demands the dual translation "anew/from above" (3:3). Nicodemus tries to fix on only one of the meanings — new birth — and thus cannot understand what Jesus is saying (3:1-11), because he does not understand that the new birth in question comes only through the one who has come from above (3:13-15; cf. 1:10-13); as the story moves along, we will see other unfortunate people who fail to understand properly where Jesus comes from (6:62, 66; 7:45-52). Nicodemus' misunderstanding is enough to keep him from staying with Jesus; it is not enough to grasp one side or the other, one must hold both together at once, and be born both "anew" and "from above." Such loaded vocabulary — word-play and double-entendre — is the stuff of John's story.

John's revelation-by-word-play strategy is demonstrated again and again in the passages that appear in the lectionary for Easter season. In John 10, Jesus announces that the shepherd enters the sheepfold through the "gate" or "door" (*thura*). He then announces that he is the "door" through which the sheep must enter to find pasture (10:7). Is it then any wonder that at the end of the story Jesus the Door is able to pass through the locked "doors" behind which disciples hide (20:19, 26)? Also in John 10, the metaphors are mixed when Jesus also proclaims himself to be not only the "door" but "the good shepherd," and this leads to reflection not only on the relation of the sheep to the shepherd, but on the shepherd's willingness to lay down his life for the sheep (10:11-18). Again, the shepherd's relation to the sheep figures in the end of the story, after the shepherd has already laid down his life and thus set the model for his followers ("Feed my sheep," Jesus tells Peter, 21:15-21). In both cases, door and shepherd, the epithets are introduced with the solemn declaration, "I am" (*ego eimi*), which is reminiscent of the divine name (Exodus 3:14), and is used absolutely by Jesus in John (John 8:58). The mixing of the two metaphors is not entirely arbitrary; Jesus as "door" opens to the "way" (14:6) that is life (10:10), and as "shepherd" leads the sheep along that way by laying down his own life. Meaning is here implied rather than explicit; the reader is left to ponder not only the shifting metaphors, but their conjunction with the absolute appellation, "I am."

One ongoing Johannine word-puzzle involves Jesus' "hour" (*hora*) of "glory" (*doxa*). When Jesus' mother asks him to do something about the wine shortage in Cana, Jesus replies rather sharply that "My hour has not yet come" (John 2:4). What he means by that statement is not yet at this point in the story clear, but when he does in fact provide the good stuff for the party, the narrator says that it was a "sign" (*semeion*) that "revealed his glory" (2:11), undoubtedly the same "glory" that he shared with his Father before the world began (1:14; 17:5). As the story proceeds, Jesus continues to speak of "my hour" or "the hour" (4:21, 23; 5:25, 28) in a manner that is both eschatological and immanent: "Very truly, I tell you, the hour is coming, and is now here, when the dead will hear the voice of the Son of God, and those who hear will live" (5:25). He could not be arrested by his enemies, "because his hour had not yet come" (7:30; 8:20). As Jesus makes his final trip to Jerusalem, he announces, "The hour has come for the Son of Man to be glorified," and continues with the image of the grain that bears much fruit when it falls to the earth and dies (12:23-24). Clearly, the hour would be avoided, except that it is Jesus' very purpose for being in the world (12:27) — the purpose being to glorify the Father (12:28; 17:1). The introduction to the footwashing makes the meaning of Jesus' "hour" explicit: it is the time for him "to depart from this world and go to the Father" (13:1). The hour is explicitly connected to the glorification of Jesus and the Father: "Now the Son of Man has been glorified, and God has been glorified in him. If God has been glorified in him, God will also glorify him in himself and will glorify him at once" (13:31-32). The disciples will scatter at that hour (16:32), though Jesus speaks to them plainly of the Father (16:25). It is as painful and joyful as childbirth (16:21).

It is a mistake to think that John limits Jesus' "glory" to his death; clearly his "hour" consists of the entire glorification of Father and Son that takes place in his death, resurrection, and ascension — not just his departure from the world but his return to the Father (13:1). The entire process is taken as one moment in time; the death, the raising from the dead, and the return to the Father are locked together as one essential act. The "hour" of "glory" is the moment to which the whole story points.

A Visit From The Gardener

The crucial question of the resurrection narratives in John is, where is Jesus? It's a twist on a question that permeates the Gospel, but is rarely fully understood by the characters who pose it. The first disciples ask, "Where are you staying?" (1:38), but do not realize the implications of their question. Knowing where Jesus is correlates with the related crucial question, where he comes from. John's prologue answers the question from the beginning: the Word was with God, and was God, and became flesh (1:1-18). Nicodemus offers uncertain testimony that Jesus comes from God, but he cannot understand the message Jesus brings from God (3:1-10). Jesus' origin is an issue in his conversation with the woman at the well (4:9), a conversation that undulates with revelation and misunderstanding. Jesus creates a ruckus when he claims to be "the bread that comes down from heaven" (6:51), but even his disciples have trouble hearing that one (6:60, 66). His enemies have even greater problems understanding where Jesus comes from — they think he merely comes from Galilee (7:45-52), and they certainly do not understand his words about where he is going to be (7:32-36; 8:14, 21-23). Knowing where Jesus is, where he comes from, and where

105

he is going — he is with the Father, comes from the Father, and goes to the Father — is essentially the same as knowing who he is (14:10-11; 1:1, 14; 16:27; 17:3; 13:1; 14:12; 17:11).

The question of Jesus' location is crucial for the disciples at the empty tomb, because Jesus himself has already answered it: "You heard me say to you, 'I am going away, and I am coming to you'" (14:28; cf. 14:18-20). Just as Jesus has come from the Father and will return to the Father, so he will leave the disciples and return to God. The arc of the story is complete in the stories of his resurrection appearances: he has kept his promise to return to his friends (15:14-15). In some sense, the resurrection in John is not so much about what happened to Jesus (he returned to God), but what happened to the disciples (Jesus returned to them).

The lesson is slow in dawning. Mary Magdalene sees the empty tomb and admits that she has no idea where Jesus is (John 20:2). Peter and the "disciple whom Jesus loved" (or the "Beloved Disciple," traditionally thought to be John, nowadays taken as the symbolic representative of the Johannine Christian community that produced, received, and preserved this Gospel) also see the empty tomb (20:3-10). Only the Beloved Disciple comes away believing, "for as yet they did not understand the scripture, that he must rise from the dead" (20:9). The theme of misunderstanding permeates even this final section of John's Gospel.

Mary Magdalene takes on a decisive role in the movement from misunderstanding to enlightenment. In contrast to the other Gospels, Mary comes alone to the tomb (cf. Matthew 28:1; Mark 16:1; Luke 24:10), and is thus afforded a more prominent role. Her report to the male disciples demonstrates both her faith and the depth of her misunderstanding: "They have taken the Lord out of the tomb, and we do not know where they have laid him" (20:2); she acknowledges that Jesus is "Lord" (cf. 13:13, "You call me Teacher and Lord — and you are right, for that is what I am"), yet she does not know the crucial facts about where he is — she thinks that some vague human instrumentation ("they") is responsible for his absence. She perhaps expresses the ignorance of the entire community when she reports that it is "we" who do not know where Jesus is. Her resistance to the truth is not dented by the appearance of two angels; she merely repeats the report that she made to the other disciples (20:11-13), with the exception that the collective "we" in her later report becomes the more personal "I": "They have taken away my Lord, and I do not know where they have laid him" (20:13). The highly personal nature of her grief is shown in that she "stood weeping outside the tomb" (20:11); she "weeps" (as Jesus had foretold, 16:20-22) because she does not yet understand. Even when she actually sees Jesus, she does not recognize him, but mistakes him for the gardener — a monumental instance of misunderstanding and narrative irony, for the reader knows what Mary does not, that Jesus stands before her (20:14-15). Jesus' question to her, "Whom are you looking for?" is loaded, for if she truly understood who Jesus was, she would not reply, "Sir, if you have carried him away, tell me where you have laid him, and I will take him away" (20:15); had she truly understood who Jesus was, where he came from, where he had been, and where he now was, she would never think that she or any human agent could "take him away." Jesus' question, "Whom are you looking for?" echoes that posed to the original disciples (1:38), because it is the question posed to every potential disciple. Only when Jesus calls her by name do her eyes open and she sees where Jesus is — standing in front of her (20:16). Now Mary's weeping has been turned to joy (cf. 16:20-22), as she recognizes the voice of the Good Shepherd calling her by name (10:3-4, 14, 16, 27), and she responds with the endearment, "Rabbouni" (cf. 13:13). Mary, having come to understanding, can now accurately report back to the other disciples, which she does (20:17-18). Mary becomes the first faithful witness to Jesus' return to the disciples.

A puzzling aspect of Jesus' return is Jesus' initial command to Mary, "Do not hold on to me, because I have not yet ascended to the Father" (John 20:17). The command could be taken either as a prohibition of what has already happened ("Stop holding me," cf. Matthew 28:9), or of intention ("Do not grasp me"). Obviously Jesus has no qualms about the disciples touching his resurrected body, since he invites Thomas to touch (20:27). Even more puzzling is the reason given for not touching Jesus at this time: "Because I have not yet ascended to the Father." This perhaps implies

107

that Jesus will actually ascend to the Father before he meets Thomas and the rest. Some scholars would make the statement a question, "Have I not ascended to the Father?" (there are no punctuation marks in John's original Greek), because Jesus' "hour" of "glory" begins with the cross, where Jesus begins the process of being "lifted up" (cf. 3:14-15; 8:28; 12:32-34). It is perhaps best to see this passage as part of the ongoing Johannine revelation-by-word-play scheme, the dialogue aimed more at the reader than at the story's characters. Jesus' "hour" of glorification, the entire movement from death to resurrection to ascension, is in God's view one moment of time, so that normal narrative and temporal patterns are in flux. Jesus is not yet ascended to the Father, because the entire process, while begun, is not complete. Mary cannot "hold" or "grasp" Jesus in this moment, because the very notion is ungraspable. To attempt to hold on to Jesus at this moment would be to interfere with the ongoing process, which must be brought to fruition if all the disciples are to understand. Ironically, they must come to understand that which cannot be completely understood by mere humans.

Sandwiched inside Mary's journey from misunderstanding to faithful witness is the footrace of Peter and the Beloved Disciple. Who actually wins the race — or whether it is a race at all — has been a matter of much discussion. Peter is the most prominent disciple in the other Gospels, and in the Gospel of John also seems to represent the others (cf. 6:66-69; 13:6-10, 36-38; 18:10-11, 15-27). The Beloved Disciple, however, takes on the foremost position in John. He appears only in the narration of Jesus' "hour" (13:21-30; 19:26-27, 35; 21:1-23), and is never identified by name (which has stopped no one, over the years, from speculating — the most prominent suspects being John the son of Zebedee, traditionally thought to be the Gospel's author, and Lazarus, the only disciple whom Jesus was said specifically to "love" [11:3]). The lack of explicit identification suggests, on one level, that John's readership would have recognized the disciple in question without a name, and on another level, that the disciple's name was secondary to his symbolic function in the story: it was not so much his identity that was important, but his relationship with Jesus. The

Beloved Disciple represents, perhaps, the community of John's readership — those who are bound with Jesus in the love that comes from the Father.

All sorts of symbolism has been read into the jogging back and forth between Peter and the Beloved Disciple on the way to the tomb — the Beloved Disciple gets there first, but Peter is first into the tomb, however only the Beloved Disciple sees and believes — but such speculation is by nature inconclusive. More important is what the two disciples see at the tomb. The Beloved Disciple can see from the outside that the linen in which Jesus' body was wrapped (19:38-42) has been left behind; Jesus, unlike Lazarus (11:44), did not come forth a mummy. Jesus has no need of burial clothes, because he has left death behind; as he himself said, "No one takes my life from me, but I lay it down of my own accord. I have power to lay it down, and I have power to take it up again" (10:18). It is Peter who first sees the detail that the head-cloth has been wrapped up by itself (20:7), but when the Beloved Disciple sees this, he believes (20:8). The symbolism of the head-cloth is subtle; it is perhaps an allusion to the veil that Moses wore to speak to the people after he had spoken to God (Exodus 34:33-35). Jesus has removed the veil of his earthly form in order to return to the Father and speak with the Father face-to-face. Seeing this provokes belief in the Beloved Disciple, but John qualifies the belief with a note of its imperfection — they did not fully understand what had happened (John 20:9). If the Beloved Disciple is supposed to be superior to Peter, he wins by no more than a nose. True faith awaits Jesus' actual return to his friends and the giving of the Holy Spirit (20:19-29).

Seeing Isn't Believing

Jesus' first appearance to the disciples as a group comes that evening (20:19). Note that John identifies the group merely as "the disciples"; they are not restricted to the Twelve (now Eleven), nor even to the males. The appearance to Mary, along with her response of faith, has already shown beyond a doubt that women are numbered among the group called "disciples" (20:16-18). In returning to the disciples, Jesus fulfills his promise: "I will not leave

109

you orphaned: I am coming to you. In a little while the world will no longer see me, but you will see me; because I live, you also will live. On that day you will know that I am in my Father, and you in me, and I in you" (14:18-20). Just as Jesus has returned to the Father (16:5), so now he returns to the disciples — they now see him. The importance of what the disciples "see" will be underlined in this section (cf. 20:29-30).

Jesus meets disciples who are in a state of not-yet-faith. Though they have received the report of Mary (20:18), and presumably a report from Peter and the Beloved Disciple (20:3-10), they have not yet overcome their resistance to the good news. They are hiding out of "fear (*phobos*) of the Jews," i.e., those Jewish leaders opposed to Jesus. This is a response of not-yet-full-faith — fear is the response of the crowds uncertain about Jesus (7:13), those afraid of legal and spiritual retribution (*phobeomai,* 9:22), Pilate (19:8), and Joseph of Arimathea, who is willing to bury Jesus but not to support him openly (19:38). Jesus himself commanded against fear (*phobeomai,* 6:20; and using not *phobos* but the synonym *deiliao,* 14:27). Indeed, the prophetic word counseled against fear: "Do not be afraid (*phobeomai*), daughter of Zion. Look, your king is coming, sitting on a donkey's colt!" (12:15, quoting Zechariah 9:9, altered by John to stress the command against fear in light of Isaiah 35:4; 40:9; Zephaniah 3:14-16). The disciples' resistance to faith is symbolized by the doors shut and locked — they do not yet realize that Jesus himself is the "door" (10:7) to a new life, without fear.

Jesus meets the disciples with a greeting of "Peace" (20:19). The greeting is standard, yet laden with overtones: "Peace I bring to you, my peace I give to you; not as the world gives, I give to you. Do not let your hearts be troubled, and do not let them be afraid" (14:27; cf. 16:33). He then gives them tangible proof of his identity and assurance of his bodily resurrection by showing them his hands and side; Jesus thus proves that he is now the same Jesus they had known before and had seen on the cross. The disciples respond, as Jesus had foretold (16:20-22), with joy (20:20); their joy proves they have now moved from disbelief into faith (3:29;

110

4:36; 8:56; 14:28-29; 15:11; 16:20-22; 17:13; note also John's alteration of the text of Zechariah 9:9 in John 12:15 from "Rejoice!" to "Do not fear" — joy is considered the opposite of fear, which is a sign of unbelief). Their belief is indicated by the title given the one they see before them: "Lord" (20:20).

In repeating the greeting of "Peace" — a greeting the disciples are able to receive in its fullest, since they now know Jesus as "Lord" (20:20) — Jesus extends it into a commission: "As the Father has sent me, so I send you" (20:21). Running throughout the Gospel are extended comparisons between Jesus and the Father, which in turn are applied to Jesus and the disciples; the relation between Father and Son is mirrored in that of the Son and his brothers and sisters (20:17). The language of "sending" (*pempo* or *apostello;* both words are used in 20:21) in particular is applied to Father and Son, Son and followers. Jesus frequently speaks of the Father simply as "the one who sent me" (*pempo,* 4:34; 5:23, 24, 30, 37; 6:38-39, 44; 7:16, 18, 28, 33; 8:16, 18, 26, 29; 9:4; 12:44-45, 49; 13:20; 15:21; 16:5). Believing in Jesus means believing that he has been sent by the Father: "And this is eternal life, that they may know you, the only true God, and Jesus Christ whom you have sent" (17:3, *apostello,* cf. 3:17; 5:36, 38; 6:29, 57; 7:29; 8:42; 10:36; 11:42; 17:8, 18, 21, 23, 25; 20:21). Jesus in his prayer for the disciples explicitly connects sending and being sent: "As you have sent me into the world, so I have sent them into the world" (17:18). The depth of his communion with the Father thus extends to his relationship with the disciples, love for love: "As you, Father, are in me and I am in you, may they also be in us, so that the world may believe that you have sent me. The glory that you have given me I have given them, so that they may be one, as we are one, I in them and you in me, that they may become completely one, so that the world may know that you have sent me and have loved them even as you have loved me" (17:21-23). The identification between Jesus and his followers is so complete that Jesus can even speak of "the one who sent *us*": "We must work the works of the one who sent us" (9:4, author's translation, using the textual variant "us" from several early witnesses; while NRSV reads "me," the plural is the more difficult reading and therefore more likely to be original).

111

The commissioning of the disciples as those sent as Jesus himself was sent is followed by the oddest thing: "He breathed on them" (20:22). This obviously symbolic action, reminiscent of the biblical act of creation (Genesis 2:7), is clarified by his next words, "Receive the Holy Spirit" (remember that the word for "Spirit," *pneuma,* can also mean "breath"). In contrast to the story in Luke-Acts (Acts 1:4-5; 2:1-4), the disciples in John do not wait long for the promised gift of the Spirit, but receive it as they are commissioned on the day of the resurrection. They have been prepared for this gift by Jesus' promise of a *parakletos* (John 14:16, 26; 15:26; 16:7); the word could be translated, "advocate," "comforter," "encourager," "exhorter," "mediator," "intercessor," "helper" — or any and all of the above, in light of the various functions the *parakletos* performs. In order to keep all the nuances in mind, many scholars simply use transliteration and speak of "the Paraclete."

In his final discourse with the disciples before his arrest, Jesus at several points speaks of the Paraclete, which he explicitly identifies with the Holy Spirit (14:26). Like Jesus, the Paraclete is sent by the Father (14:26) in Jesus' name; like the disciples, the Paraclete is sent by Jesus himself (15:26; 16:7) from the Father (the Paraclete can be said to be sent by both the Father and Jesus because the two are completely united in their work, cf. 5:17, 19; 10:30, 37-38). The Paraclete's primary function, like that of the disciples, is to "testify" or "witness" (*martureo*) to Jesus (15:26-27) and thus to glorify him (16:14). This reflects Jesus' own "witness" in his works and word (5:36; 8:14, 18; 10:25; 18:37). The Paraclete is "the Spirit of truth" (14:17; 15:26), because Jesus himself is the truth (14:6); the Paraclete is a "guide," "one who leads the way" (*hodegeo,* 16:13), because Jesus himself is the "way" (*hodos,* 14:6). The Paraclete functions to teach the disciples, and to remind them of what they have seen for themselves (14:26); John portrays this process at work as he tells the story, noting that the disciples after the resurrection did in fact remember what Jesus had said and done (2:22; 12:16). The Paraclete, by reminding the disciples of Jesus' teaching rather than offering new teaching, passes on what Jesus has received from the Father (16:14-15). The Paraclete's teaching function is expressed in language similar to the words that Jesus

112

used to describe his own mission: "He will guide you into all the truth; for he will not speak on his own, but will speak whatever he hears, and he will declare to you the things that are to come" (16:13; cf. 8:28; 14:10). Thus the Paraclete is given as a sort of Jesus-substitute, or even a Jesus-enhancer; Jesus speaks while he is still with them (14:25), but the Paraclete will continue to teach them (14:26; 15:26) and be with them to teach them forever (14:16). The Paraclete is going to be the new mode of Jesus' presence with the disciples, no longer bound by time, place, or circumstance, in order to ensure that the ongoing community will be able to hear Jesus' words afresh (cf. 20:31). The close communion between Jesus and the Paraclete is indicated by Jesus' promise that the Father will give the disciples "another Paraclete," i.e., besides Jesus himself (14:16), who will "remain" (*meno*) with them (14:17), just as Jesus himself remains with them (15:4). Jesus actually portrays his death as an improvement of the disciples' situation, because it permits the coming of the Paraclete (16:7). The presence of the Spirit sets the disciples apart from those who oppose Jesus: "This is the Spirit of truth, whom the world cannot receive, because it neither sees him nor knows him. You know him, because he abides with you, and he will be in (and/or "among") you" (14:17). Thus the Paraclete, in unity with Father, Son, and disciples, empowers the disciples from the inside by teaching and guiding them in the way shown by Jesus himself. The Paraclete provides the ongoing presence of Jesus in the community, making Jesus' love available without temporal or spatial limits. In John's Paraclete we do not have the fully-developed doctrine of the Holy Spirit found in later Trinitarian theology, but we certainly can see the seeds of it.

The presence of the Paraclete in and among the community of disciples is probably how we should account for Jesus' final words in his commission to them: "If you forgive (or "release," *aphiemi*) the sins of any, they are forgiven them; if you retain (or "hold," *krateo*) the sins of any, they are retained" (20:23). While this is the only mention of "forgiving sins" in the Gospel of John, the other Gospels remind us that only God can forgive sin (Mark 2:7) while extending that authority to Jesus himself (Mark 2:10). Nevertheless, John's perspective is not to be confused with that of other

113

Gospel writers (even though this saying may have its roots in a tradition similar to Matthew 18:18). Cultic language of sin and forgiveness is used when Jesus is called "The Lamb of God who takes away the sin of the world" (John 1:29), and portrayed as the Paschal Lamb who is sacrificed for sin (19:32-36; cf. Exodus 12:46). The sacrificial imagery of the Temple is shifted to Jesus. Thus, in the Gospel of John, sin and forgiveness of sin is focused on belief in Jesus himself; sin is not so much a moral failing but a theological mistake (cf. 3:19-21; 8:21-24; 9:39-41; 15:22-24). In the continuing mission of the disciples to the world, it is the Paraclete who will "expose," "convict," and/or "reprove" (*elencho*) the world of its sin (16:8; NRSV "prove the world wrong about sin"). Here John uses the language of the legal system to portray the Paraclete as a prosecuting attorney against those who oppose Jesus (the "world," *kosmos,* here and so often in John, is not the created order *per se*, but those creatures who stand opposed to God, cf. 1:10, 29; 3:16-17; 7:7; 8:23; 12:31; 12:47; 14:30; 15:18-25; 17:1-26; 18:36). The Paraclete both brings the sin of the world into the open, and holds the world accountable for that sin. Sin is defined in terms of unbelief — the world sins because it does not believe in Jesus (16:9; cf. 8:24; 15:22-24). Righteousness is seen in terms of Jesus' hour (16:10, "because I am going to the Father and you will see me no longer"). The judgment of the world is also defined in Jesus' hour, "because the ruler of this world has been condemned" (16:11; cf. 12:31; 14:30). Thus, the sins which the Paraclete convicts the world of, and which the disciples are given authority over, are focused on belief in Jesus as the one who is sent by, and returns to, the Father. In their unity with Jesus and the Paraclete, which stems from the unity of Jesus with the Father, the disciples now have the power to "release" (*aphiemi*) or "hold" (*krateo*) the sins of the world, because the world will either believe or disbelieve based on their witness in the power of the Paraclete. Again, this power is given to the entire community of disciples, not to a select group within it.

Unfortunately, one important member of that community is absent — in fact, he stands in for all those absent because they have yet to see the signs that point to Jesus' true nature. "Thomas (who was called the Twin), one of the twelve, was not with them when Jesus came. So the other disciples told him, 'We have seen the Lord.' But he said to them, 'Unless I see the mark of the nails in his hands, and put my finger in the mark of the nails and my hand in his side, I will not believe' " (John 20:24-25). Thomas' biblical nickname *Didymus,* "Twin," (cf. 11:16; also 14:5; nobody knows whose twin he was) is traditionally secondary to his popular moniker, "Doubting Thomas." However, he doubts no less than the other disciples did before they had come to faith (20:15, 19), and he himself comes to faith through the same path as Mary and the others — faith comes through a direct encounter with the risen Lord ("We have seen the Lord," 20:25; cf. 20:16, 20).

Thomas' encounter with Jesus is more dramatic than that of the others, just as his disbelief is expressed more forcefully. The drama is increased by the time scheme; a week goes by before Jesus returns with the same greeting of "Peace" (note that this time the narrator does not mention locked doors or fear, since only Thomas remains in unbelief at this point). Jesus does not wait for Thomas to speak, but cuts right to the heart of the matter, using the same words in which Thomas had expressed his disbelief: "Put your finger here and see my hands. Reach out your hand and put it in my side. Do not doubt but believe" (20:27). Note that Jesus does not criticize or condemn Thomas for his lack of faith; his words are in no way a rebuke — he simply gives Thomas exactly what he gave to the others, exactly what he needs to come to faith. Thomas does not continue for a moment in disbelief, nor does he continue to seek physical reassurance (he does not actually touch Jesus). His answer is a confession of faith in the unity of Father and Son: "My Lord and my God!" (20:28; cf. 1:1; 14:7, 9). Note that this sequence is no more than a dramatized version of the first encounter with the others: the greeting of "Peace," demonstration of the resurrected body, and confirmation of faith. The heightened drama stresses the complete transformation that has taken place: Jesus is not dead but risen, and not just risen, but restored to the glory he had with the Father before the foundation of the world, and the disciples are not scattered in disbelief, but together in belief with their Lord and their God.

115

Unlike the previous appearance to the disciples, this incident does not conclude with a commission, but a blessing. "Have you believed because you have seen me? Blessed are those who have not seen and yet have come to believe" (20:29; cf. 1:50-51). The first sentence could be punctuated as a statement rather than a question, but either way the meaning is clear. Jesus both acknowledges the basis of their faith (he does not disparage it) and notes that it does not provide a paradigm. One need not be a first-generation witness of these events in order to be a part of the community. These disciples believe because of the direct physical presence of the risen Lord, but future generations of believers — in fact, the readers of this Gospel — will believe despite having not seen. These readers deserve the blessing.

The appeal to readers is made explicit by the narrator, in a summary that many scholars believe was the ending of the original Gospel: "Now Jesus did many other signs in the presence of his disciples, which are not written in this book. But these are written so that you may come to believe that Jesus is the Messiah, the Son of God, and that through believing you may have life in his name" (20:30-31). The narrator acknowledges that these stories are not to be considered random incidents, but as "signs" (*semeia*) that lead to faith (cf. the "signs" in 2:11; 4:54; 12:18). Further, this is a selective group of signs, culled from a larger pool of those things Jesus did "in the presence of his disciples" after the resurrection. The purpose of the signs is to produce belief in Jesus as Messiah and Son of God, with an ultimate goal of providing "life in his name." There is some debate over the tense of the first instance of the Greek verb "to believe" (*pisteuo*), due to textual variations among ancient hand-copied manuscripts. Some manuscripts read the aorist tense, which would signify a single act of belief, as in a conversion (thus NRSV "come to believe"). Other manuscripts read the present tense, which would indicate continuing action, "continue to believe." One variant would perhaps indicate that the book was written to evoke faith where none was present, while the other, that the intention was to confirm already-existing faith. The argument could be made either way, and it would be silly to pigeonhole the Gospel based on a copyist's error. Not only is John's Gospel an evangelistic tool, useful for evoking faith in those, like Thomas, who are in disbelief, but it also serves to strengthen and encourage the faith of those who have already come to believe.

Postscript (?) On Sheep And Fish

John 21 is often considered to be a later appendix to the Gospel of John. The usual arguments are that 20:30-31 provide a fitting climax to the Gospel as a whole, that chapter 21 seems an anticlimactic ending, far too focused on later church concerns, and that the language of chapter 21 seems sufficiently different from that of the rest of the Gospel to warrant the hypothesis of a later editor.

While certainly John, like the other Gospels, shows signs of multiple sources, there are reasons to think that John 21 is more of a piece with the whole than many believe. The apparent ending at 20:30-31 could be considered simply a conclusion to the stories found in chapter 20, which function as "signs" of Jesus' true nature; the narrator's intrusion is but one of many such editorial comments that interrupt the story to explain the significance of certain events (cf. John 2:22; 11:51-52; 12:16, 33; 18:32; 19:35). There is certainly no manuscript evidence that the Gospel ever circulated without chapter 21, and the slight differences in language can be explained by the subject mater. And while it may seem loosely connected to chapter 20, the concern for the ongoing community of disciples in chapter 21 echoes the concerns expressed in Jesus' final prayer (17:6-26), as well as Jesus' many references to the nature of the community to come (14:12; 15:12-27; 16:2-3; 17:17-18, 20; 19:26-27). If chapter 21 is a postscript, it nevertheless ties up some loose ends.

Jesus' appearance by the Sea of Tiberias (another name for the Sea of Galilee) brings the Gospel full circle. As in chapter 1, there are two unnamed disciples present (21:2; cf. 1:35) along with Simon Peter (cf. 1:40) and Nathaniel (cf. 1:45). Nathaniel, with the others, will now see the "greater things" he was promised in 1:50. As in chapter 1, the episode is highly symbolic; whereas in chapter 1 we see the "Lamb of God," in chapter 21 Jesus speaks of "my lambs" (21:15). There are allusions to other parts of the Gospel as well. The references to sheepherding also hearken back to the "Good Shepherd" of chapter 10 (10:11-18), while the fish recall the miraculous feeding in chapter 6 (6:9). The responses of Peter and the Beloved Disciple echo their actions at the tomb in 20:1-10; Peter's overeagerness in dressing to go swimming — wanting to greet Jesus with proper respect, yet arrive immediately — is in keeping with his rash promise to follow Jesus to the cross (21:7; cf. 13:36-38). The disciples recognize the stranger on the shore as Jesus in light of the abundant gifts he offers; this reflects earlier stories such as the wedding at Cana (2:1-11) and the feeding of 5,000 (6:1-14). The narrator underlines the revelatory nature of this appearance through the threefold repetition of the verb "to show oneself" or "to reveal" (*phaneroo,* 21:1, 14; cf. 1:31; 2:11; 9:3; 17:6); the purpose of this scene, as throughout the Gospel, is for us to see Jesus and what he shows us.

The web of imagery suggests that the disciples have not reverted to their previous lives in deciding to go fishing (21:3). While John does not include the story found in the other Gospels of the call to fisherfolk to leave their nets and follow him — indeed, John does not specify the pre-call occupation of Simon Peter and the rest, perhaps because it was irrelevant to their new life as disciples of Jesus — this story obviously means more than it says. This is evident from the long night of zero success (21:3), the change from darkness to light (21:4), the call of the mysterious stranger from the shore resulting in an overabundant catch (21:4-6), the sudden recognition of the caller as Jesus (21:7), the impetuous response of Peter (21:7), the ongoing awe in the presence of Jesus (21:12), and even the number of fish caught in the unbroken net (21:11; the actual significance of the number 153 is elusive, but it is obviously symbolic).

The symbolic narrative's twofold significance is clarified in the story of the meal and conversation that follows. First, the fish that result from following Jesus' instructions help form the basis of a communal meal, along with the food he has directly provided (he already has bread, and some fish on the fire, 21:10). Jesus invites his family to a meal (he calls them "children" in 21:5, using a synonym of the word used in 13:33; cf. "brothers," 20:17). As giver of gifts and source of life, Jesus calls together his community (cf. 4:13-14; 6:35, 51; 7:37-38; 10:9). The sacramental nature of the meal is implied by the language used: "Jesus came and took the bread and gave it to them, and did the same with the fish" (21:13; cf. 6:11). While the nature of sacramental theology in John's Gospel is a subject of debate, the meal is clearly linked by this language to the feeding of the 5,000 (6:1-14). In that chapter, Jesus responds to the people who follow him in hopes for another meal, using vivid imagery:

> *"I am the living bread that came down from heaven. Whoever eats of this bread will live forever; and the bread that I will give for the life of the world is my flesh ... Very truly, I tell you, unless you eat the flesh of the Son of Man and drink his blood, you have no life in you. Those who eat my flesh and drink my blood have eternal life, and I will raise them up on the last day; for my flesh is true food and my blood is true drink. Those who eat my flesh and drink my blood abide in me, and I in them. Just as the living Father sent me, and I live because of the Father, so whoever eats me will live because of me."* — John 6:51, 53-57

This language seems clearly sacramental; John understands the eucharist as Jesus' gift to believers and a reflection of the believers' ongoing relationship to him. The nature of the sacrament is played out in the Gospel's final chapter: the disciples come in from their labors to share a meal with each other and with the awesome risen Lord.

Secondly, the disciples move from their common fellowship meal to a common mission. The meal becomes fuel for yet another venture into the ongoing work, which in turn will provide the basis for the next meal. While the imagery is slightly incongruous — we don't normally think of sheep as eating fish — it is hard to miss the connection between the meal the disciples have just eaten with the command to "Feed my sheep." The disciples' work is to provide for the communal meal. The catch the disciples made at Jesus' direction was so great that they were hardly able to "haul" (*helko*) it in (21:6); the same verb is used at 6:44, "No one can come to me unless drawn (*helko*) by the Father who sent me," and 12:32, "And I, when I am lifted up from the earth, will draw (*helko*) all people to myself." The catch is thus symbolic of the mission the disciples share with Jesus. Just as the risen Lord provided the miraculous catch for the meal, but the disciples had to do the dirty work of hauling it in (21:8), Peter is commanded to return to the work of providing sustenance for those under the care of the Good Shepherd. As with Jesus, the work itself provides the sustenance (cf. 4:31-34, "My food is to do the will of him who sent me and to complete his work").

The work springs from the disciple's love for the Shepherd. Jesus shows that he is worthy of that love as the Good Shepherd in that he calls this particular sheep by name, "Simon, son of John" (21:15, 16, 17; cf. 10:3; 1:42). He commends to Peter — and to all of "these" his disciples (21:15) — the love he himself has demonstrated: "Just as I have loved you, you also should love one another" (13:34, cf. 13:35). That love is expressed in the charge Jesus gives Peter along with the others: "Feed my sheep." To love Jesus is to love his sheep as he has loved them (cf. 10:11-18). The threefold repetition in 21:15-17 of the question, answer, and command (with slight variations between "lambs" and "sheep," along with two Greek synonyms for "love," *agapao* and *phileo*) helps to dramatize the situation (cf. the three appearances of Jesus in chapter 20, and the three denials of Jesus in 18:15-27).

Jesus' final interchange with Simon Peter is poignant not only for the agony it gives Peter (21:17), but because its threefold structure echoes Peter's denials (18:15-27); it concludes with a very personal word concerning the cost of discipleship (21:18-19) that recalls Peter's initial boast, "I will lay down my life for you" (13:37). The earlier words drew a rebuke, "Will you lay down your life for me? Very truly, I tell you, before the cock crows, you will have denied me three times" (13:38). Jesus now indicates in cryptic fashion that Peter will get the chance to fulfill that earlier promise: "Very truly, I tell you, when you were younger, you used to fasten your own belt and to go wherever you wished. But when you grow old, you will stretch out your hands, and someone else will fasten a belt around you and take you where you do not wish to go" (21:18). Just in case we did not get it, the narrator tells us that "He said this to indicate the kind of death by which he would glorify God" (21:19); Peter has been traditionally considered a martyr by crucifixion ("you will stretch out your hands"). Note that Peter's death in witness to Jesus, like the death of Jesus himself, is considered an act that brings glory to God (cf. 7:39; 12:16; 13:31-32; 14:13; 17:1-5). There is pain in the ongoing work of hauling the unbroken net, pain that may lead to death, but there is also glory to the God who gives the marvelous catch.

The final encounter with the risen Jesus in the Gospel of John ends, appropriately enough, with a word about the Beloved Disciple (perhaps understood to be one of the unnamed disciples mentioned in 21:2). Peter, on seeing the Beloved Disciple behind them, asks his fate (21:20-21). Jesus' answer is more cryptic than usual: "If it is my will that he remain until I come, what is that to you? Follow me!" (21:22). The narrator finds it necessary to quell the rumors that arose from this answer (21:23); Jesus did not say that the Beloved Disciple would not die, but would "remain" (again, *meno*). The Beloved Disciple may not, in contrast with Peter, die as a martyr, but he would perform the duty assigned to all disciples, to stay with Jesus to the end.

Finally, the narrator assures the reader that this selection from the words and acts of Jesus are from a reliable witness (21:24-25). The Beloved Disciple himself is cited as the source ("This is the disciple who is testifying to these things," 21:24). Yet the narrator of the Gospel is cast as someone else, the "we," in "we know that his testimony is true" (21:24; cf. 1:14-18). Thus the Beloved Disciple is portrayed as the eyewitness of these events but not the actual author (cf. 19:35). The "we" of the author's community is in fact that ongoing community blessed by Jesus in 20:30-31 — those who have not seen, and yet who have believed on the basis of what the Beloved Disciple saw. The Gospel concludes by humbly acknowledging that this witness is but one of many possible (21:25).

However, the words of the Gospel that ring clearly as its true final word are those of the risen Lord himself. The NRSV uses only an exclamation point to indicate the emphatic imperative directed at Peter; it should perhaps be translated more literally, "*You* follow me" (21:22). Jesus' word to Peter is a word to all the readers of John's Gospel, reflecting the purpose for which the book was written (20:30-31). The book is not about what happened to the Beloved Disciple (indeed, by camouflaging his true identity, the narrator ensures that seeking his fate could take us nowhere but a blind alley). The book is not about what happened to Simon Peter (his fate is only prophesied). The book is about Jesus, but not just Jesus. It is also about us, the readers of the book, and how we respond to Jesus, regardless of how those around us believe and act. The imperative to Peter is a call to all from the living Lord, "*You* follow me."

Seeing Isn't Believing

Easter 2, Year C — John 20:19-31
April 23, 1995

While this particular sermon was preached at Emmanuel Episcopal Church, a small parish in Quakertown, Pennsylvania, its genesis goes back a few years earlier, to a story I heard on the radio about memory and perception and the funeral of President John F. Kennedy. The gist of the story was that memory is slippery, sometimes as much creative as mnemonic. At the time, I thought it was a perfect illustration of a Johannine theme. As you will see, subsequent events have either proved the original thesis, or shown that I never heard it properly in the first place (or perhaps proved that the guy on the radio did not know what he was talking about).

Perhaps most preachers do not have quite the luxury I have had in reusing examples like this. As an intentional interim minister, I rarely have to deal with the same passage twice with the same congregation. Since this particular illustration works so well with the text, there really has been no reason not to reuse it. I've found it works well in a variety of different contexts, with different supporting examples (I think the first time I used it, I talked about the new "morphing" graphics technology used in the movie *Terminator 2*, which now could be done on almost anyone's personal computer). This sermon is filled with contemporary topical references to politics, movies, and current events. If I were to use the example again in a different context, it would require a number of changes.

The moral for preachers is that listeners do not hear a sermon but sermons, and that the lectionary always comes around to roost (in the case of this reading, once a year, at Easter 2). Generally speaking, whole sermons cannot be repeated in different contexts, since they were originally composed for a particular congregation and situation; the effort in revising them often outweighs the work of producing an entirely new sermon. However, I have no objection to preachers reusing illustrations and examples, on occasion

123

even with the same congregation. You might want to preface a repeat story with "I know I've told you this before, but it's worth telling again...." Just as we get a certain amount of delight in hearing an old song on the radio once again, congregations may appreciate a familiar tale now and again.

The preacher will want to take care, however, in recycling illustrations culled from outside sources like radio, television, magazines, and the ubiquitous pulpit helps (not to mention books like this one). While sermons do not require footnotes, a brief acknowledgment that this is borrowed material is usually needed for honesty's sake, and this can be minimal. For example, you usually don't need to say, "As I. M. Mouth writes in *The Pulpit Compendium,* page 14," or even as much as, "The famous preacher I. M. Mouth once said," but perhaps only, "I read this story...." Use your best judgment; the explicit attribution is usually only meaningful to the congregation if the person you are quoting is well-known (I was perhaps optimistic in citing Bishop Stephen Neill at the end of this sermon). Be careful about putting yourself into someone else's story. There is nothing more disconcerting than hearing a preacher tell a riveting tale about being trapped in a cave, only to hear the next week a completely different preacher in a different church use exactly the same words to tell how the same thing happened to him!

Be wary of pretending that the old is new, or that you've never addressed a certain issue before. A congregation's memory for sermons can be quite long. I remember hearing a sermon one Sunday morning on the feeding of the 5,000, in which the preacher pulled out that tired old rationalist chestnut, "Maybe the people were inspired by the example of the little boy sharing his lunch, and they all pulled out the food they had been hiding for later, and shared it with their neighbors. The only miracle was the miracle of sharing." One crotchety gray-haired man who always sat on the first pew came up to me after the service and said, "The preacher pulled a new one on us, huh?" I replied that it was a long-discredited explanation that dated back to the early nineteenth century. He just shook his head and said, "Everyone's trying to take something away from Jesus."

Three years later the train had come all the way around the track. Same church, same text, same preacher, same crotchety old guy sitting in the front pew. The preacher, however, had had a change of heart. "We shouldn't try to rationalize these stories. We shouldn't try to explain them away by naturalistic means, the way some people do." "Yeah," the old fellow said in a voice loud enough for the back pew, "it's happened right here in this church!"

And always remember, memory being what it is, people may well remember not what we said, but what they thought we said.

Seeing isn't believing.

What they can do with computers these days.

Have you heard about digitized pictures? Give a computer a picture and it turns it into ones and zeros. Then you can take those ones and zeros and put them together with any other set of ones and zeros and make a picture of, say, Hillary Clinton kissing Newt Gingrich. You can make any picture you want. It's frightening.

This is the year of Gump. Tom Hanks shaking hands with Nixon, Johnson, and Kennedy. Gary Sinese without any legs. All done on computers and celluloid. It's really quite amazing the way they can make you believe in something that never happened. Life is like a box of chocolates — you never know what you're going to get.

Of course, we knew this, that seeing isn't believing, in the days before the digital. I heard one expert on the radio put it this way. If you're old enough, you remember John Kennedy's funeral. You watched it on television. Remember how as the procession went past the first family, his little son saluted his father's coffin? No, you don't. That was a picture in *Life Magazine*. It was never on television. But we all think we saw it, says the expert.

You know, I've used that example for years, and people always nod their heads and insist they saw it on television, and I tell them, no, no. One day a few months ago I was flipping through the channels, and they had a documentary on the Kennedys, and there was the funeral, the flag-draped coffin moving past the First Family, and then little John made his famous salute, right there on the screen. Did I hear it wrong? Was the expert wrong? Or was I watching film and not the tape of what was broadcast that day? Who knows?

Memories can be faulty, and so can perceptions. It's a bunt, and the kid on first runs to second and — oh no! he's heading for third. The first baseman throws him out easily. Afterwards the coach says, "What were you doing?" The kid says, "I thought the throw to first was wild." But that was no baseball he saw behind first base, just a piece of white paper fluttering in the wind.

Seeing isn't believing, not these days, not that it ever was.

Which doesn't say much for Thomas. He insists on seeing, on touching. "Let me see the marks of the nails, let me put my hand in the wound."

Nowadays, a Thomas would think it was just another special effect. But when Thomas the Twin saw Jesus alive, he confessed the creed of a Christian: "My Lord and my God!"

What are we going to do with this guy? Today, more than ever before, seeing isn't believing. How can we even relate to Thomas, who got to see for himself?

Oh, I know that there are some who are convinced, who "know," who think they've seen just like Thomas, and I don't want to disparage them.

But for most of us, it's not that easy. At the most basic level, life is an act of faith. It's an act of faith to get up in the morning, to get dressed. It's an act of faith to believe that what we are doing has meaning. Because even if seeing were believing, at best we see in a mirror darkly. The evidence for God in this world is, let's face it, ambiguous. If it were clear, everyone would believe.

So what do we do? Fortunately, Jesus gives the answer.

"Have you believed because you have seen me?" he says to Thomas. "Blessed are those who have not seen and yet have come to believe."

I always feel proud when I come to this part. Because he's talking about me. Jesus shifts the action from the stage to the audience; it becomes participatory theater. He's talking about us. "Blessed are you who have not seen."

And here's how it works. According to John, when Jesus appeared to the disciples he breathed on them and said, "Receive the Spirit." There's a pun there in John's story, because the word "spirit" also means "breath." And in a very real way, the Spirit is the Breath of Jesus. He told the disciples, "It's better for you that I go. Because after I go, my Spirit will come."

The coming of the Spirit means that the Word has jumped the fence. The boundaries of the mission are open. We can believe. It's not just first century Palestinian Jews. Not just those who saw — Mary Magdalene at the tomb, Peter and James and John, Thomas — people who could say, "We have seen the Lord." We who hear those words through the Spirit now also can say, "My Lord and my God!"

This does not mean that the Thomas in us just disappears.

Face it, we live with doubt. We can't trust our eyes or our ears, and we just don't know what's going to happen next. The lesson of Oklahoma City along with all the bullets and traffic accidents and heart attacks that clutter our television, newspapers, and gossip is that your life is not your own. It's gone, it's changed, just like that.

127

The point of religion is not, as some would have it, the narcotic numbing of mind and body to the razored edge of life. We do not eliminate doubt, or deny the sting of living. Believing in God means believing in one who loves us consistently, no matter what happens. God does not help us avoid life. God leads us through life with all its changes.

The interesting thing about the word "faith" in the Gospel of John: It's always a verb. "Faith" is never a noun. That's because for John, faith is not a thing, something you can touch or hold. As Jesus said to Mary, "Do not hold me." Like a running river, there's nothing to hold on to.

I'll never forget when I was in college, I was in a Christian campus group, and we had a dispute. The problem was one of our members whose theology was changing, and so he wasn't comfortable with the official positions of that group anymore. Some people wanted the group to throw him out: "He just doesn't believe anymore," they said. But the wisest among us just sat back and quoted the words of the seeker to Jesus: "Lord, I believe; help me with my unbelief."

Faith is always a verb — it's always a process. We're never quite there. Faith goes on.

Bishop Stephen Neill once said that about three mornings a week he woke up and said, "Of course it couldn't possibly be true." But then he realized that it was true, and with some annoyance he found himself saying, "Thou only art Holy, thou only are the Lord."

Seeing isn't believing, and besides, we don't see. We don't see, and that's why we have the Spirit. Because even the best of us need help.

"Lord, I believe; help me with my unbelief." That's our cry. Jesus answers: "Blessed are you. Blessed are you — and you, and you, and you, and you — Blessed are you who have not seen, and yet believe."

128

The Unsnatchables

Easter 4, Year C — John 10:22-30
May 3, 1998

Analogy can be one of the preacher's most powerful tools. Part of the job of the sermon is to make a connection between modern life and the biblical text, and the right analogy can take the preacher a long way toward Sunday morning. This has long been recognized but often applied too narrowly: the preacher is advised, for example, to determine the historical situation that brought the text to life in a certain community, and then to look for a modern example of that situation. Anyone who has struggled with modern parallels to "eating meat offered to idols" (1 Corinthians 8-10) knows how precarious that sort of procedure can be. The unfortunate alternative taken by many preachers, however, is to use the Bible solely as a source for phrases and images used in a brainstorming process, so that the subsequent sermon is related to the original text only by a couple of catchwords (in which case, why preach on the Bible? *Roget's Thesaurus* would be a more promising source).

There is another way, however, and it involves both the free application of analogy to the text and careful attention to what the text actually says and does. I would argue that a good analogy comes only from careful attention to the entire text. In the biblical text selected for this sermon, the image is that of the shepherd. The question is not so much, What images of the shepherd can I conjure up? (though that's a good starting place), but What will produce thoughts and feelings that correspond to the image of the shepherd as used in the text? Simple pastoral scenery will not do, when what John emphasizes is the danger inherent to both sheep and shepherd. John's Good Shepherd provides comfort only because the danger is real. So the analogy that opens this sermon was chosen because it points out a real modern danger that puts the congregation in a position similar to that depicted in the text. The goal is to make them feel the danger, so that by the end of the sermon, they can feel the comfort.

This sermon was preached at Christ Episcopal Church, Avon, Connecticut, a middle-sized church in an affluent suburb of Hartford.

The faces on the flyers and the milk cartons tend to stare right past
    me, they are such a cliché.
    But this one was different.
    The child's picture I expected. "Missing since 6/15/97."
    But the ValueMail flyer also had the picture of a man with the
    same last name.
    Then it hit me. I checked the calendar. 6/15/97 was a Sunday.
    Weekend visitation.

The problem made the headlines last week in the case of William
    Martin.
    Palm Beach socialite, owner of an oceanfront home and a red
    Ferrari, a regular on the black-tie circuit, a father who ap-
    parently doted on his two daughters but who never seemed
    to work.
    Turns out that William Martin was really Stephen Fagan,
    wanted in Massachusetts since 1979 for kidnapping his
    two daughters from his ex-wife.
    He had told the little girls that their mother had died in a car
    accident.
    It's the slightly upscale version of an all-too-common solu-
    tion to a custody dispute.

And it's the monster under the bed for parents, divorced or
    otherwise —
    The idea that anyone, stranger or ex-, would snatch our chil-
    dren away — well, that's top-of-the-line nightmare.
        This is why we go through safe-kid training, we teach them
        to shout, "stranger."
        Because we know that no one is immune.

And it's not just children.

A few years back, the boogeyman was carjacking.

More recently it's home invasion, where they actually come into your house while you're home and hold you hostage while they rip you off.

And this morning there was a report from upstate New York, about some people who kidnapped a retarded woman and her daughter, and lived off their Social Security checks for ten years.

To judge from the books and articles and movies on the subject, I'd say we have a perverse fascination with the darkest nightmare.

Jacqueline Mitchard wrote a novel about child abduction, *The Deep End of the Ocean;* it was a big hit, Oprah's Book Club.

A friend of hers read the first draft and said, "Oh, how could you write something like this?" but kept reading anyway.

They all kept reading.

The thing about books and articles and movies is that they have endings, often happy endings. If we're going to think about the monster under the bed, we want to have a story.

The problem is, in real life, sometimes it's just episodes, not a story. No happy ending, maybe no ending at all.

There is no safe place, except in fiction. No place where we and the people we love are not in danger of being snatched.

No place, that is, but one.

Jesus said, "I am the Good Shepherd."

Most of us, when we hear this, conjure up a certain picture: a pastoral scene, green hills, verdant pastures, fluffy white animals, the shepherd sprawled lazily on the grass, playing a zither.

131

Jesus' friends and enemies would have thought of something else. They would have pictured palaces and thrones. The image of David the Shepherd-King was a powerful force in Jewish thought — you remember David: shepherd boy, slingshot, Goliath, King of Israel. And from David's house would come the last great King of the Jews, the Messiah. To say that you were a Shepherd with a capital "S" was to invoke some of the most powerful political and religious language at hand.

This is where we pick up the story today in the Gospel of John. His enemies want him to drop the metaphor and speak plainly. "Stop with the suspense," they say, but we could just as easily translate that, "Stop annoying us."

Jesus' answer: "I've told you plainly." He has. You can't get any plainer than the language of the Shepherd-King the likes of David.

The reason you have not heard, Jesus tells his enemies, is that you are not sheep. "My sheep hear my voice."

Jesus makes some remarkable statements about his sheep:

I know them, he says.

They follow me.

I give them eternal life.

They will never perish.

And he makes a remarkable statement about himself.

"I and the Father are one."

Over the years, theologians have taken these words and woven some elaborate theologies over them. It's a classic proof text for the doctrine of the Trinity.

But the Gospel of John wasn't really saying anything that complicated; John wasn't talking about essence or nature.

Jesus and the Father are one in action. You cannot tell God's
work from Jesus' work. The one does exactly what
the other does.

And this is why the sheep are safe with the Shepherd.

"No one will snatch them out of my hand. What my Father has given me is greater than all else, and no one
can snatch it out of the Father's hand."

Mind you, the metaphor is against him. There was no more
precarious profession than sheepherding. You've got
your wolves, you've got thieves, you've got rocks and
cliffs and ponds and all sorts of potential natural dangers, *and* you have the dumbest animals in the world
wandering around at will. Not a low-risk operation.

But Jesus says that no one will snatch his sheep; he is
holding on. The sheep are unsnatchable.

Because when Jesus holds, the Father holds with him.

"I and the Father are one."

Years ago I was talking with one of my high-school friends about
her Uncle Al.

She went to a rather strict church, and she insisted that her
Uncle Al had lost his salvation.

He didn't come to church anymore, he didn't show any interest in God, didn't read his Bible or pray, he just didn't
care.

Even Uncle Al himself admitted that it was true, he had gone
back to smokin' and drinkin' and dancin' and cattin' around,
that he once was found but now was lost.

Everyone said Uncle Al was a goner.

I would be willing to grant the point, if Christianity were a matter
of climbing the stairway to heaven.

Uncle Al may have turned his back on God, but God did not
go away. God does not go away.

133

Like children shutting their eyes and pretending they're invisible, we can fool ourselves into thinking it's all in *our* hands.

When the truth is, it's a matter of being in *God's* hands.

And salvation means simply opening our eyes and seeing what really is.

Remarkably, God knows how we are, this way — "I know my sheep," says Jesus. It may be the most important thing he says today: "I know."

"I know them," he says — every crusty edge of Uncle Al's heart, every detail and every deception and every last dusty unkempt corner —

Jesus knows all about Uncle Al, all about us.

Yet Jesus was and still is willing to hold on.

If the Gospel of John is right, we'd have to pry Jesus' fingers loose, while God's hand was closed over Jesus' fist.

No one, not even Uncle Al, is *that* strong.

Sheep's Life

Easter 4, Year A — John 10:1-10
April 28, 1996

When people talk about "liturgical sermons," they seem to have in mind sermons that address various aspects of Sunday worship. I myself have never been particularly impressed by the kind of sermon that begins, "Today is the Fourth Sunday of Easter, and by this time in the Easter season we feel...." To begin with, the "we" is silly; few if any but the preacher come to church having any feelings at all about the liturgical season. But what's really silly is to think that liturgical preaching involves talking about the liturgy. To preach liturgically is to base the sermon on the readings appointed for the day; the liturgy is merely the context in which those texts are read.

In the case of the Gospel of John, and in the case of Easter, the interconnection of text and liturgical context is crucial. As we have seen, the lectionary treats practically the whole of the Johannine Gospel as Lenten and Easter material. In this instance, the connection between text and context is made through John's emphasis on eternal life. For John, the resurrected life of the Christian begins with belief in Jesus as the Son of God. Life is defined not just quantitatively, but qualitatively, as "abundant." The sheepfold metaphor gives the preacher an opportunity to stress the communal aspect of new life. Easter is not about just the eternal life of individuals, but that of a community.

This sermon was preached at Emmanuel Episcopal Church, Quakertown, Pennsylvania.

The woman woke up to a cry for help.
> She thought that it was her husband talking in his sleep. But no, there he was, snoring.
> She was about to go back to snoring herself when she heard it again. "Help me. Help me."

She got out of the bed and went wandering into the dark house
in search of the voice.

It got louder, "Help me, help me," it said.

"Where are you?" the woman asked.

"In here," said the voice.

The woman walked into her living room.

"Over here," said the voice.

The woman flipped on the lights.

And there in the living room, in the fireplace, hanging upside
down, was a head.

"Who are you?" the woman asked.

"Lady, who do you think is hanging from your chimney at
3:00 in the morning? I'm a burglar," he said.

The police had to take the chimney apart to get him out.

"Anyone who doesn't come in by the door," says Jesus, "is a thief
and a bandit."

Anyone who comes in by the fireplace is either Santa Claus or
a bandit.

Jesus, of course, was talking about a sheepfold, so we call it
the "gate," but it's the same word he would have used for
the door to your house, or the door to your church, anything you have to open to get in.

No one who has any business being there comes in through
the fireplace or the window or a hole in the wall. The home-
owner walks in the door, and the farmer and the sheep
come in through the gate.

When the disciples don't understand his parable, Jesus explains
it to them.

"I am the gate," he says. "Whoever enters by me will be
saved."

If you want to get in, he says, you've got to go through
me.

Some people, of course, try to skirt around him.

"Maybe we can slip past," they say. "Maybe we can get in without shaking his hand."

Every now and then we get a check in the mail marked "Church Dues."

As if the church were a club you could join — pay your dues, just the minimum amount, don't let them cheat you.

But the church is not a club, it's a sheepfold. And we're not here to be fleeced.

A woman once came to me very upset because she found out that the church where I worked would perform weddings only for church members. "You're wrong," she said. "You should do weddings for anyone who shows up at the door. The church is here to *serve*."

But I have to tell you, no —

K-Mart is here to serve.

McDonald's is here to serve.

The church is here to call people into a relationship with God.

And you can't get in our door unless you're willing to deal with Jesus.

What Jesus gives can't be found on the shelves of the K-Mart.

It's not listed on the menu of McDonald's.

He gives what any sheep would expect to find behind the walls of the sheepfold — safety, comfort, protection against a world of wolves, thieves, bandits, and certain death.

Jesus puts it simply: "I came that they may have life, and have it abundantly." Jesus brings life.

He brings life, and he brings lots of life — abundant life.

I don't limit that to just time — long life, eternal life, years and years and years. The life Jesus brings can't be tested by pulse or brain waves or whether you can see breath on the mirror.

Nor do I think he was talking just about the quality of an individual person's life. It's not about being more prosperous, or wealthy, or happy in this life. I know this is what you hear from the television evangelists, but I don't think it's necessarily true. Jesus *may* make you a better businessperson, or a richer person, or a happier person. Or he may not.

But when Jesus says he brings lots of life, I think we can safely say that he was talking about sheer numbers.

There are lots of sheep in the sheepfold.

Let's change the metaphor here for a moment.

A friend of ours just had her fiftieth birthday party.

One of the presents was a piece of Tupperware.

It was marked: Special Bagel Keeper, and there was a little sign on it: "This bagel was sealed in this special container fifty years ago. We guarantee that it is as well-preserved as you are."

She opened it up, and inside there was — a Cheerio.

Which is to say, that a human being is like a bagel. Seal it up for fifty years all by itself, and it will come out dry, brittle, and puny. Just like a Cheerio.

The theologian Frederick Buechner gives this test for life:

"Have you wept at anything during the past year?...

"... do you really *listen* when people are speaking to you instead of waiting for your turn to speak?

"Is there anybody you know in whose place, if one of you had to suffer great pain, you would volunteer yourself?"

"If your answer to all or most of these questions is No," he says, "the chances are that you're dead." (Frederick Buechner, *Wishful Thinking*, 51)

The only thing I can add to Buechner's test is that all his questions require community. They involve persons, plural. You can't pass the test sealed up by yourself.

Or to go back to the sheepfold metaphor, yes, the sheep smell. Yes, they take up your space. Yes, they eat your food and Yes, they baa baa baa incessantly. But if it weren't for the rest of the sheep in the sheepfold, you wouldn't have a life to speak of. Certainly not the life Jesus called abundant.

The test for life is life together.

Jesus is the gate.

And behind the gate is — surprise! the rest of the flock.

If you're looking for life abundant, just look around at the fuzzy faces of your fellow sheep.

Coming Home

Easter 4, Year B — John 10:11-16
April 20, 1997

This is another variation on the sheep/shepherd imagery of John's Gospel. Again, John uses this imagery to establish the ongoing presence of the risen Jesus among successive generations of believers. John's story almost always is operating on more than one level. Here, Jesus explicitly says he has other sheep in the sheepfold besides those standing in front of him. Most commentators take that statement to be a reference to the Gentiles, but it is allusive and elusive enough to allow for other possibilities, one of which John states clearly near the end of his Gospel: the ongoing community of those who continue to treasure his words (20:30-31) and believe without having seen Jesus (20:29).

In this instance, John's imagery is filtered, somewhat ironically, through a very personal sieve. While keeping in touch with the biblical imagery, the sermon juxtaposes it with modern references, in order to give it a reinterpretation for the present day, while honoring its ancient origins. In a society that is by-and-large unfamiliar with sheep, the image is all too easily co-opted by sentimental pastoral pictures. My goal was to get the congregation to rethink the sheep imagery in terms more familiar to suburban New York City.

This sermon was preached at St. Luke's Episcopal Church, Katonah, New York.

Let me begin with a disclaimer.

In my case, Shepherd is a name and not a title.

I know you New Yorkers probably think everyone who comes from Indiana was raised on a farm, but I can probably count the times I've been up-close and personal with a sheep on one hand.

No, make that one finger, and that one time was in rural Connecticut, not Indiana.

I was a city boy, even if it was a small city.

So the only thing I really know about sheep is from books.

The books say: Sheep, well, they're wooly, and they're cute, or at least they are in pictures.

But you probably wouldn't keep one as a pet, like a dog or a cat.

For one thing, they are supposed to require a lot of supervision.

You can't just let a sheep wander around, they're relatively defenseless, they'll get lost, they'll get hurt.

Herding sheep calls for diligence and endurance, a careful eye cast over the flock.

Supposedly in Jesus' day, the search for pasture led the sheepherder to take the flock far and wide across the countryside, and then back to the stone-walled sheepfold, where several sheepherders would keep their flocks by night in safety.

Most of all, sheep are supposed to be lacking in common sense, if not downright stupid.

Think of the expressions "to get fleeced," or "to pull the wool over his eyes."

But as I say, I don't know from personal experience.

For all I know, it may be like the movie about Babe the pig, where he tries to learn to be a sheepdog, and the other sheepdog tells him, "You just have to go and bark and snarl at the sheep, they're real dumb and will do anything you tell them to."

But when Babe goes and tries to bark and snarl, the sheep just laugh at him.

And Babe breaks down and says to the sheep, "Why do you listen to the dogs and not to me when I bark and snarl?"

The sheep say, "Dogs are mean and stupid; we expect better from you. If you want us to do something, why don't you just ask politely?"
I know that you can get a long way with a lot of God's creatures if you just ask politely.

I'd like to think that sheep are smarter than we give them credit for.
I'd like to raise the IQ of sheep for strictly religious reasons.
Because according to Jesus, we are the sheep.
"I am the good shepherd," says Jesus, and that makes us the sheep.
And I know that we human beings aren't always that smart.
We don't always ask politely.
We tend either to be too suspicious or too naive.
We trust people we shouldn't trust and we suspect those who are most trustworthy.
We either believe in Mom, baseball, and apple pie, or we're totally disillusioned by Watergate and Whitewatergate, and we want a special prosecutor for every tax return.
We go for false prophets in droves, while the messenger of God sits unnoticed on the curb.
But I still look for some clue, some glimmer of hope that we're not as dumb as we appear to be —
That we're not as dumb as sheep.

But all I know is what I read —
And while the Bible is not a textbook on animal husbandry, I do notice a few clues, if not to real sheep, at least to the metaphor Jesus uses.
For one thing, the sheep hear his voice.
"My sheep listen to my voice," says Jesus.
Now that's no mean feat.

Anybody who's ever tried to use a computer to take voice dictation knows how tough it is to get a dumb machine to understand what you say.

And yet even a toddler can pick up a phone and recognize Mom or Dad or Aunt Beth.

And the sheep know the shepherd when he calls.

If sheep have voice recognition, they at least have something going for them.

They're not total dummies, if they can hear his voice.

And Jesus is also clear on another point:

The sheep do know the shepherd.

"I know my own and my own know me," he says.

And then he moves a step away from the sheep metaphor: "I know my own and my own know me," he says, "just as the Father knows me and I know the Father."

There are two important words here:

The first word is "know."

When Jesus says he knows the Father, he's not talking about an intellectual achievement.

It's not really a matter of being smart or stupid; it's more along the lines of asking politely.

This is recognition, personal recognition, to "know" someone in the sense of "I know Dan, or Jill, or the guy who runs the corner store."

To know people is to have some sort of personal, ongoing relationship with them.

The second important word Jesus uses is "Father" —

It's a relational term, Father.

It's not some impersonal deity out there, a watchmaker who set the gears going and went away to let them wind down on their own.

This is the relationship of a parent with a child —

143

A mother with a baby at the breast, a father playing catch
with a son, Grandma baking cookies as the kids sip
their milk at the table —
Or, a sheepherder, who looks on his flock as if they were
his own children.
The sheep are not totally dumb; at least they know the shepherd, and they have some ongoing relationship with him.
What Jesus is telling us is that we are safe at home, and we are
loved.
To be a sheep is to know the Shepherd with that same intimacy that God shared with Jesus himself.
Jesus is the Good Shepherd not just because he knows the
sheep and the sheep know him, but because of his relationship to God.

"And," he says, "I lay down my life for the sheep."
It's the one qualification, and the hardest part of the job
description.
"The good shepherd lays down his life for the sheep," he says.
Contrast the hired hand, who runs away when the wolf howls.
The good shepherd puts his own life on the line, says Jesus.
And he's very clear that this is no accident.
It's not that the wolf snuck up on him, or that rustlers
conked him on the head when he wasn't looking.
Jesus lays down and takes up his own life voluntarily.
There's no force here, no breaking and entering, no abuse
of the weak.
Jesus gives it up of his own free will.
He gives up his life — no, he gives it away willingly.
He gives his life for us and to us.

And not just us here today, but the whole flock.
"I have other sheep that do not belong to this fold," Jesus tells
his disciples, hinting at what is to come next in the story,

144

how the community will spread across the land and abroad through their efforts, crossing ethnic boundaries from Jews to Greeks and Romans and everyone who listens to his voice.

"I have other sheep," he says, "I will bring them too, and they will listen to my voice."

Ultimately there will be one flock under one shepherd — one very large flock, one very great shepherd.

Which is how it should be.

Again, all I know is what it says in the books.

But it seems to be the case that sheep are supposed to travel in flocks.

Sheep are supposed to be together, under the leadership of the sheepherder, knowing if they know anything that the only way they can get through life is to stick together, to stick with the sheepherder, to do what the sheepherder says and go where the sheepherder says to go.

And indeed, here we are.

It's like coming home —

Home in the most ideal sense, home as the place you know you were meant to be.

You got here listening to the voice of the Good Shepherd —

Like the voice of your mother calling you home at dusk, home for dinner.

You go through the door into the house, where it's cozy, the lights are on, and you get your face washed with a warm damp washcloth before you sit down to dinner —

It's home, you've been called home.

The voice of Jesus, calling us home.

6. Preaching Resurrection In Acts

To turn to the Book of Acts from the Gospel of Luke is to experience *déjà vu*. Once again the mysterious Theophilus is addressed, in much the same words as before: "In the first book, Theophilus, I wrote about all that Jesus did and taught from the beginning ..." (Acts 1:1; cf. Luke 1:1-4). It has long been accepted that Acts is the second volume of the Gospel of Luke, and stylistic studies show beyond a doubt that the two books come from the same hand (thus we speak of the author of Acts as "Luke"). It was common practice in Greek and Roman literature to begin a book with a prologue (often addressed to a patron) and to signify the continuation of that book with a similar prologue. The maximum length of these ancient writings was determined by the practicalities of the scroll, which could only be so long (the codex, or book form, came into widespread use shortly after the New Testament books were written, in part because of its adoption by Christians, who could now have all of their sacred books in one volume). Luke needed two scrolls to tell his whole story. Luke and Acts are really of the same piece, one book in two volumes; thus biblical scholars typically speak of the entire work as Luke-Acts. For some of us, it seems odd to come to the last page of Luke and see on the next page the beginning not of Acts, but of John; a professor once suggested we get looseleaf Bibles so we could arrange the books properly!

Indeed, all that I said in the chapter on Luke could be repeated here. The same themes are present: the link with the Old Testament as a continuation of the biblical history (Acts 1:19-20; 2:17-21, 25-28, 31, 34-35; 3:18; 4:11, 25-26; 7:1-53; 8:32-33; 13:26-

27, 33-35, 41, 47; 15:1-35; 17:11; 18:28; 24:14; 26:6, 22; 28:23, 26-28); references to God's "plan" (*boule,* 2:23; 4:28; 5:38; 13:36; 20:27) and divine necessity (*dei,* 1:16; 3:21; 4:12; 9:16; 14:22; 17:3; 23:11; 27:24); the story of the prophet and the people, with Jesus as the prophet like Moses (7:1-53), the disciples as the new generation of prophets (2:43; 5:12) who seek to re-form the divided people of God (1:15-26; 2:41, 46; 5:14; 6:7; 9:31), which now includes the Gentiles (Acts 10-28); the preaching of the forgiveness of sins (2:38; 3:19; 5:31; 8:22; 11:18; 13:24; 17:30; 19:4; 20:21; 26:20) through the power of the Holy Spirit (1:5, 8; 2:1-13; 4:1-22; 5:12-42; 6:8-10; 8:4-40; 10:44-48; 11:27-28; 13:1-2; 4-12; 16:6-10; 18:24-28; 19:1-7; 19:21-22; 20:17-38; 21:1-14; 23:9; 28:25) to the ends of the earth (1:8).

For lectionary preachers (and their listeners), the *déjà vu* experience that is Acts is literally an Easter experience. The only time those who follow the lectionary read the Book of Acts in church is Easter, when it pinch-hits for the Old Testament. Liturgical planners recognize that Acts is an Easter book; the centrality of the risen Jesus comes through more clearly nowhere else in the New Testament, with the possible exception of the writings of Paul. And whereas Paul employs the resurrection as a factor in his pastoral care for the churches in his charge, Acts tells a story about what the risen Jesus has been up to in those churches — and in particular, how those churches came to be in the first place. This important witness is available to the worshiping community only during the Easter season; smart liturgists and preachers will make sure the message is heard.

What Jesus Began

The prologue to Acts is very clear: it is about what Jesus did next. "In the first book, Theophilus, I wrote about all that Jesus began (*archomai*) to do and teach from the beginning ..." (Acts 1:1, author's translation). Many translations (such as NRSV, which reads "Jesus did and taught") miss the significance of the word "began" — *archomai* is not simply a helping verb, but has inceptive force — thus the sentence means, "Jesus *began* to do and teach." The first book, the Gospel of Luke, begins the story of Jesus' deeds

148

and teaching. The implication is that this second volume, the Book of Acts, is about what he did next. Jesus will personally continue his work into the second book.

This is not mere metaphor on Luke's part. Jesus really does appear to do things and teach in Acts. Of course, he is there at the beginning, "giving instructions through the Holy Spirit to the apostles whom he had chosen" (1:2). Jesus takes this time to continue his work among them. "After his suffering he presented himself alive to them by many convincing proofs, appearing to them during forty days and speaking about the kingdom of God" (1:3). He also gives final instructions: "Wait for the promise of the Father" (1:4), "You will be baptized with the Holy Spirit not many days from now" (1:5). He stays with them until he is taken up into a cloud to heaven (1:11).

But this is not Jesus' final personal appearance in Acts. He keeps popping up again — for he is still alive; this is the central message of the resurrection preaching. He appears in Peter's first sermon as one who is alive and sitting exalted at the right hand of God (2:33). He appears in that same place to Stephen just before his martyrdom: "Filled with the Holy Spirit, he [Stephen] gazed into heaven and saw the glory of God and Jesus standing at the right hand of God. 'Look,' he said, 'I see the heavens opened and the Son of Man standing at the right hand of God!' " (7:55-56). Jesus speaks from heaven to Saul: "Now as he [Saul] was going along and approaching Damascus, suddenly a light from heaven flashed around him. He fell to the ground and heard a voice saying to him, 'Saul, Saul, why do you persecute me?' He asked, 'Who are you, Lord?' The reply came, 'I am Jesus, whom you are persecuting' " (9:3-5). Later, the Lord Jesus appears to Paul in a vision: "One night the Lord said to Paul in a vision, 'Do not be afraid, but speak and do not be silent; for I am with you, and no one will lay a hand on you to harm you, for there are many in this city who are my people' " (18:9-10). What Jesus began to do and teach in the Gospel of Luke, he personally continues in Acts.

Jesus also acts through intermediary characters. Foremost among these is the Holy Spirit. The connection between the Spirit and Jesus is so close that Acts calls it the "Spirit of Jesus" (16:7).

The Spirit comes according to Jesus' promise (1:8; 2:1-4) to empower the witness of the disciples "in Jerusalem, in all Judea and Samaria, and to the ends of the earth" (1:8). What many do not realize, until they have read Luke-Acts very closely, is that the Spirit is not confined to working through human proxies, but actually functions as a character in the narrative. This is evident in Luke's Gospel (Luke 1:35; 2:26-27; 3:22; 4:1; 10:21; 12:12), but abundantly clear in Acts.

The Holy Spirit in Luke-Acts functions as does any character in any story: it acts, and it comes into conflict with other characters. Acts presents the Spirit as an actor in the story: the Spirit "speaks" through scripture (Acts 1:16; 4:25; 28:25) and independently (8:29; 10:19-20; 11:12; 13:2; 21:11). The Spirit even "testifies" (20:23) and "forbids" (16:6-7), as well as giving words to others (2:1-4). It travels from one location to another (8:39-40; 19:6; cf. Luke 3:22). It appoints leaders (13:4; 20:28). This way of speaking of the Spirit draws on long precedent, as it is quite frequent in the Old Testament (cf. 2 Samuel 23:2; 1 Kings 22:24; Nehemiah 9:20; Psalm 143:10; Isaiah 63:10, 14; Ezekiel 2:2; 3:24; Zechariah 7:12; Wisdom 7:7, 22; 9:17).

As an actor in the story, the Spirit also comes into conflict and/or agreement with other characters. Ananias, in holding back part of his goods, has lied to the Spirit (Acts 5:3), and his wife Sapphira has tested or tempted the Spirit (5:9), with disastrous results. The Spirit does battle with magicians (8:9-25; 13:4-12). Even Paul and his companions butt heads with the Spirit (16:6-7). Thus prodding, pushing, resisting, and propelling, the Spirit continues the work of Jesus in a very personal way. When James says, "It seemed good to the Holy Spirit and to us" (Acts 15:28), one can almost picture the Spirit sitting in an easy chair among the disciples as if it were the most ordinary thing in the world.

The disciples, of course, are the ones who act most often on Jesus' behalf in Acts. Everything they do is done "in the name of Jesus" (2:38; 3:6; 4:7-10, 18, 30; 5:28, 40-41; 8:12, 16; 9:27-28; 16:18; 21:13). The disciples even take on the characteristics of Jesus, who for Luke is the prophet-like-Moses promised long ago (Acts 7:35-37). They, too, are prophets — sometimes explicitly characterized so (11:27-28; 21:9-10), but more often described in prophetic terms by Luke. Thus the disciples see visions and dream dreams (2:17; 7:55-56; 9:3-10; 10:3, 10-16; 11:5; 16:9-10; 18:9; 27:23). They are "filled with the Holy Spirit" (2:4; 4:8, 31; 5:32; 6:3, 5, 8; 7:55; 9:17; 11:24; 13:9, 52) to make "bold" proclamation (4:13; 13:46; 28:31) of the "good news" (5:42; 8:4, 12, 25, 40; 11:20; 13:32; 14:7; 15:35). Most important, they are "witnesses" (2:32; 10:41; 13:31; 22:20) who work "signs and wonders" (2:19; 4:16, 22, 30; 5:12; 6:8; 8:6, 13; 14:3; 15:12) among the "people" (3:22; 4:1; 6:8; 13:15). All this language draws on Old Testament prophetic imagery, particularly that of the prophet-like-Moses (Deuteronomy 34:10-12; Exodus 7:3, 9; 11:9-10; Deuteronomy 4:34; 6:22; 7:19; 11:3; 26:8; 29:3; Psalm 78:43; 105:27; 135:9). The disciples, like Jesus, act as prophets; they carry on his prophetic work among the people.

Toss Of The Coin

Jesus prepares the disciples personally for this continuing work by remaining with them for forty days, giving them proof of his bodily resurrection, and teaching them further about the kingdom of God (Acts 1:3). He reiterates the "promise of the Father" (Acts 1:4, cf. Luke 24:49), the gift of the Holy Spirit: "For John baptized with water, but you will be baptized with (or "in") the Holy Spirit not many days from now" (Acts 1:5; Jesus once again proves himself a prophet, since his words come true at Pentecost, 2:1-4). Jesus reiterates and extends John the Baptist's use of the term "baptize" (*baptizo*), which essentially meant "to dip"; the disciples would experience an overwhelming immersion in the Spirit soon (cf. 11:16; 19:1-7).

Since they have not yet experienced this total immersion of prophetic power, they are still a bit confused about what is happening: "Lord, is this the time when you will restore the kingdom to Israel?" (1:6). They do not realize that they are being formed as the basis of an entirely new Israel, one of a different order. They think of Israel as a political territory in space and time, while Jesus thinks of Israel as the people of God. The kingdom is God's rule over human hearts, and it will involve the proclamation of the prophetic word in the power of the Spirit and the formation of a new community around that message (2:41-47; 4:32-37). Jesus' reply steers them away from "times or periods" (1:7) toward their mission: "But you will receive power when the Holy Spirit has come upon you; and you will be my witnesses in Jerusalem, in all Judea and Samaria, and to the ends of the earth" (1:8). The disciples will indeed take on the name Jesus gives them, "witnesses" (cf. 2:32; 3:15; 5:32; 10:39, 41; 13:31; 22:15). The expression is double-edged; the disciples both witness to Jesus, and function as his representatives ("*my* witnesses").

Jesus' final word also sets out the geographical plan of Acts, and has often been seen as an outline for the book (1:8). Acts picks up where the Gospel left off, the center of the two-volume narrative is Jerusalem. Soon the disciples take their witness to the rest of Judea, and into Samaria (Acts 8), and then into the wide-ranging travels of Paul. There is some debate as to the significance of "the ends of the earth." Many believe that it refers to Paul's final trip to Rome (Acts 28), and thus signifies the actual end of the book. More likely, it refers to the extreme limit of the inhabited world, leaving the story to continue beyond the book's end. In fact, some ancient authors considered Ethiopia to be "the end of the earth," and in perhaps a sly allusion to that tradition, an Ethiopian is converted rather early in Acts (8:26-40). The story of the Ethiopian eunuch is but one instance of a character who is sent along from the pages of Acts to be a part of a larger untold story (Acts 8:39). But it is not necessary to go all the way to chapter 8 to find the disciples preaching to the inhabitants of far-off places; they do so immediately on receiving the Spirit at Pentecost, as the crowds that were gathered in Jerusalem for the festival hear the good news proclaimed in their native tongues: "Parthians, Medes, Elamites, and residents of Mesopotamia, Judea and Cappodocia, Pontus and Asia, Phrygia and Pamphylia, Egypt and the parts of Libya belonging to Cyrene, and visitors from Rome, but Jews and proselytes, Cretans, and Arabs — in our own languages we hear them speaking about God's deeds of power" (2:9-11).

The physical removal of Jesus himself from the sight of the disciples is reminiscent of Old Testament stories about the transition of prophetic power: Moses transmits his "spirit of wisdom" to Joshua (Deuteronomy 34:9), and Elijah is carried away in front of Elisha (2 Kings 2:9-12). Luke pictures Jesus similarly taken into heaven before the disciples (Acts 1:10-11). Once again, the prophetic mantle has been transferred. As they stand there gawking, two heavenly messengers assure them that they have not seen the last of him. As the King of Israel, enthroned at the right hand of God, he will be with them in a new and more powerful way (cf. 2:24-36; 7:55). As with Joshua and Elijah, the departure of the prophet makes way for the disciples to gain their share of the prophetic Spirit (1:8; 2:14; cf. Deuteronomy 34:9; 2 Kings 2:9).

The first order of business, however, is to re-form the community in light of its recent loss. That the narrative does not proceed directly to Pentecost is a sign of how important the next scene is; the story about the choosing of Matthias is not an awkward insertion. Rather, it is imperative for Luke's overall purpose. Judas' defection was not just a personal failure; it was a betrayal of his office as an apostle (everything about Peter's speech in Acts 1:15-22, which is quite different from Matthew's account of Judas' end [Matthew 27:3-4], points to Judas' defection from the Twelve). If Israel is to be re-formed on a new basis as the obedient people of God, it must also stand in continuity with Israel of old. The new Israel is not formed from scratch, but from the believing remnant, those who have accepted God's new prophetic visitation. Jesus himself had told them the plan: "I confer on you, just as my Father has conferred on me, a kingdom, so that you may eat and drink at my table in my kingdom, and you will sit on thrones judging the twelve tribes of Israel" (Luke 22:29-30). This Israel, like that of old, must have twelve leaders to represent the twelve tribes; the symbolism was essential. Thus the necessity of replacing Judas.

Peter uses the language of divine necessity: "One of these must (*dei*) become a witness with us to his resurrection" (1:22). All this is happening in accordance with God's plan ("the scripture had to be fulfilled," 1:16), and so confident are the disciples that God is at work here, that they are able to leave the final decision to the

153

casting of lots (a frequently-used decision-making tool in the ancient world, cf. Leviticus 16:8; Numbers 26:55; 33:54; Joshua 19:1-40; Jonah 1:7-8; Micah 2:5). Note, however, that there were criteria other than bald fate: Peter sets out absolute qualifications (it must be someone who was there from the beginning, Acts 1:21-22), cites scripture (1:20), and the entire community engages in prayer (1:24-25). The lot simply allows God to make the choice between two equally-qualified candidates.

Tongues On Fire

The promise of the Father (Luke 24:49), given first by John the Baptist (Luke 3:16) and reiterated by Jesus (Acts 1:5), comes to the band of disciples on the day of Pentecost: "When the day of Pentecost had come, they were all together in one place. And suddenly from heaven there came a sound like the rush of a violent wind, and it filled the entire house where they were sitting. Divided tongues, as of fire, appeared among them, and a tongue rested on each of them. All of them were filled with the Holy Spirit and began to speak in other languages, as the Spirit gave them ability" (Acts 2:1-4).

Pentecost was a harvest feast, but it may have been connected with the giving of the Law to Moses. Pentecost means simply "fifty," since the date was calculated as the fiftieth day after Passover. Originally the celebration of the spring harvest, the Feast of Weeks, Pentecost (along with Passover and Tabernacles) was one of the major feasts that brought pilgrims to Jerusalem to worship at the Temple (cf. Exodus 23:14-17; 34:18-24; Deuteronomy 16:16; 2 Chronicles 8:13). Later, the rabbis began to think of Pentecost as celebrating the giving of the Law, and as a covenant-renewal feast. Thus it was sometimes connected with the fire on Mount Sinai, and with flaming speech and speaking flame. Fire was often a symbol used for the Law, and also was connected with the presence of God (cf. Exodus 3:2; 13:21-22; 14:24; 19:18; 24:17). As enticing as these images may be in light of Acts 2, and Luke's ongoing comparison between Jesus and Moses, there is little evidence outside Luke-Acts that this connection between Pentecost and Sinai was made in Luke's time.

The crowds that hear the disciples' message are presumably from the large group of pilgrims who would normally gather for the feast, though Luke's statement that they were "living in Jerusalem" may indicate that they were permanent residents of that cosmopolitan city. The exact place is unspecified; Luke mentions only a "house" (2:2), perhaps the same house with the "upper room" of the previous scene (1:13). But this episode seems to happen out in the open, since the crowd gathered for the festival can hear them (2:5); this would eliminate the "upper room." Many have suggested somewhere in the Temple as a sensible locale, given the presence of the crowd, but this would be stretching the sense of "house"; Luke is at best unclear. Also unclear is the number of disciples who are present. In the upper room, there was a crowd of about 120 persons (1:15); however, in this scene, the only ones explicitly mentioned are Peter and the eleven (2:14) — but is the rest of the community implied by the scriptural references to sons, daughters, young men and old (2:17)? Throughout Acts, disciples other than the twelve receive and are empowered by the Spirit (e.g., 19:1-7), but at least on one other occasion the giving of the Spirit is connected exclusively to the original apostles (in Samaria, 8:14-17). Luke left loose ends in his narrative; some scholars have speculated that Acts is in some respects a not-quite-polished draft. Luke may have had theological reasons, however, to blur lines where the story touches on the Spirit, perhaps because he believed with John that "the Spirit blows where it chooses" (John 3:8).

The tangible aspects of the Spirit's appearance help stress its character. The designation of time, "suddenly," and place, "from heaven," highlight divine and not human control of the Spirit's action. Luke, like John, uses word-play to enhance the narrative, since "Spirit" (*pneuma*) can also mean "wind." In this case, there is a certain urgency, even violence, connected to the Spirit, since the sound coming from heaven is like the rush of a violent wind (Acts 2:2; note that Luke refers only to a sound — he does not say that wind actually rushed). The comparison with the wind also highlights the unpredictable nature of the Spirit. The sound "filled" the whole house, much as the Spirit would "fill" disciples to empower their witness (cf. 2:4; 4:8, 31; 6:3, 5, 8; 7:55; 9:17; 11:24;

155

13:9, 52; also Luke 1:15, 41, 67; 4:1). There are visible signs of the Spirit, "divided tongues, as of fire" (as with the wind, there is no actual fire, just a comparison). "Tongues of fire" (2:3) alludes not only to the audible tokens of the Spirit's empowerment (the disciples will speak in other languages, 2:4), but to John the Baptist's promise of baptism with the Spirit and fire (Luke 3:16; Acts 1:5). The prophecy that the disciples would be baptized with the Spirit is thus confirmed, as is the prediction that they would "be my witnesses in Jerusalem, in all Judea and Samaria, and to the ends of the earth" (Acts 1:8; cf. Luke 12:12), because the disciples immediately begin preaching to representatives of "the ends of the earth": "Now there were devout Jews from every nation under heaven living in Jerusalem. And at this sound the crowd gathered and was bewildered, because each one heard them speaking in the native language of each" (Acts 2:5-6). The catalog of nations that follows (2:7-11) has a slightly archaic flavor ("Medes, Elamites, and residents of Mesopotamia"), which lends a certain air to its allusion to "the ends of the earth."

Speaking in other languages (literally, "other tongues," *heterai glossai*) is one sign of the Spirit's presence in various stories throughout Acts (cf. 10:46; 19:6). In each case, the gift of other tongues has a clear and definite purpose in the narrative. Here, it enables the disciples to preach to the representatives from the ends of the earth. In the case of the centurion Cornelius, "speaking in tongues and extolling God" (10:46) confirms that the Gentiles have been given full admission to the people of God; Peter later will argue that the act of God giving the Spirit before he could even finish his sermon was sure proof that the movement toward the Gentiles was divine: "If then God gave them the same gift that he gave us when we believed in the Lord Jesus Christ, who was I that I could hinder God?" (11:17). In the case of the disciples of John the Baptist found in Ephesus, "they spoke in tongues and prophesied" (19:6) to signify that they had finally received John's promise of baptism in fire and the Spirit.

It is impossible to make Luke's picture of tongues-speaking and the gift of the Spirit into systematic theology. The coming of the Spirit is sometimes connected with the laying-on-of-hands

(8:17; 19:6), but not always (2:4; 10:44); it is definitely connected with baptism (2:38; 19:6), but may precede it (10:44). The coming of the Spirit sometimes results in speaking in tongues (2:4; 10:45; 19:6), but not always (8:15-17). Luke is certainly nowhere near as systematic when it comes to this spiritual gift as Paul (cf. 1 Corinthians 12-14). It is clear that for Luke, the primary function of the Spirit is to empower the disciples for their witness to Jesus, sometimes through extraordinary actions (Acts 1:26; 8:29, 39-40; 13:4; 16:6-7), but most often by inspiring the disciples' speech (Acts 1:8; 2:4; 4:8, 31; 5:32; 6:3, 5, 10; 7:55; 9:17; 11:24, 28; 13:9; 15:28; 21:4, 11). The Spirit in Luke-Acts is primarily the prophetic Spirit, which inspires the witness to Jesus.

There is some debate whether the speech of Pentecost was a miracle of speaking or hearing (this is somewhat related to the wider debate, beyond the scope of this book, about whether tongues-speaking, ancient or modern, has actual linguistic structure or is only ecstatic unstructured utterance; most linguists think the latter). On the one hand, Luke asserts that the disciples spoke in "other tongues," as if they were actually speaking the various languages of the Parthians, Medes, et al. On the other hand, the crowd is said to be bewildered, because "each one *heard* them speaking in the native language of each" (2:6); if one places the emphasis on the verb "heard," then we are talking about miraculous hearing as much as miraculous speaking. The picture in the first case here would be of a veritable Babel, with each disciple speaking a different language, and it would be hard to see how anyone could hear anything through all that noise; the second scenario, with the disciples speaking in harmony, and each ear translating for itself, makes for a cleaner picture. However, Luke clearly portrays the disciples, not the crowd, as inspired by the Spirit, and the portrait of disciples speaking the good news in many languages fits in well with Luke's overall story of the proclamation to the ends of the earth. The disciples' inspired speech in languages they have not learned foreshadows the universality of the Christian mission.

As we have already seen, Luke's narrative portrait in this scene is not without its rough edges — he even pictures the whole crowd speaking the same words in unison! This should not bother us too much; Luke's narrative is stylized, and conforms to the standards of historical writing of his day, where speeches often were used to put events into perspective for the reader. Speeches of ancient historians often were a form of authorial commentary, pointing the readers to the true meaning of the story; they were not meant so much to portray the actual words spoken, but the general feeling of the situation. In this, Luke succeeds admirably.

Peter's speech in the power of the Spirit sets the tone for the story that follows. With the eleven standing in support behind him, he debunks the notion that the work of the Spirit represents drunken speech (2:14; cf. 2:13). Not only is it too early in the morning to be drinking, what has happened here is the fulfillment of scripture: "In the last days it will be, God declares, that I will pour out my Spirit upon all flesh, and your sons and your daughters shall prophesy, and your young men shall see visions, and your old men shall dream dreams" (2:17-18; cf. Joel 2:28). Peter's sermon is littered with other references to scripture, reflecting Luke's conviction that this is the fulfillment and continuation of the biblical story (2:17-21, 25-28, 31, 34-35); it is part of "the definite plan (*boule*) and foreknowledge of God" (2:23). The sermon is a concise summary of Luke's view of the whole: Jesus was attested a prophet by "deeds of power, wonders, and signs" (2:22), was "killed by the hands of those outside the law" (2:23), but raised by God from a death that could not keep him in its power (2:24). The disciples are witnesses of this resurrection, proclaimers of his exaltation to the right hand of God, and receivers of his promise of the Holy Spirit (2:32-33). Their message is simple, and repeated again and again throughout Acts: "Repent, and be baptized every one of you in the name of Jesus Christ so that your sins may be forgiven; and you will receive the gift of the Holy Spirit" (2:38; cf. 3:19; 5:31; 8:22; 10:43; 11:18; 13:38; 17:30; 19:4; 20:21; 26:18, 20). Peter speaks for all the others, and his words echo through the entire book; at last, the tongues of the disciples have caught fire, and the world will be turned upside down for it (17:6).

The rest of the world will have to wait a bit, however. Peter directs this particular message to "the entire house of Israel" (Acts

2:36). The target market is Israel; the goal is the re-formation of the people of God. Though their leaders had rejected the prophet on his first visitation (2:36, "this Jesus whom *you* crucified"), they now have received a second chance to recognize God's work among them: "Save yourselves from this corrupt generation" (2:40). The promise of God has come to Israel, "for you, for your children" (2:39); yet there is an ever-so-gentle hint of the universal mission to come, for the promise is also "for all who are far away, everyone whom the Lord our God calls" (2:39).

Peter's speech leads immediately to the formation of a new community: "Those who welcomed his message were baptized, and that day about 3,000 persons were added" (2:41). The community grows exponentially (and it is beside the point to ask how they could baptize so many people in one day — Luke simply indicates tremendous and immediate success among the people). The community begins at once to take on the characteristics of their new reality: "They devoted themselves to the apostles' teaching and fellowship, to the breaking of bread and the prayers" (2:42). As good Israelites, they gather daily in the Temple (2:46). The prophetic community continues to experience "many wonders and signs being done by the apostles" (2:43). In sharing their possessions, the community creates a new social order as well (2:44-46), to which new members are added daily (2:47). Thus Luke depicts the successful beginning of the new Israel, with the apostles at its spiritual head; the entire community shares the gift of the empowering Spirit, as well as their material goods. The faithful remnant has responded to God's visitation and become a community of prophets themselves.

Where We Ended

The sense of *déjà* vu increases as one reads through the Book of Acts. Paul seems to mimic Peter, who both mimic Jesus. Peter gives a grand speech to the people of Jerusalem (2:14-36); Paul gives a similar speech to the synagogue in Pisidian Antioch (13:16-41). Peter follows his speech with healing the lame man at the Temple (3:1-10); Paul follows his with the healing of the crippled man at Lystra (14:8-18). Both follow the pattern of Jesus, who

159

followed his big speech at the synagogue in Nazareth (Luke 4:16-30) with cures of "any who were sick with various kinds of diseases" (Luke 4:40). These "signs and wonders" accompanied by the prophetic word mark Luke's stereotypical use of the biblical tradition of the prophet, which is the model for all the heroes in Luke-Acts. The risen Jesus continues his work through his disciples, who act in the same prophetic manner as he did.

It is Paul, of course, who gets most of the attention in Acts, once he appears on the scene. From his first appearance as coatholder at the stoning of Stephen (Acts 7:58), and his subsequent role as persecutor of the church (8:1-3), through his call by the risen Jesus (9:1-31) and his appointment directly by the Holy Spirit (13:1-3), Paul ever so gradually takes over the story. While there had been a few forays by Christian missionaries into Gentile territory (11:19-20), it is Paul who becomes the apostle to the Gentiles, preaching in town after town first to the synagogue, then to the entire city (cf. 13:46; 18:6; 28:28). On this point at least, Luke's portrait of Paul is consistent with that found in Paul's own letters (cf. Romans 1:16). As the Book of Acts moves along, it becomes more and more the story of how a small Jewish messianic movement became a Gentile religion, and thus it becomes more and more a story about Paul.

But Peter, not Paul, makes the crucial move toward the Gentiles. Luke's ultimate concern is to show how God had fulfilled the promises to Israel, and he needs Peter for that. Luke is careful to trace the connection between the restored people of Israel in the early chapters of Acts and the largely Gentile Pauline church in the later sections of the book, lest anyone conclude that God has actually abandoned Israel by turning to the Gentiles. No, it is exactly as Paul had said: the promise was offered first to the Jews, who were divided in their response to God's prophetic visitation, but since it had been offered, God was now free to expand the promise to all nations, which had been the plan all along. It is Peter who provides the link between a gospel preached only to the Jews, and one given to the Jews first, then the Gentiles.

Peter resists at first. Even though the universal mission had been promised by Jesus himself (Luke 24:47; Acts 1:8), it was not something that a faithful Jew could easily grasp. When the hungry Peter sees a bevy of ritually unclean food laid before him in a vision, he is aghast at the suggestion of the voice from heaven that he eat; he has never broken kosher in his life! The threefold vision is a matter of some puzzlement for Peter, until he receives a message to come to the house of a certain Italian centurion named Cornelius. Though "it is unlawful for a Jew to associate with or to visit a Gentile" (Acts 10:28), Peter is encouraged by his vision to respond to Cornelius anyway. He is further amazed to hear Cornelius' own story of a vision of an angel of God, and even more amazed that Cornelius and his party receive the Holy Spirit before he can even finish his sermon (10:1-48). Peter is finally convinced: "Can anyone withhold the water for baptizing these people who have received the Holy Spirit just as we have?" (10:47).

The extent of Peter's perceived transgression is made apparent immediately, when the believers in Judea criticize him, not for the preaching *per se* — it would have been perfectly acceptable for Peter to convert some Gentiles to messianic Judaism — but for his table fellowship with them: "Why did you go to uncircumcised men and eat with them?" (11:3). Luke notes that Peter recounted the entire story of his vision and meeting with Cornelius, "step by step" (*kathexes*, 11:4). Peter's compelling story is successful in silencing his critics (11:1-18). The end result is in fact a sort of awe: "Then God has given even to the Gentiles the repentance that leads to life" (11:18).

Unsurprisingly, this episode is not the end of the matter. When Paul and Barnabas find success among the Gentiles in Syrian Antioch, they are faced with a contingent of their fellow messianic Jews from Judea, who claim, "Unless you are circumcised according to the custom of Moses, you cannot be saved" (15:1). The debate spills back into Jerusalem and the so-called "Apostolic Council" (15:4-35). Here again, the power of story asserts itself. Peter stands and retells his own story: "You know that in the early days God made a choice among you, that I should be the one through whom the Gentiles would hear the message of the good news and become believers" (15:7). Peter thus enables the community to hear Paul and Barnabas tell their story "of all the signs and wonders that God had done through them among the Gentiles" (15:12). The prophetic community has been at work even among the Gentiles! The community concludes that they must welcome the Gentiles, while laying down some rules for table fellowship between Jewish and Gentile Christians (15:19-21).

It is hardly a surprise that Luke would present the early Christian community as swayed by the story of the prophetic community at work, because that is exactly what Luke is trying to do with his two-volume work. This he told us from the beginning, in his original dedication to Theophilus: "Since many have undertaken to order a narrative (*diegesis*) of the events that have been fulfilled among us, just as they were handed onto us by those who from the beginning were eyewitnesses and servants of the word, I too decided, after investigating everything carefully from the very first, to write step-by-step (*kathexes*) for you, most excellent Theophilus, so that you may know certainty (*asphaleia*) concerning the things about which you have been instructed (*katecheo*)" (Luke 1:1-4, author's translation).

While "Theophilus" means "friend who loves God," and thus could be a literary fiction, it is just as likely that Theophilus was a real person — probably Luke's financial patron — who had already been given official instruction in the Christian faith (*katecheo* is the root from which we get the word "catechesis," cf. Acts 18:25; Romans 2:8; 1 Corinthians 14:19; Galatians 6:6). Luke thus writes for an audience who is already instructed in and persuaded by the Christian faith.

Luke is quite clear about the purpose of his writing: it is to provide "certainty" (*asphaleia*). Many translations miss the significance of this word (cf. NRSV, "that you may know the truth"). *Asphaleia* does not mean "truth" as opposed to "falsehood." In ancient times, it was used as a legal financial term for "written security"; elsewhere in Luke-Acts, it refers to securely-locked doors (Acts 5:23), and the adjectival form is usually translated "safe, steadfast" (Philippians 3:1; Hebrews 6:19). Luke's stated intention is not to give Theophilus knowledge of the truth — he already has been taught that — but security, or assurance; Luke intends to assure Theophilus of the truth he already knows.

The truth Theophilus already knows is precisely the truth of Luke's story, the "things that have been fulfilled among us" (Luke 1:1): that God has visited the people with a prophet-like-Moses, who showed by signs and wonders that it was time for a new Israel to be formed, based not on territory or lineage, but on the response of faith to what God was doing among the people. But the leaders of the people rejected the prophet, and like so many prophets before him, put him to death. God proved that this was no run-of-the-mill prophet by raising him from the dead and exalting him to God's own right hand. Thus the people were given a second chance to respond to God's visitation. Once the people had been given that chance, God would fulfill the long-delayed promise to bring the good news to all nations.

Why does Theophilus need "assurance" of this? One need only look at his Greek name, or the last half of the Book of Acts. The community Theophilus came into was overwhelmingly Gentile. Yet God's promises were to the Jews! If the historical Jewish people were not in possession of the promise, how could anyone believe that God was faithful to any promise? If God's word could fail the Jews, could it not also fail the Gentiles? The problem Luke was dealing with was the problem of theodicy: how to account for the justice of God in an imperfect world. Luke's answer is that God *did* fulfill the promise, first to Israel, then to the nations. Only, the Jewish community was divided over God's visitation; some believed in the prophet-like-Moses, others did not. God remains faithful despite the division, and that faithfulness is shown precisely in the turn to the Gentiles: that which had been promised for so long, good news to all the nations, was now fulfilled.

And how is Luke to bring this assurance to Theophilus (and by extension, to all who read this story)? We have already seen the power Luke attributes to a story well-told. In Acts 11-15, the repeated narratives given by Peter, supplemented by the stories of Paul and Barnabas, win the day. The conviction of Peter's story came in his careful telling "step-by-step" (*kathexes*); Luke uses the same word to describe his own writing (Luke 1:3; cf. 11:4). Luke, like Peter, is setting forth a narrative (*diegesis*), and in that narrative he shows us again and again the power of narrative itself (cf. his use of the verb form, "to narrate," *diogeomai,* to describe convincing stories, Luke 8:39; 9:10; Acts 8:33; 9:27; 12:17). The orderly story, set forth step-by-step, shows us that God's plan has been moving step-by-step itself, in order that all of God's promises may be fulfilled.

So in the end we understand Luke-Acts by understanding its beginning. When Paul finally stands before the Jews of Rome at the end of Acts, he finds them just as divided as the people of God have been throughout the narrative: "Some were convinced by what he had said, while others refused to believe. So they disagreed with each other" (Acts 28:24-25). For Paul, this is merely a sign that the promises of God in scripture had been fulfilled (28:25-27). Paul announces God's next move: "Let it be known to you then that this salvation of God has been sent to the Gentiles; they will listen" (28:28). Does this close the door on the Jewish people, and Paul's hope that they will recognize the new visitation of God? By no means! This is simply the announcement he has made in city by city, as he went from one place to another preaching the good news first to Israel, then to the nations (cf. 13:46; 18:6). There is no reason to think that Paul would have varied that pattern in the next town.

We never learn what happened next, because the story ends with Paul spending two years in Rome, "proclaiming the kingdom of God and teaching about the Lord Jesus Christ with all boldness and without hindrance" (28:31). The Book of Acts famously ends without ending; we never learn the ultimate fate of Paul, or the result of his trial (though speculation abounds). I believe Luke's ending is of a piece with his overall plan. The ending is open because it must be; the narrative is unfinished because the plan is yet to be fully realized. God is a faithful God, who will assuredly bring the entire promise to fulfillment. The Spirit will continue to work among both Jews and Gentiles. The risen Jesus will continue all that he began to do and to teach, until the good news really has been carried literally to every corner of the ends of the earth. For Luke, there can be no closure of the story, as long as there is gospel left to preach.

Jolt For Jesus

Easter 3, Year C — Acts 9:1-19a
April 26, 1998

The Book of Acts presents us with a series of conversions; one can hardly leaf past a page without running across a story about mass baptism (2:41), mass healing (5:12-16), the positive response to the gospel of an entire group such as the Samaritans (8:6), the Lystrans (14:8-18), or the Beroeans (17:10-12), or the conversion of individuals such as the Ethiopian eunuch (8:26-40), Apollos (18:24-28), or even entire families such as that of Lydia (16:14) or the Philippian jailer (16:25-34).

In some Christian communities the moment of conversion is distinctive, and considered the most important time of one's life, a "spiritual birthday." In other communities, baptism is honored in this way, sometimes apart from, sometimes in addition to, any moment of personal enlightenment. Some communities allow for various degrees of conversion over a lifetime; it does not make sense, for example, to "convert" someone who has grown up amid the symbols and rituals of the church and never strayed from them. One could point to the Bible itself for a wide understanding of how people come to a mature Christian faith, ranging from Paul's dramatic conversion (Acts 9:1-29) to Timothy's quiet acceptance of Christianity on the knee of his mother and grandmother (2 Timothy 1:5). One may even point to variety in the retelling of Paul's own conversion, which is given in three distinct and differing versions in Acts (9:1-29; 22:3-21; 26:9-20), in addition to Paul's allusions to it in his own writings (e.g., Philippians 3:4-11; 1 Corinthians 15:8-10).

But whether a particular community stresses conversion, or whether it contains folk who can point to such valued religious experience alongside with people who see faith more as a given (or perhaps as an evolution), most Christian communities would agree that faith is expressed in an ongoing commitment rather than a single moment. Thus I believe it is important to stress that Paul's conversion was even more so a call. Not everyone can relate to the drama that brought Paul to faith, but this is not the aspect of Paul's encounter with Jesus that provides a model for all of us — it is not Paul's conversion but his call that is a normative example. We do not all come to faith through a dramatic reversal of our lives; we are all called to serve Jesus in the lives we have been given.

I don't remember where I got the wacky opening story, but I believe it was from an irreverent ecclesiastical website called "Ship of Fools" (www.ship-of-fools.com), which provides a constant catalog of Christian absurdities. Preachers can find plenty of humorous sermon fodder here, though one must remember that there can be too much of a good thing; what seems hilarious to pulpiteers who must deal constantly with the Church's failings is not necessarily funny to those who take time out of their week to hear a serious word from God.

This sermon was preached at Christ Church, Avon, Connecticut.

I don't know if this is true, but there is supposedly a minister in
    Florida who was accidentally shocked by the battery while
    working on his car.
The experience was so profound that he took it as a sign from
    God.
So he invented a new ritual, not baptism but "zaptism."
He hooks people up to car batteries and "zaptizes" them into
    the kingdom.

Come to think of it, I know a few people who could use a jolt for
    Jesus.
But the idea of God as an electric experience is not a new one.
The writer Dan Wakefield wrote a spiritual biography called
    Returning, which talked about what happened one night
    when he was a young boy.
He had the sensation that his whole body was filled with
    electric light.

166

"It was a white light of such brightness and intensity that it seemed almost silver. It was neither hot nor cold, neither burning nor soothing, it was simply *there*, filling every part of [his] body from [his] head to [his] feet." (Dan Wakefield, *Returning,* 40)
He believed that the light was Christ.

Years later, when Wakefield went to college and became an atheist, he didn't know what to do with his experience of being zapped; it was the kind of thing you could not deny, but it also did not fit with being an atheist.
He stumbled across a book by William James, called *The Varieties of Religious Experience.*
James talked about experiences called "photisms."
It turns out that lots of religious people — mystics, saints, preachers, even ordinary people — have this experience of blinding light.
"Was blind but now I see."
Ironically, learning about photisms gave Wakefield a way out.
He could explain his zaptism psychologically — just a hallucination, happens all the time.
You could see the light without necessarily seeing God.

The Book of Acts is not going to let us off the hook so easily.
Saul on the road to Damascus has the quintessential photism.
There is the blinding light, flashing from heaven, so intense that no one can see anything.
It's so bright that Saul himself was blinded for three days afterward. He has to be led around by the hand.
But it's not just light, there's also a voice, "Saul, Saul, why do you persecute me?"
Saul does not seem to understand whom or what he is dealing with.

The words we translate, "Who are you, Lord?" could simply be a polite form of address, "Who are you, sir?" Saul only unwittingly confesses the truth.

The answer comes from above, "I am Jesus, whom you are persecuting."

At these words, Saul goes into serious reevaluation of his life, neither eating or drinking, just praying, for three days.

Let's be clear about what's at stake here.

This is the same Saul that held coats while the mob stoned Stephen, the first Christian to die for his faith.

The Book of Acts tells us that Saul was "breathing threats and murder against the disciples of the Lord."

This guy was a terrorist. "Breathing threats and murder" — he exhaled death, his life's breath was spent in hatred.

The letters of extradition he gathered were probably not even legal.

But he was determined that "if he found any who belonged to the Way, men or women, he might bring them bound to Jerusalem."

Is it any wonder that Ananias, the disciple and prophet from Damascus, objects?

I'd object; I'd be hiding in the basement.

"Go to the street called Straight, look in the house of Judas for *Saul*?"

Are you kidding? Do I look like a fool? Are my pants on backward? "I have heard about this man," Ananias says to the risen Jesus, "the evil he has done, how he's here to do more."

But Jesus answers, "He is my chosen instrument. He will bring my name to Gentiles and kings and all the people. And I myself will show him how much he must suffer for my name."

It is a little rhetorical trick the Book of Acts plays here, using the conversation between Ananias and Jesus as a preview of coming attractions.

It's a summary of the story from here on out, how Saul will carry forth the mission to Gentiles and kings and the ends of the earth, with no little suffering along the way.

He's been zapped, but the point is not the zapping, the point is what comes next.

If you read William James closely enough, you'll find that the experience of blinding light usually brings with it a divine demand. It is not the opiate of the people; Saul gets blindness, not bliss. What's important is what's next.

Ananias lays hands on Saul and something like scales fall from his eyes, and you don't need me to explain that symbolism.

This man named Saul we know better by his Greek name, Paul; he is the same Paul who wrote a third of the New Testament.

I do not for one minute believe that everyone is going to get zapped by God. There's a good reason that William James called his book *The Varieties of Religious Experience.* We're not all the same. We're not all going to have the same experience. Not everyone is struck by blinding light.

But I do believe that we are all called to follow the path set for Saul *after* he saw the light.

It is the same path Ananias followed into the terrorist cell armed with nothing but the Word of the Lord and the water of baptism.

It is the path Jesus himself followed.

Dan Wakefield wrote about this path near the end of his book, *Returning* —

>You didn't think I was going to leave him back there an atheist, did you?

No, Wakefield came back, and told the story of being at a retreat with his pastor, a man named Carl.

Carl seems to be a man who renews himself by giving himself, Wakefield said.

>He watched Carl talk to a troubled man at the retreat. This man was going through a nasty divorce; he had moped through the weekend.

>Carl said how great it was to have the man with them.

>*Are you kidding?* thought Wakefield. *What a loser.*

>Carl told the man he'd like to have lunch someday back in the city, if the man could spare the time.

>*You liar, Carl. No one would like to have lunch with that guy.*

>But then Wakefield looked at the man's face.

>Scales fell.

To follow Jesus means more than seeing the light.

>To follow Jesus is to act like him, to give yourself away daily.

The last time I saw a photism was at the movies.

>*Phenomenon.* John Travolta looks up and sees a blinding light streaking toward him.

The movie plays out various explanations for his experience.

But we don't find out the truth until the end, when he looks into his girlfriend's eyes and says, "Will you love me for the rest of my life?"

"No," she says. "I'm going to love you for the rest of my life."

When *we* look at Jesus and ask if there are any limits, the answer showers scales from our eyes.

170

Voices Of Hate, Voice Of Love

Easter 3, Year C — Acts 9:1-19a
April 30, 1995

Here is another take on the story of the conversion/call of Paul, this time in a very different historical context.

On April 19, 1995 a car bomb exploded at the Murrow Federal Building in Oklahoma City, killing 187 people. America's rage was palpable: "We will find those who did this, and we will bomb their country back to the stone age," was the cry on talk radio. Drastic measures to protect our borders and limit our freedoms were under consideration. Rage turned to shock days later when an American citizen, Timothy McVeigh, a military veteran who claimed to be a patriot, was arrested and proved linked to the bombing. The President promised to seek the death penalty. America applauded.

McVeigh is now dead by lethal injection, but his death did not bring closure, safety, or comfort. America still reels under the threat of hatred, and still threatens and demands retaliation, even when the object of our retaliation would have to move up to get into the stone age. The cycle of violence spirals downward.

Current circumstances do influence how people hear sermons; people sometimes referred to this sermon as the "anti-death-penalty sermon," even though it was not particularly that, and more than that. I suppose it will be heard quite differently today, in the aftermath of even more devastating terrorist attacks.

This sermon was preached at Emmanuel Episcopal Church, Quakertown, Pennsylvania.

Here is a man who is angry.
He puts on camouflage, he trains in weapons and self-defense.
He calls together his troops.
Here is a man who kicks in doors, dragging men and women
out of their homes, throwing them in jail to await the pre-
dictable verdict of a kangaroo court.

171

No, this man is not a member of the Michigan Militia, or the Aryan Nation, or even the Bureau of Alcohol, Tobacco, and Firearms.

The name of the man is Saul. He lived in Jerusalem about 2,000 years ago.

We don't know why he was so angry.

Why does anyone burn so fiercely inside that he takes to guns and bombs and paramilitary training?

But angry he was — enraged at an obscure little group of Jews who called themselves "The Way." This little group claimed to have found the Messiah in a crucified Galilean peasant who (they said) was still alive.

We know that Saul was in his own words a Hebrew of Hebrews and a Pharisee of Pharisees. He was impeccably religious, extremely zealous for the traditions of his ancestors. Everyone knew that those traditions said nothing about a Messiah from Galilee, and pronounced a curse on one who hung from a cross.

Wherever his anger came from, however religious he may have been, Saul's actions were those of a terrorist. "Saul, breathing threats and murder against the disciples of the Lord, went to the high priest and asked him for letters to the synagogues at Damascus, so that if he found any who belonged to the Way, men or women, he might bring them bound to Jerusalem."

This was his last act as a terrorist.

What did it take to get him to stop?

Did the early Christians rise up in arms against him? Did they recruit the National Guard to block the road? Did they unleash the FBI, vote to repeal the Bill of Rights, legislate against everyone remotely connected to Saul and his friends?

No. You see, their Galilean carpenter had told them to love their enemies, to pray for those who persecuted them.

They believed that violence was not the answer. "Shoot straight for the head" was not an option. They knew that violence solves nothing.

But, oh, you say, didn't the Bible say, "An eye for an eye...?" Well, just look at how well that's worked for the modern state of Israel.

Or maybe you'd rather live where car bombs are everyday dangers, where school teachers carry Uzis on routine field trips, where the hate smoulders overhead like the noxious fumes above a burning garbage dump.

Violence solves nothing. All violence does is breed more violence.

But maybe you'd rather live in a land where the only certainty is that your neighbors hate you, and your neighbors' children hate your children, and their children's children your children's children.

The early Christians refused the way of violence. Saul breathing threats and murder did not prompt them to arms. They did not answer rage with rage.

Instead they followed the advice of their Lord. They prayed for their enemies.

Jesus answers the prayer in person.

He appears to Saul on the road to Damascus in blinding light.

He turns Saul with one question, and one answer. "Saul, Saul, why do you persecute me?"

"Who are you, Lord?"

"I am Jesus, whom you are persecuting."

Saul finds himself completely blind. Bright light can do that to you. In this case, the bright light exposed Saul to the bone, the physical blindness being symbolic of the state of his heart. Saul has been so blind — blind to his rage, his hatred, his self-righteousness.

Like so many people, he had chosen to live by his worst instincts and yet call them his best instincts. It doesn't take much to go blind — to fool yourself, to think that the hate in your heart is justified, and that anything you do out of that hate is good for you, God, and country.

In that moment of blindness — the minute you fool yourself into thinking that you can solve the problem by force — in that moment is born a terrorist.

I suspect that most of us, in our most honest moments, know how tempting it is to turn to rage, and how hard it is once we've turned to rage to stop ourselves from turning to fists, knives, and guns.

There are in our hearts and along the road many voices calling to us. Only one is the voice of Jesus. And the voice of Jesus does not say, "Shoot for the head."

Saul the terrorist had listened for oh so long to the wrong voice. But even after years of mistaken, misguided, hurtful living, he was changed the minute he heard the voice of Jesus — so powerful is the voice of Truth over the many voices of evil.

There remains for Saul one last step in this conversion.

Repentance requires restitution and reconciliation. To say "I forgive but I won't forget" is never to forgive at all.

So Saul must become a part of the community he has up to this point terrorized. That's the way God works.

There was in Damascus a disciple named Ananias. The Lord appeared to Ananias and said, "Get up and go to the street called Straight, and at the house of Judas look for a man of Tarsus named Saul."

But Ananias said, "Lord, are you kidding? I have heard about this man, how much evil he has done to your saints in

174

Jerusalem; and here he has authority to bind all who invoke your name."

Ananias is the sensible Christian — Lord, let's not get too idealistic here. People don't change overnight. How do we know we can trust this guy? And don't we need to make him pay, and pay good, for his crimes? God, are you sure you know what you're doing when you bring this terrorist scum into our pews?

But Jesus said, "Go, for he is an instrument whom I have chosen to bring my name before Gentiles and kings and before the people of Israel; I myself will show him how much he must suffer for the sake of my name."

You see, Jesus turns the tables entirely. Yes, Saul is a terrorist. Yes, he has caused much suffering. He will suffer for it. But he will suffer *in my name.*

God will do what God always does: turn evil to good, change those who do harm into those who bring good news to the people.

Ananias went to the street called Straight and laid his hands on Saul. The scales fell from Saul's eyes, and he went on to become the man we now call Saint Paul.

These are difficult days to be followers of Jesus.

The voices raised in hate are loud and raucous.

It's a very small quiet voice that calls us to put aside hate as a way of life, to disassemble our guns and turn them in to be melted down and fashioned into plowshares, to wield those plows for the good of all people, and to use fertilizer for nothing more than to refresh our fields.

Those who refuse to yield to the voice of hate may not be popular. Society tends to rally around the like-minded, and our society does not seem to understand that violence is the problem, not the solution. The voice we follow tells us, as it told Saul, that we will suffer in his name.

175

Living in Truth has its price.

But what does it cost us to live in hate? What is the price of hate?

Jesus calls us to live in love.

How can we afford anything less?

The Lord Of All Choices

Easter 7, Year B — Acts 1:15-26
May 11, 1997

One way to sustain anticipation in a sermon is to promise something at the beginning, but make them wait for it. This I do in the opening sentences. The tactic is risky, because you really have to come through on the promise, and you have to keep them interested enough along the way so that they will still be with you at the conclusion. The reader can judge how well I did that.

This sermon is an attempt to deal with the complex issue of Christian discernment in the short space of a sermon. Acts 1 provides the perfect opportunity to do that, because it portrays the early Christian community in the process of making a decision. It is disarming in a way, because the decision seems fairly inconsequential on the face of it — the choosing of an apostle that no one ever heard from again. The text is surprisingly deep; on the surface it seems to involve no more than a roll of the dice, but the underlying process involves much more. It is also a forbidding text, because it bristles with strange and foreign elements; it is not clear to modern folk why the choice of Matthias was worth so much ink, nor do most people resonate with Peter's method of scriptural interpretation, and as for the process of choosing by lots, that's usually reserved for deciding who gets the ball first in a football game.

But it is precisely because of its obscurity and seeming irrelevance that the text is such a convenient jumping-off point. It presents us with a community making a decision not our own; we can be perfectly objective here, because there is nothing of our own at stake (try, for example, to do a sermon on discernment using the example of whether to abort a deformed fetus, and see how far you get). It also presents us with a God who thinks and acts on a plane different from our own; there is no danger of confusing our will with the deity's. This is an instance where the historical conditioning of the biblical text offers us an opportunity to hear a word from outside our own historical and social context, and thus gives us a token of that Word which comes from outside history altogether.

This sermon was preached at St. Luke's Episcopal Church, Katonah, New York.

Preview of what is to come:

Before the morning is over, I will explain to you the will of the Lord.

But first, let's set the scene.

Jesus is gone, but there is no reverential silence.

You have to expect a little noise when you have people jammed in like commuters on a train at rush hour.

Imagine 120 people crammed into your living room, the clatter of plates and coffee cups, the children playing in a corner, the din of dozens of little conversations going on at once, every cushion and chair filled, every nook and cranny pulsing with protoplasm.

Finally Peter rises and quiets the crowd. He speaks.

Seems there needs to be an election.

One of the apostles is missing — that symbolic twelfth apostle that fills out the number to match the ancient sons of Israel.

You couldn't start this new movement in Judaism with fewer than twelve tribes, anymore than you could leave the flag with 48 stars once Alaska and Hawaii joined the union.

We've got to have a new apostle to replace Judas, according to Peter.

So let's try the Lotto approach.

They cast lots to choose the winner.

They cleared out some floor space against the wall and shot craps.

But of course, there's more to it than that.

Peter begins by appealing to scripture, in the conviction that God has already spoken to the issue in the words of the Old Testament.

"The Holy Spirit spoke through David," he says, and he quotes from the Psalms.

For that matter, even the idea of casting lots probably came from the Bible.

The ancient high priests determined the will of the Lord by using something called Urim and Thummin —

Nobody knows exactly what the Urim and Thummin were, but some people think they were just a set of dice.

Now it may seem odd to us today that Peter could at will pull out a Bible verse that fits.

But you have to remember that he had extensive knowledge of the scriptures.

These people ate, drank, and slept Bible.

This is not, by the way, that practice of treating the Bible like an oracle — where you let it fall open to a page and point.

Like the guy who was wondering what God wanted him to do, and he let his Bible fall open to Matthew's story about what happened to the traitor: O God, what do you want me to do? Plunk: "Judas went out and hung himself."

Well, that can't be right; try again: "Jesus said, Go and do likewise."

How about another: "What you do, do quickly."

It's beyond me how anyone can believe they can know what God wants them to do by remaining ignorant.

And yet, they come to me and say, "These people come to my door with all these Bible verses and I don't know what to tell them...."

Well, why don't you know the Bible at least as well as they?

If Episcopalians spent half as much time ...

And yet for Peter and the 120, there was more to it that just knowing the Bible.
There was also a value placed on the wisdom of experience.
They weren't going to put just anyone in Judas' place.
It wasn't a matter of taking volunteers or grabbing the first
warm body.
Peter asks them to nominate someone who's been with them
the whole time, from day one with John at the baptism in
the Jordan River, to the day Jesus took off and left them
for good.
What we need, says Peter, is someone who's seen it all: a
witness to the resurrection.
Someone who's seen him alive, seen him dead, and seen
him alive again.
We require someone who from the beginning has been
one of us.
One of my fundamentalist friends once told me that I think
too much —
That thinking was dangerous,
Experience was dangerous —
"You just have to believe the Bible."
I can reply only by describing a poster put out by the Episco-
pal Ad Campaign a few years back:
A man with duct tape over his mouth: "In some churches,
there are no questions."
It wasn't that way for Peter and the 120 in that room.
There were questions, and the main question was, "Who
was Jesus, really? Dead man? Or living Lord?"
They read their Bibles in light of their answer.
For them, the Bible was filtered through their experience
of Jesus' resurrection.
So they needed a leader who shared this resurrection
experience —
Someone who would understand.

There wasn't anything in the Old Testament that in and of itself anyone would have understood to be about Jesus unless and until they had met Jesus.

Everything they read was changed because of Jesus.

It was like looking through a magnifying glass and seeing the details you never noticed before.

You see, there is no unmediated Bible.

It is impossible to read anything without interpreting, including especially the Bible.

Anyone who tells you otherwise is either extremely naive, or a bald-faced liar.

With the duct tape ripped from your mouth, not only can you ask questions, you can also pray.

Prayer is the other thing these 120 disciples do.

They pray: "Lord, show us the one you have chosen."

They follow the example of their Master, in that last moment before his betrayal.

According to the Gospel of John, Jesus prayed for those very same disciples.

"Protect them," he says. "Guard them, help them do their jobs."

I know, it's hard to believe when all around us people treat prayer as a kind of spiritual grab bag, magic that provides all our wants, which we call "needs."

I hear people talk about how they were driving around, praying for a parking space, and Behold! God gave them a parking space.

Does it ever even occur to them just to park the car and get on with what God has called them to do?

The audacity of Jesus to pray that his disciples might be empowered to do God's will.

And here in Acts, God is answering that very prayer, providing a twelfth for apostleship.

181

So we come full circle, to the craps shoot, the casting of lots —
Which now looks more like a tie breaker, drawing straws.
Two candidates survive the tests of scripture, experience, and
prayer.
So flip a coin.
Matthias is elected.
It's not a random choice.

How do you find out the will of God?
I will now explain it to you.
I can tell you, if the Book of Acts is any indication, you don't
find it alone.
It took a whole room crammed full of people to discern
the will of God.
And you don't find the will of God without education, without
experience, without reason.
These early disciples valued scripture and accumulated
wisdom.
They demanded someone who had been around.
And you aren't going to find the will of God without asking.
Prayer was at the heart of the early Christians' decision-
making process.
And we are talking here about that very human process of choos-
ing this one or that, the process of making a decision.
The will of God is not going to float down from the sky,
any more than it did for Peter and the 120.
The disciples' decision is a reflection of who they are, their
knowledge and experience, what they pray for, what
was deep down inside.
They can recognize the will of God when they see it, be-
cause they've given their lives for it.
What is the will of God?
There is no easy answer.
There is only the ongoing process of giving ourselves to
the Lord of all choices.

The Real Thing

Easter 6, Year A — Acts 17:22-31
May 9, 1999

Sometimes the best resources for introducing unfamiliar material lie close at hand. In this case, novelist Tom Wolfe paints a vivid portrait of a modern person in a contemporary predicament who turns to the ancient Stoics for comfort. Wolfe's story provides a springboard for understanding Paul's sermon to the Athenians, since the two are connected by Stoic ideology.

As Wolfe makes Epictetus come alive by giving him a contemporary embodiment, so the preacher can give scripture a contemporary edge by using analogy and story. Literature, along with the media, and material drawn from conversations with friends (used delicately) can enlighten the Bible and enliven the sermon. In addition to Wolfe, I have drawn from novelist Amy Herrick, *At the Sign of the Naked Waiter*, for the image of life as a makeshift boat. Media, news reports, and popular culture figure prominently in my preaching; this sermon is peppered with references to current events, which have lost none of their punch. Finally, I am indebted to an anonymous friend for one personal story, and to a homiletics colleague for the concluding story.

This sermon was preached at Christ Episcopal Church, Avon, Connecticut.

In Tom Wolfe's novel, *A Man in Full*, there's a fellow called Conrad.
Conrad is a little guy who's been kicked around all his life.
He has to quit junior college when his girlfriend gets pregnant.
Instead of applying to U. C. Berkeley he goes to work in a
frozen food warehouse, lifting eighty-pound blocks of cardboard and ice while stalactites droop from his mustache.
When he gets laid off from that job, he finds himself pushed
into a fight over his car, and he ends up in prison for felonious assault.

Incarcerated in a dark, dirty prison cell in Northern California, he receives a tattered book called *The Stoics*.

Now this is not about people who are long-suffering and grim-faced.

The book contains the writings of the first-century Roman philosopher Epictetus.

Epictetus taught that one should live through reason and self-control.

We should be free and independent of the ins and outs of fortune, said Epictetus, our happiness not depending on that which we cannot control.

And the only thing we can control is our own self, our own will. "The body is a vessel of clay and a quart of blood," he said, "Life is just on loan."

The only thing we can ever really own is our character, and even character is a spark from Zeus.

Epictetus believed that Zeus controlled our fortune, and so we need not worry. Don't be driven by fear, necessity, and desire, he said. "Did you ever see an old beggar on the street?" he asked. "He must have found food and a place to sleep. Three-hundred sixty-five days a year. If he can find food, surely you can. What more do you need?"

Conrad in prison is dumbstruck by these words.

He comes out of jail a changed man. He calls himself a Stoic, a worshiper at the Church of Zeus. He becomes an evangelist, a messenger.

I can't tell you the whole story today, only to say that he ends up taking the words of the ancient Roman philosopher Epictetus across the country to the least likely place —

The richest part of Atlanta, Georgia —

Winding streets, rolling lawns, Scarlett O'Hara mansions complete with uniformed servants:

Epictetus in Buckhead.

On the other side of the world and a couple thousand years earlier,
Paul stood in front of the Areopagus in Athens.

Epictetus was not yet in diapers, but his future teachers were
out in force.

Luke tells us that the Stoics gathered to debate with Paul, along
with the Epicureans, who denied divine judgment and said
that what you could see here on earth was all that there was.

Still, these Greek and Roman philosophers loved to listen to
Paul, the proclaimer of foreign divinities.

Luke tells us that all the Athenians and their friends would
gladly spend their time "in nothing but telling or hearing
something new."

But before Paul jumped into the debate, he did one very important
thing.

He told them what he had done:

He said that he had "gone through the city and looked around
very carefully."

That "looking around carefully" is crucial.

It's what we so often forget to do; what we overlook, especially when things seem so familiar.

If you looked carefully around your city, your town, your neighborhood, what would you see? What would you find out?

I read in *Newsweek* that the father of one of the shooters in
Littleton, Colorado, had a collection of vintage BMWs.

Yet he didn't notice that his son was stockpiling weapons
and building bombs.

I think that says a lot.

What would you see, if you looked around carefully?

Paul in Athens ran across an altar with the inscription, "To an unknown god."

That's what I think we're going to see nine times out of ten:
the altar to the unknown god.

If we look carefully, we will find altars and objects of worship
that are barely recognized as such.

Epictetus was right — most people are driven by fear, necessity, and desire.

They don't realize what's important. They haven't figured it
out yet.

One of my old friends was raised in Atlanta, not far from
Buckhead.

She once told me why she got married right out of
college —

Not because she really wanted to.

It was just what you did.

You graduated from college and married your boyfriend.

That's what everyone did.

You didn't stop to think about what you *really* wanted to
do.

Paul told the Athenians that the first step is to recognize your place
in the world:

Rather than worship what you do not know, meet the God who
made the world and everything in it.

This God does not live in shrines made by human hands, be
they altars, mansions, or BMWs.

God gives life and breath to all.

Not so different from the words that Conrad carried from prison
to Buckhead.

Paul met the Athenians right where they lived — he was even
willing to quote their own poets: "In him we live and move
and have our being," "We too are his offspring."

As far as it goes, according to Paul, the poets and philosophers spoke the truth: What we have, we have from God.

If we think otherwise, we are deluding ourselves.

How could anyone think otherwise, who saw the images this
last week from Kansas and Oklahoma, the half-mile wide

swath that looked like a war zone, every house reduced to rubble by Force Five twisters?
We cannot control this. No one can.
"Safe at home" is an illusion.
Sooner or later, we're going to have to deal with the truth.

The truth, Paul said in Athens, is that we cannot worship gold, silver, stone, image, or imagination.
Because we are God's offspring —
So God cannot be a thing — an object — anymore than we are.
The one true God has commanded all people to repent.
God has fixed a day to have the world judged by the appointed person.
And God has testified to all this by raising that person from the dead.
Needless to say, the philosophers were not happy to hear Paul talking about things like Judgment Day.
Some in the crowd scoffed, Luke tells us. Some wanted to hear more.
A few — just a few — became believers.
It is one thing to recognize that life is a little boat made of a twig, a leaf, and a wadded-up piece of gum.
It is quite another to acknowledge that it's not even your gum.

And yet God is nothing if not persistent.
God keeps pushing us to move from ignorance to faith —
To abandon the worship of the unknown god in order to come face to face with the real thing —
If only we could see.

Years ago there was a little girl named Jennifer.
She was in the store with her mother when she spotted a necklace of plastic pearls.

187

She became enchanted. She had never seen anything so beautiful. "Mommy, can we buy them?"

Mom looked at the price tag. A dollar ninety-five, plus tax. "That looks like something you'll have to save up for," she said. "Maybe you could do some extra chores, and Grandma always gives you a dollar for your birthday."

Jennifer went home and emptied out her piggy bank. She had seventeen cents.

But the necklace was gorgeous.

So she started doing extra chores. She went over to the neighbor's house to see if they had any chores for her. A quarter here, a dime there.

When her birthday came, and Grandma handed over the dollar bill, she was over the top.

She ran to the store and bought the plastic pearls.

She wore them everywhere — to school, to church, she even slept with them on.

The only place she didn't wear them was the bathtub, because her mother told her they would make her neck turn green.

Over the weeks and months to follow she was never without her pearls, she was meticulously careful with them, and even though the plastic changed color and got dirty and chipped here and there, she thought they were the most beautiful thing she had ever owned.

One night her mother came to tuck her in her bed, looked thoughtfully at her, and said, "Jennifer, do you love me?"

"Yes, Mommy, I love you."

"Would you give me your pearls?"

"Oh, no, Mommy, anything but my pearls. You can have my Rainbow Pony. It's the nicest one in my collection."

"That's okay, Jennifer," said Mom.

The next night her mother came in and said, "Jennifer, do you love me?"

"Yes, Mommy, I love you."

"Would you give me your pearls?"

"Oh, no, Mommy, anything but my pearls. Why don't you take my dolly? She talks and eats and even wets."

"That's okay, Jennifer."

The next night when her mother came in, Jennifer was sitting cross-legged on her bed, nearly in tears. Her hands were clutched around the string of plastic pearls, which she held out toward her mother.

"If you really want them," she said, "you can have them." Jennifer's mother took the pearls and put them in a pocket. From another pocket, she took an ancient blue velvet box. She opened the box, and inside was a gleaming string of genuine pearls.

"These pearls belonged to my mother," she said, "and now I want to give them to you."

How long are *we* going to clutch the beloved counterfeit — When God is waiting, just dying, to give us the real thing?

7. Preaching Resurrection In Paul

It is hard to isolate Paul's teaching on the resurrection. For one thing, Paul is not a systematic theologian, no matter how hard Christians have tried to make him one over the years. He is an occasional, pastoral theologian. His letters to individuals and churches deal with specific problems that are still familiar to pastors: personality conflicts, doctrinal insecurity, financial need, and even personal attacks. To be sure, Paul's answers to these questions are deeply theological; they are rooted in his experience of following in the steps of the Crucified One. But there is no real system here, simply thoughtful answers to issues one-by-one as they come up.

A second problem is determining just what we mean when we say "Paul." Tradition ascribes thirteen letters to the apostle (plus, in some quarters, the Letter to the Hebrews). Modern scholars have not been so generous, usually attributing direct authorship to only Romans, 1 and 2 Corinthians, Galatians, Philippians, 1 Thessalonians, and Philemon. Of the others, there is varying debate over which come from the hand of Paul. Colossians, Ephesians, and 2 Thessalonians are considered the most likely to be Pauline, based on the degree they share common language and themes with the others; 1 Timothy, 2 Timothy, and Titus, least likely. All of this is by its very nature hypothetical, with sound arguments standing side-by-side with shaky speculation. Largely it is a matter of how one sorts and groups the various letters. Certainly there is a Protestant theological prejudice which puts Romans and Galatians in a prime position; based on congruence with the great theme of justification by faith found in these two letters, 1 Thessalonians (or for that matter, Philemon) does not deserve to be in their company. However, 1 Thessalonians does fit in rather well with the chronology of Paul's life as found in Acts and the other letters, and so it gains admittance with the others, while 1 Timothy, 2 Timothy, and Titus require a speculative approach to Pauline chronology, and thus are excluded. But once one admits 1 Thessalonians, is there really a good reason to exclude 2 Thessalonians, which presupposes it, and is so similar in style? Colossians is so similar to Ephesians that it is hard to include one but not the other, unless one speculates that a disciple made a close copy of a Pauline original. When 2 Timothy is lumped with 1 Timothy as one of the "Pastoral Epistles," it is necessarily excluded, but what if it were taken by itself, or read with Philippians, which also claims to come from a captive Paul? To some extent, judgment must be made according to the theological as well as literary characteristics of each letter; those letters considered to be post-Pauline are often said to reflect later theological developments, such as a hierarchical church order — but it is entirely possible to read these passages in a different way (or for that matter, to find hierarchy in the seven so-called genuine letters).

But another problem is that — whether we take a maximalist or minimalist view of the Pauline authorship of these writings — Paul's view on the Easter event can hardly be separated from the very fabric of his being. The Pauline letters are littered with references to "resurrection" (*anastasis*) of Jesus (Romans 1:4; 6:5; 1 Corinthians 15:12-13, 21, 42; Philippians 3:10; 2 Timothy 2:18; also the related *exanastasis,* Philippians 3:11; and the verb form, *anistemi,* 1 Thessalonians 4:14, 16). Just as often, Paul testifies that God "raised" (*egeiro*) Jesus (Romans 4:24-25; 6:4, 9; 7:4; 8:11, 34; 10:9; 1 Corinthians 6:14; 15:4, 12-17, 20, 29, 32, 35, 42-44, 52; 2 Corinthians 1:9; 4:14; 5:15; Galatians 1:1; Ephesians 1:20; Colossians 2:12; 1 Thessalonians 1:10; 2 Timothy 2:8; the related *exegeiro,* 1 Corinthians 6:14). Paul routinely speaks of the foundation of his faith being "the power of his resurrection" (Philippians 3:10). Christians are those who "believe in him who raised Jesus our Lord from the dead" (Romans 4:24) in order to secure "our justification" (Romans 4:25). Belief in the resurrection is part and parcel of salvation: "If you confess with your lips that Jesus is Lord and believe in your heart that God raised him from the dead, you will be saved" (Romans 10:9). The resurrection of Jesus authenticates him as the Son of God (Romans 1:4). Paul admits that his entire message would be nonsense if the resurrection were not true: "If Christ has not been raised, your faith is futile and you are still in your sins" (1 Corinthians 15:17). God's action in raising Jesus provides assurance that we too will be raised at the last day (2 Corinthians 4:14).

Nevertheless, there are two passages in the Pauline letters which zero in most keenly on the meaning of the resurrection of Jesus, and which are of great interest and importance to Easter preachers and their congregations. They also come from two letters of undisputed Pauline authorship. The two passages are 1 Corinthians 15 and Romans 6.

In A Twinkling
Paul's first letter to the Corinthians is largely a question-and-answer session. "Now concerning the matters about which you wrote ..." (1 Corinthians 7:1; cf. 8:1; 12:1; 15:1; 16:1). Paul had a long and complicated relationship with the community that he established in this cosmopolitan Roman city; the Book of Acts tells us that he spent eighteen months with them (Acts 18:1-11; cf. 1 Corinthians 4:15), and various clues to their stormy relationship pop up between the seams of his letters. Presumably the letter from Corinth that Paul is responding to here is the report from "Chloe's people" about the various "quarrels" among them (1 Corinthians 1:11); it seems to contain questions that the community had raised in Paul's absence. Since we do not have a copy of the letter the Corinthians wrote to Paul, we can only guess at its contents; it is much like listening to only one end of a telephone conversation. One may end up like Linus in *Peanuts:* "We're studying the Epistles of Paul in Sunday school ... I feel like I'm reading someone else's mail."

Well, we are reading someone else's mail, with only one-half of the discussion. Trying to reverse-engineer the questions to Paul's answers is a popular interpretive game, often referred to as the

193

"mirror method": whatever Paul said, his opponents must have said the opposite. While there is some legitimacy to this method in the case of 1 Corinthians, since Paul often tells us exactly what he is responding to in the Corinthians' mail, we need to be aware that our hypotheses about the Corinthians need to be tested against what Paul actually says — it is all too tempting to create elaborate interpretations based merely on a speculation about what was going on in Corinth.

As to resurrection, Paul is clear that "some of you say there is no resurrection of the dead" (1 Corinthians 15:12). It is hard to move from this negative statement, "there is no resurrection," to determine what some of them actually believed about resurrection. Most scholars reject the notion that there were in the Corinthian church outright deniers of the resurrection — given that the resurrection of Jesus was so central to the early church (and not an unusual notion in a pre-scientific culture), how could there actually be such skeptics in Corinth? However, it is important to note that Paul's argument is directed precisely against this sort of skepticism; his argument begins not with the means but the fact of resurrection. His argument is based on the fact of Jesus' resurrection (15:1-34); only later does he get around to how resurrection takes place (cf. 15:35-57).

Attempts to get a clearer picture of the issue at Corinth often point to other possible clues within Paul's discourse. Some speculate that the Corinthians were worried that those who died before Christ came again would miss out on the Second Coming (usually signified in Paul simply as "his coming," *parousia*); they point to Paul's mysterious allusion to "baptism for the dead" (15:29), which may have signified a vicarious baptism for loved ones who have passed on. In this concern for those who have passed on, the Corinthians are like the Thessalonians (cf. 1 Thessalonians 4:13-18). However, this interpretation may be entirely too indebted to the analogy with 1 Thessalonians, and no one really knows what Paul meant by "baptism for the dead."

Another interpretive possibility takes its clue from 1 Corinthians 15:35: "But someone will ask, 'How are the dead raised? With what kind of body do they come?' " If Paul says, "someone will ask," so the reasoning goes, someone must have really asked, perhaps in the very letter that Paul is answering. Thus the Corinthians' question concerned the mode of resurrection, and how there could be continuity between our earthly bodies and those of the resurrected life. This "mirror method" interpretation fails to account for the literary method Paul uses so often, known in ancient rhetoric as the "diatribe." In the diatribe, one has an imaginary opponent raise an objection, so that you can knock it down. Paul frequently uses the diatribal style (cf. Romans 6:1, 15; 7:7, 13). It is hard to attribute historical significance to something that is so obviously a factor of literary style.

By far the most dominant hypotheses among scholars as to the theological leanings of the Corinthians is that they held to some sort of proto-gnostic ideology. Gnosticism (from the Greek word for knowledge, *gnosis*, which Paul uses with some irony in 1 Corinthians 8:1-11) was a rather complicated theological system that held to a dualism between the inferior material realm and an exalted spiritual reality; the body was essentially evil, but could be overcome by attention to the divine spark of spiritual enlightenment. Until recently, it was considered to be a Christian heresy, a perversion of the teachings of Paul himself; lately there have been some scholars who have argued that Gnosticism was a religious strain that existed independently of Christianity.

There is a good deal of debate over whether Gnostic ideology can be traced prior to the time of Paul with any but the vaguest congruency with later, full-blown Gnosticism. But many hold that one aspect of gnostic (small "g") thought may have been at work among the Corinthian Christians: the notion of "realized eschatology." The Corinthians, under this view, may have believed that the teachings of Jesus had already brought them into a new age. Having been spiritually enlightened, there would now be no need of a literal resurrection; they had already been resurrected in their hearts! The Corinthians felt no need of a future bodily transformation, for they were experiencing the full advantages of resurrected glory in the present. Already they were rich rulers (1 Corinthians 4:8). The advantage of this hypothesis is that it would help explain some of the other problems apparent in the Corinthian church, such as their overemphasis on ecstatic spiritual gifts (1 Corinthians 12-14), their willingness to flaunt their spiritual prowess and their superior knowledge (*gnosis,* 1 Corinthians 8:2) even when it bordered on idolatry (1 Corinthians 8-10), and their tolerance of carnal sin (1 Corinthians 5, 11), coupled with an apparent sexual asceticism (1 Corinthians 7) — if the body were secondary to the spiritual, one could either indulge or abstain from physical pleasures with no spiritual harm, while luxuriating in distinctions between one's "spiritual" and "unspiritual" friends. It would also explain why Paul spent a good deal of this particular section dealing with the mode of the resurrected body, which would be at best irrelevant under a realized eschatology.

Paul's approach to resurrection, by contrast, was rooted in the notion of the unity of body and spirit. Paul did not think of the body (*soma*) as something evil (his frequent references to "flesh" [*sarx*], as a principle opposed to God, refers not to bodily functions but human nature). The human being was for Paul a single entity, not a clash of warring factions. The clash came between the human desire to have its own way, and God's desire to transform us, body and soul, through the Holy Spirit (cf. Romans 8:1-11). That transformation, while begun in the present life, is completed only at the end of time (*telos,* 1 Corinthians 1:8; 15:24).

Paul begins his discourse on resurrection with a reminder. This teaching is nothing new, it is simply "the good news that I proclaimed to you, which you in turn received" (1 Corinthians 15:1). More than that, in this news they "hold firmly" and "stand" (1 Corinthians 15:1-2); without it their faith would be in vain (*eike,* 15:2). The good news culminates in a process, that of "being saved" (a progressive verb — the response to the good news does not result in a static condition but an ongoing way of life, 15:2). It was and is news of "first importance" (1 Corinthians 15:3) which Paul begins to summarize in a creedal form: "that Christ died for our sins in accordance with the scriptures, and that he was buried, and that he was raised on the third day in accordance with the scriptures" (1 Corinthians 15:3-4). Paul goes on to list specific appearances, some of which are familiar from the Gospel accounts, others which appear only here: to Cephas, to the twelve, to 500 at once, to James and all the apostles (understood to be a different group from the "twelve"?), and finally to Paul himself, "as to one untimely born" (1 Corinthians 15:8). While Paul obviously has access to traditions about resurrection appearances that differ from those found in the Gospels, he shares with Luke-Acts the conviction that Jesus continued to make appearances to his disciples — particularly to Paul himself — even after his ascension.

So fundamental is this tradition that Paul is amazed that any of the Corinthians could deny belief in the resurrection. His argument is *reductio ad absurdum* — the reduction of a proposition to its inevitable absurd conclusion (1 Corinthians 15:12-18). If there is no resurrection, Jesus was not raised, and a faith based on his resurrection is worthless (15:14, "in vain," here using *kenos,* which means literally "empty"). More than that, such proclamation in the face of a contrary reality is no more than a lie, and the Corinthians are thus still in sin, and those who have died have truly perished. The entire structure of the Corinthians' faith, so predicated on the spiritual gifts that could not be given were Christ not alive, is on shaky grounds indeed if there is no resurrection of the dead. "If for this life only we have hoped in Christ, we are of all people most to be pitied" (15:19).

But of course, in Paul's view, Christ has indeed been raised by God, "the first fruits of those who have died" (15:20). Paul draws upon an agricultural metaphor; in Old Testament law, the first fruits of the harvest were those offered to the deity (cf. Exodus 23:16, 19). This leads to a comparison between Christ and Adam, the first human and the last (15:21-22; cf. Romans 5:12-21), followed by an extended description of the last days: Christ, the first fruits, is followed by all those who belong to him at his coming (*parousia*). Then comes "the end" (*telos*), where Christ receives the kingdom, having destroyed his spiritual enemies, the last of which is death itself (15:26). Thus all things are subjected to the Son, who in turn subjects himself to God the Father, "so that God may be all in all" (15:28). Paul's teaching on the last day puts to rest any possibility that the Corinthians have arrived at spiritual completion and are now ruling in Christ's kingdom (cf. 4:8). The kingdom is not yet complete, any more than the Corinthians are truly risen.

Paul's outline of the end of days hovers over his everyday life; for if there is no resurrection, "why are we putting ourselves in danger every hour?" (15:30). Paul alludes to his own troubles in preaching the good news about Jesus' resurrection (one wonders whether to take him literally when he says, "I fought with wild animals at Ephesus," 15:32). But if there is no resurrection, such a life would make no sense; one might as well agree with the fool who says, "Let us eat and drink, for tomorrow we die" (cf. Isaiah 22:13). Paul is not above shaming the so-called "spiritual" Corinthians on this point, calling them to true knowledge ("a sober and right mind," 15:34).

To the question of what kind of body is involved in resurrection, Paul offers a comparison to the sprouting of a seed (cf. John 12:24), and even indulges in a little natural history, comparing the various types of bodies found in nature (15:35-41). The language of metaphor is the only language that lends itself to matters hidden by the veil of the future. The spiritual body (*soma pneumatikon*, 15:44) of the resurrection must be quite different from the physical body (*soma physikon*) fashioned from dirt; Paul returns to the Adam/Christ typology (15:42-29): "Just as we have borne the image of the man of dust, we will also bear the image of the man of heaven" (15:29).

Paul concludes his argument with a paroxysm of doxology: "Listen, I will tell you a mystery! We will not all die, but we will all be changed, in a moment, in the twinkling of an eye, at the last trumpet" (15:51-52). This is one of those passages that seem to indicate that Paul expected Jesus to return in his own lifetime (cf. 1 Thessalonians 4:17), but the promise in which he exults is certainly not limited by his time and place. Christians over the centuries have found their voices joined with Paul, "Where, O death, is your victory? Where, O death, is your sting?" (15:55; quoting Hosea 13:14).

For Paul, the conclusion of the argument involves not only the praise of God, but the practical consequences inherent in the truth that is proclaimed: "Therefore, my beloved, be steadfast, immovable, always excelling in the work of the Lord, because you know that in the Lord your labor is not in vain (again, "empty," *kenos*)"

(15:58). The Christian's labor is not empty (*kenos*), because Christian faith is not empty (cf. 15:10, 14; also 15:2). Sound theology makes for sound practice.

Baptized Into Death

The Letter to the Romans, by contrast with the Corinthian correspondence, is not part of a larger extended conversation between old friends. Paul had not yet been to Rome, and did not know the Roman Christians except by reputation ("Your faith is proclaimed throughout the world," Romans 1:8; cf. Acts 28:14-15). "I am longing to see you," he says. "I have often intended to come to you but thus far have been prevented" (1:11, 13). Paul does not give any hint of problems within the Roman church, and speaks of contentious issues in only a general way (cf. chapter 14), so in contrast to the Corinthian correspondence, he is not writing to correct some deficiency in their faith or practice. Instead, he wishes to be "mutually encouraged by each other's faith, both yours and mine" (1:12), and to "reap some harvest among you as I have among the rest of the Gentiles" (1:13). Paul's expressed desire is simply "to proclaim the gospel to you also who are in Rome" (1:15).

Which of course has not prevented speculation on what his true motives might have been. Romans is obviously more than a friendly hello, as it contains Paul's most systematic attempt at theology and a summary of the essence of his preaching. Some, of course, hypothesize that Paul was making a theological statement against his enemies and misinterpreters, but once we understand that the various questions and objections raised in the letter are features of the rhetorical style known as the diatribe, rather than attempts to refute actual enemies, this thesis becomes less than compelling. A more popular view is that Paul writes a defense of his preaching for the Roman empire at large, proving that it is no fly-by-night cult but a respectable religion, and as such is no threat to Roman power (Romans 13:1-7, "Let every person be subject to the governing authorities ..." is in this view the well-disguised climax of the letter).

A better approach would be to take seriously Paul's stated purposes, not only at the beginning of the letter, but at its end. Paul concludes as he begins, with a compliment to the Roman church, "I myself feel confident about you" (15:14). "Nevertheless on some points I have written to you rather boldly by way of reminder" (15:15). Paul then goes on to describe himself as "a minister of Christ Jesus to the Gentiles" (15:16), mouthpiece of Christ's work in word, signs and wonders (15:18-19), and preacher where others have not yet preached (15:20-21). He elaborates on his plans to come see them and to visit Spain: there is nowhere else new to go (15:23), but his job carrying a collection to Jerusalem takes precedence (15:25-29). In short, Paul is writing a letter telling them of his travel plans.

His letter has a particular purpose with regard to those plans, stated ever so subtly: "For I do hope to see you on my journey and to be sent on (*propempo*) by you, once I have enjoyed your company for a little while" (15:24). Paul uses the language of the travel professional; he wishes to be "sent on" or "sped along" (*propempo*) by the Romans, as if they were underwriting his expedition (cf. 3 John 6). He uses similar subtle innuendo when he asks to be "refreshed" (cf. Philemon 7) by them (15:32). "And I know that when I come to you I will come in the fullness of the blessing of Christ" (15:29). It is clear that Paul hopes the Romans will finance his mission to Spain; the "blessing" he hopes for is a very tangible one. In this light, Paul's opening statements take on new meaning. The "harvest" (1:13) could not refer primarily to new converts — Paul did not seek to preach "where Christ has already been named" (15:20) — rather, he hoped to reap among them financial support. The "mutual encouragement" (1:12) included money. Paul would offer his spiritual gift (1:11) in exchange for more tangible support for his search for unplowed mission fields in Spain.

Thus Paul is really writing a letter of introduction and recommendation for himself (cf. 2 Corinthians 3:1). He does not know the Romans personally. They have never met him. Rumors about him, many bad, abound. Yet he expects them to fund his work; he expects to be "refreshed in your company" (15:32). He therefore finds it necessary to write to them in depth, explaining himself and his work. The entire letter is an elaborate fund-raiser. It is not systematic theology; by no means does it touch on every theological idea Paul ever had. But it does contain the essence of the mission that would bring him to Rome and, he hoped, beyond to Spain. It is designed to let the Roman church know the details of his proclamation of "salvation to everyone who has faith, to the Jew first and also to the Greek." Thus the Romans would know Paul — and would be able to decide for themselves whether and how to support him — on a first-hand basis.

The great advantage of this interpretation is that it allows us to explain the final chapter of Romans, which is little more than a list of names. It seems jarring to have this list of greeting appended to a letter sent to a community from one who claimed to be a stranger. Some have speculated that Romans 16 was actually a loose leaf from some other letter (perhaps Ephesians) that got attached to Romans, but there is no textual evidence for this thesis. But if Paul were writing a letter of introduction, which was intended to be read aloud to the whole church for the purpose of inculcating tangible support for his work, what better way to conclude than to capitalize on every personal connection with that community. When one keeps in mind the mobility possible under the *pax Romana* — the "Roman peace" that resulted from the empire's widespread rule — and that the Roman church was already well-established, is it any surprise that many of the people Paul had worked with during his journeys had migrated to the capital of the empire? In light of Paul's purpose, it is significant that the first person Paul mentions is his "benefactor" (or "helper," *prostatis*) Phoebe, the deacon of Cenchreae (Romans 16:1); the word *prostatis* had the same financial connotation as "benefactor" does today. Paul asks the Romans to be her "helpers" or "benefactors" in turn (16:2), which has led some scholars to speculate that Phoebe might have been leading Paul's advance team, in charge of organizing his mission to Spain.

The foundation of Paul's self-introduction is what most scholars take to be the theme sentence of the entire letter, "For I am not ashamed of the gospel; it is the power of God for salvation to everyone who has faith, to the Jew first and also to the Greek. For in it the righteousness of God is revealed through faith for faith; as it

201

is written, 'The one who is righteous will live by faith' " (Romans 1:16-17; quoting Habakkuk 2:4). Paul writes to explain his gospel of salvation by faith. By "faith" (*pistis*), Paul means the positive human response to the call of God, as demonstrated in Abraham (chapter 4), and most particularly in Jesus (3:21-26; 5:1-12). Faith for Paul is practically synonymous with obedience; he speaks of the "obedience of faith" (1:5; cf. 5:19; 6:16; 15:18; 16:26) in such a way as to make the two terms practically define each other — he uses faith here in the sense of "faithfulness." Jesus in his death is the supreme example of this faithful and obedient response to God, which is why Paul commends "the faith of Jesus" (*pistis Iesou*, Romans 3:22, 26; cf. Galatians 2:16; 3:22) that is, the obedient response to God that Jesus demonstrated (the expression *pistis Iesou*, "faith of Jesus," which can mean either "faith in Jesus" or "faith like Jesus' faith," is usually misinterpreted by NRSV and others as if it were solely *pistis eis/en Iesoun*, "faith in Jesus," which is also commended by Paul, but is something else entirely [Galatians 2:16; 3:26; and among the disputed letters, Ephesians 1:15; Colossians 1:4; 1 Timothy 3:13; 2 Timothy 1:13; 3:15]). Thus the "righteousness of God is revealed through faith for faith (*ek pisteos eis pistin*)" (1:17), that is, through Jesus' obedient response for the sake of ours; the "righteous one" who "lives by faith" cited from the Book of Habakkuk is first of all Jesus himself, and secondarily all who follow him to share in the righteousness of God. This "righteousness of God" that is revealed through faith involves both God's righteous nature, and the activity of God in establishing human beings in a right relationship with God (3:26). Paul is concerned in particular with how the faith of Jesus, and thus the righteousness of God, comes first to the Jew and only later to all nations. The priority of the Jewish law, and Jesus as the answer to the conundrums introduced by the law, is foundational. This is his entire justification for the pattern of preaching first to the Jewish people, then to the Gentiles (cf. Acts 13:46; 18:6; 28:28). Chapters 9-11, which offer Paul's explanation for why the church of his day was dominated by Gentiles and not Jews, are actually the climax of the book (they are not, as some have held, an excursus).

One of the conundrums of life under Jewish law leads to Paul's extended analysis of the place of resurrection in the Christian life. Sin, in Paul's view, was introduced into the world from the beginning, with Adam (5:12). But under Moses, sin abounded. "But law came in, with the result that the trespass multiplied" (5:20). The more rules there are, the more chances they will be broken. Sin proliferated. Paul speaks of this unfortunate consequence using a political metaphor; sin and death have established a "reign" or "dominion" over human beings (5:14, 17, 21). Fortunately for us, "where sin increased, grace abounded all the more" (5:20). That is, Jesus through his faithful obedience brings "justification and life for all" (5:18), so the net effect is that many, many sins are forgiven, and that "grace might also exercise dominion [or "reign, be a king," *basileuo*] through justification leading to eternal life through Jesus Christ our Lord" (5:21).

Paul, writing in the diatribal style, has his imaginary opponent raise a logical objection. If more sin brings about more grace, why not indulge in sin in order to be deluged with grace? "Should we continue in sin in order that grace may abound?" (6:1). Paul's answer is emphatic, "By no means!" (*me genoito*, 6:2, literally, "May it never ever be"). That is to say, for the Christian to indulge in sin is a logical impossibility. "How can we who died to sin go on living in it?" (6:2). The gift of the righteousness of God through the faith of Jesus is not simply an accounting procedure; it actually changes those who accept the gift. The obedience that is faith has transforming power; it is literally a new life. In Paul's view, the believer has died to even the possibility of continuing to live in the disobedience to God which he calls sin.

Paul explains himself with reference to baptism: "Do you not know that all of us who have been baptized into Christ Jesus were baptized into his death?" (6:3). To understand Paul's claim here, one has to understand both the symbolic and theological meaning of baptism. The symbolism is clear from Paul's following statement: "Therefore we have been buried with him by baptism into death, so that, just as Christ was raised from the dead by the glory of the Father, so we too might walk in newness of life" (6:4). The imagery clearly refers to baptism by immersion; the head of the new believer goes under the water, symbolizing death and burial, and just when we think it's all over, and that nobody could hold his breath that long, the new Christian is raised sputtering to take a fresh breath. We now expect the baptized person to live in a different way, to "walk in newness of life," the resurrected life.

But this is not mere symbolism for Paul; it is clear from what he says next that he truly believes that baptism is an act of God. God does something to the newly baptized — God unites the believer to Jesus in death and resurrection. "For if we have been united with him in a death like his, we will certainly be united with him in a resurrection like his" (6:5). For Paul, baptism has ontological significance. The believer's sin really is dead in Christ. "Our old self was crucified with him so that the body of sin might be destroyed, and we might no longer be enslaved to sin. For whoever has died is freed from sin" (6:6-7). Paul will go on later to explore the metaphor of sin and slavery (6:15-23), with death as one possible method of freedom from slavery (7:1-6); here he builds on his earlier contrast between Christ and Adam (5:12-21). The "old self" (literally, the "old man," *palaios anthropos,* a reference to universal sin as embodied in the "first man," Adam) hangs on the cross with the body of Jesus; the "body of sin" (*soma tes hamartias* — the human being as characterized and dominated by resistance to God) is dead. As with Christ, the death of the principle of sin in the human being is followed by resurrection — a human being governed not by the sin characteristic of Adam, but the righteousness brought by Christ. "But if we have died with Christ, we believe that we will also live with him" (6:8). Paul is not referring to a future resurrected life, with new spiritual bodies, as in 1 Corinthians 15; here Paul speaks of the tangible benefits of Christ's resurrection in the new life to be led by Christians (and perhaps here we can see the germ of the mistaken "realized eschatology" in Corinth). Paul expects the baptized Christian to live according to the spirit of the resurrected Jesus, because baptism brings with it the power to live a resurrected life.

204

Paul's view of the Christian life is rooted in his perception of Christ's resurrection. He need not repeat his defense of the resurrection tradition delivered to the Corinthians; a simple "we know" will suffice: "We know that Christ, being raised from the dead, will never die again; death no longer has dominion over him" (6:9). For Paul, it is simply a matter of who's in charge: death or Christ. With his resurrection, death is no longer able to "have dominion" (or "lord it over him," *kyrieuo*). Dead is dead, but if death itself is destroyed, life rules (cf. 1 Corinthians 15:26). Christ's death is an irrevokable victory over sin; the rule of sin is irretrievably broken. The result is life under a new rule: "The death he died, he died to sin, once for all; but the life he lives, he lives to God" (6:10).

Paul's view of Christ's death and resurrection as a death to sin resulting in new life under God has practical consequences for the believer, once one realizes that baptism unites the believer to a resurrected reality. "So you also must consider yourselves dead to sin and alive to God in Christ Jesus" (6:11). God has made it so in Christ; now the believer must believe it to make it so in his or her own life. Christ's resurrection is thus made the theological foundation of an exhortation: "Therefore, do not let sin exercise dominion ["be king," *basileuo*] in your mortal bodies, to make you obey their passions" (6:12). The Christian is presented with a choice, whether to submit to the dominion of the old dead body, or to offer oneself to God in resurrected life: "No longer present your members [that is, the parts of your body] to sin as instruments [or "weapons," *hopla*] of wickedness, but present yourselves to God as those who have been brought from death to life, and present your members to God as instruments of righteousness. For sin will have no dominion ["have no lordship," *kyrieuo*] over you, since you are not under law but under grace" (6:13-14).

Years ago, a youth leader presented my high-school group with an image based on this passage, as a method for avoiding sin: "Picture your grave, with a tombstone over it; the stone has your name, and the words, 'Dead to sin.'" I would add today one image: as you examine the grave closely, you will see that the tomb is empty. If we are united with Christ in his death to sin, it is only because we are united with him in the new resurrected life. Baptism is an

205

act of God that brings Christians into this relationship with Christ's death and resurrection; in it, our disobedient selves die with him on the cross, so that we might be raised from the dead with him. Our job is simply to consider God's act to be so, and present ourselves to God in that way of new life.

Life In The Big House

Easter Vigil — Romans 6:3-11
April 4, 1998

While this particular sermon was preached at Christ Episcopal Church, Avon, Connecticut, I have used the opening story many times at Easter Vigil, because I believe the image of baptism by immersion best conveys Paul's understanding of baptism as uniting the believer in the death and resurrection of Jesus. But what if your church does not baptize by immersion? Perhaps only the imagination can span the resultant gap. The story goes that someone asked a well-known biblical scholar if he believed in infant baptism. His reply was, "Believe in it? Why, I've seen it!" Keep in mind that most Episcopalians have never even *seen* baptism by immersion, thus the need to tell the story.

But sermons are always heard in context, and I have been vexed on a number of occasions when this story was heard (often by those who come from baptism-by-immersion tradition) as a criticism of immersion! Perhaps the problem is the first-person orientation. While I have been loathe to give that up — it is, after all, a story about *my* surprised Episcopal reaction — I have found myself trimming the story down to its essentials, omitting a good deal of the details — the preacher actually wore a waist-high rubber fishing suit under his robe — and thus a considerable amount of humor, since people took it not as funny but as condescending. Of course, the point of the story is quite the opposite; immersion is of the utmost continuity with Paul's understanding, and as far as I'm concerned, we ought to build baptismal fonts into Episcopal churches, or at least march every baptismal candidate down to the river! But good intentions are not good communication, so the story has over the years been whittled to its present form, and if I ever tell it again, I'll probably put it into the third person, just to be safe.

———

My brother was in high school when he decided to get baptized at the Church of God, Anderson, Indiana.

You had to say it that way, Church of God Anderson Indiana, because that's where their headquarters were, and to distinguish them from all the other Churches of God.

Now my brother had already been baptized, but the Church of God Anderson Indiana told him it didn't take until you were old enough to profess a faith of your own, so my brother was going to do it again, and he asked me to come along.

There I was, totally unprepared by the Episcopal Church for what was about to happen.

It was the end of the service, my brother and the preacher had disappeared, when suddenly the curtains at the front of the church opened.

My brother and the preacher were there, walking deliberately — wading, I realized, in hip-high water — the curtains had opened to reveal a pool full of water.

Immediately the preacher grabbed my brother, one hand on his nose, the other behind his back, and WHOMP! pushed him back under the water, held him there almost long enough to drown him, and brought him up sputtering. WHOMP! he did it again. WHOMP! he did the third time. Father, Son, and Holy Spirit.

No one in that church had any doubt that my brother had been baptized.

Sometimes I think that we might be doing ourselves a favor if we installed one of those baptismal pools in every Episcopal Church.

Or at least went down to the river for baptism like the good-ole days.

Because I never quite understood the sixth chapter of Paul's letter to the Romans until I saw it for myself.

"Do you not know that all of us who have been baptized into Christ Jesus were baptized into his death? Therefore we have been buried with him by baptism into death, so that just as Christ was raised from the dead by the glory of the Father, so we too might walk in newness of life."

For Paul, baptism is a kind of death by drowning, followed by resurrection.

Going under the water is a symbol of burial; coming up again into the light again stands for being raised from the dead.

The whole act of putting someone under water and bringing him back up points to Jesus being buried and being raised from the dead.

But for Paul, it's not just figurative, not empty symbol.

This is exactly what God has done.

It is Paul's fundamental take on reality: to be baptized is to join in Christ's death and resurrection. It is to walk with him in newness of life.

This is why I have trouble when people talk about "christening."

"I want to schedule my new baby's christening."

I can't help myself, I always picture a champagne bottle slamming against the prow of a ship, "I hereby christen you, *U.S.S. Enterprise*."

Baptism is not a naming ceremony — or at least, not the baby's name.

For Paul, the name in question is the name of Jesus.

Baptism imprints identity, yes, but it is the identity of the dead and risen Christ.

Jesus' death and life mark out the essential pattern of Christian life.

Paul says we Christians can't go on living in sin, any more than Jesus can stay in the tomb.

We have died to sin. There's a tombstone with our name on it; the inscription says, "Dead to Sin."

Because sin means closing us off to God's gift; to accept the gift is to live in faith.

There's no other option.

You can't die to sin without being raised to new life.

You can't go under the water without coming back up.

Paul switches images to make his point:

"We know that our old self was crucified with him," he says, "so that the body of sin might be destroyed, and we might no longer be *enslaved* to sin. For whoever has died is freed from sin."

Paul pictures sin as the slave owner.

We all know that when the slave dies, ownership ceases.

And you have died with Christ, Paul says —

The chains are broken, the leg irons have been removed. You can move out of the slave quarters and into the big house. Emancipation Proclamation. You are free.

But the proof is in the pudding.

The early Christians had another baptismal ritual, where they put on new clothes after coming up out of the water, clean white robes.

Paul was known to tell people to "put on" the new life, like a new suit.

"Consider yourselves," he says to the Romans, "dead to sin and alive to God in Christ Jesus."

God has already given you newness of life, now give yourselves over to it.

We are called to put our faith into action, day after day after day.

Faith is a process, not an accomplishment; a verb, not a noun.

It means making faithful, faith-filled decisions day-by-day.

Even here, God has not left us high and dry. God has given us help. That's why we've always associated baptism with the coming of the Holy Spirit.

God has already done unto you as God would have you do.
You've been given your freedom, and the power of the Spirit.
Now, act like it.

Tonight we have observed the ancient Christian festival of death
and resurrection.
We have moved from darkness into light, from under the deep
waters up into the light of the sun.
We have renewed our own baptismal vows — something we
are called to do day after day.
And in the end I don't think it makes any difference whether
you were forced under water until your lungs burst, or
flicked with a drip from a medicine dropper in the name
of the Father, Son, and Holy Spirit.
If Paul is right, then baptism is not something we do, but something God has done to us, uniting us to him in death, uniting us to him also in newness of life.
What we do is live the life given us. Walk the road to freedom.
Leave our chains behind, and move into the big house.

8. Preaching Resurrection Intertextually

In my beginning preaching classes, I have always taught students to deal with one biblical text carefully and thoroughly. Sometimes, though, students from lectionary churches are expecting to learn how to integrate all the Sunday texts into the sermon. "That's advanced preaching," I say.

Whether you're dealing with two, three, or all four texts from a lectionary selection, or choosing two or more passages on your own, preaching more than one biblical text — what I call "preaching intertextually" — is definitely advanced preaching. It would be folly for the preacher to address any text without thorough background study — so at the least, an intertextual sermon on three texts would require three times the study that a single text would require. Fortunately for lectionary preachers who save their study notes, that time can be spread over the years; there will always be a chance to study the Gospel this year, and save the Epistle for three years from now.

Other than the extra time involved, an intertextual preacher will have to engage in a more difficult and sophisticated interpretive process to bring more than one text to congregation. Truly intertextual preaching bears no resemblance to those sermons which skim across the surface of a concordance, drawing prooftexts haphazardly from across the Bible, but setting none of them in context.

Some may question all that work: why put texts together, when one will do nicely? There are two reasons: first, the sermon is always an intertextual endeavor, and second, the Bible itself is an intertextual book. First, the sermon always straddles at least two texts, though one of them is not the kind of text made up of words on a page — it is the text of our lives. The sermon always confronts a gap between the biblical text and modern life, between the times of the Bible and the times of our lives. The problem with modern life is that it is much less contained than a short passage from scripture. We must interpret life; we must bring some order to it, give it a story or a theme or a reason. In that act of interpretation, we have given our lives the shape of a text, which then is expressed literally as a text in the words of our sermon. The basic movement of preaching is in that sense intertextual.

Second, just as modern life is multivalent — that is, we can bring multiple understandings of it into our lives, and even into our sermons — the Bible itself is composed of material of great diversity, being not "The Book" but "The Books," compiled over centuries by various authors and editors, with varying literary, historical, theological, anthropological, and sociological backgrounds. The diverse perspectives that can be found in the Bible remind us that God is not contained in any one situation or understanding, including our own. It also gives us hope that we can hear a word from God in our situation as readily as those who were part of the biblical stories. Preaching intertextually helps us discern the voice of God among diverse witnesses.

There are various ways of putting biblical texts together in a sermon, some of them very similar to how we might use material from modern life in our sermons. One can, for example, give two or more biblical texts equal weight in the sermon, both contributing their support to a single theme. By contrast, one could play off two texts as opposites (as we have already seen, the diversity of New Testament writings easily allows this); there is no reason to think that we will always agree with every biblical text, when they don't necessarily agree with each other. One could also use one text in support of another, perhaps to confirm a point, perhaps as an illustration or example. Too many preachers miss the chance to use an illustration that is sitting right under their noses, in the morning's lectionary!

There are also ways not to put texts together; one must beware of manipulating texts or making artificial use of them. Some lectionary preachers forget that the lectionary is itself artificial;

somebody has chosen those texts to fit together. Usually only the Old Testament has been selected to fit with the Gospel reading; the Epistles are read serially, or "in course." In fact, churches have been moving toward reading the Old Testament in course as well, as a way of avoiding the overemphasis on typological interpretation that sometimes seems to be at work in lectionary selection. The Old Testament can be read in and for itself, without always having to have a New Testament analogy. At any rate, biblical interpretation for preaching must always take each individual text seriously; it is not a matter of reading the minds of the lectionary authors, in order to discern the supposed links between and among texts. Other pitfalls for the intertextual preacher include the temptation to turn the sermon into three or four sermonettes, covering one text after another, and thus violating the unity of the sermon; or stretching too far to connect diverse texts, and thus pulling them all out of shape.

Despite the pitfalls, and despite all the hard interpretive work, intertextual preaching is great fun. Here is a chance to join a conversation that has been going on for ages, includes some of the most influential thinkers of history, and involves the great issues of life and death. Humbly, the preacher joins the discussion, but with a smile. Enjoy!

A Hand From The Tomb

Easter Day — Acts 10:34-43; Colossians 3:1-4; Luke 24:1-10
April 12, 1998

This sermon was preached at Christ Church, Avon, Connecticut, to the 8:00 service, which is usually quiet, reserved, gray-haired, traditional, and lightly attended.

Over the years, I have evolved in my thinking about the 8:00 sermon. I used to try to condense the "big" sermon into a short sound bite, often sans stories, illustrations, and anything that seemed remotely extraneous — the "no-frills sermon" (an example appeared in an earlier section). But too often I had the feeling that such sermons were not so much "no-frill" as "lite" — some substance was missing. One day my wife said, "Why short-change people just because they come early?" I began to preach the same sermon I would use at the later service.

Easter Day in Avon introduced one variation on the 8:00 tradition: we actually had music at the early service — the 8:00 crowd permitted singing, just this one time per year. Also different on this day was that the sermon was composed particularly for this audience (I was going to do a children's sermon at the later service). It is fairly straightforward, as befits the service, using the three readings in a stepping-stone sequence to show how Jesus' resurrection is the foundation for the Christian's new life.

Back before I realized I was a hopeless case, I used to read books about how to remember people's names.

I once worked for a priest who could meet you at the back door before the service and then say your name as he put the wafer in your hand, but I've always been the kind who could walk by his best friend on the street and wonder if I've met that guy.

I used to read memory books, which didn't help much.

I did find one good piece of advice, though.

216

Always pay attention when they introduce themselves.

Most of the time, we don't remember the name because we didn't hear it in the first place.

If you want to remember, you have to be there.

This is common sense, but it may lead us to an entirely new picture of Jesus and his disciples.

Remember, the two men in dazzling clothes say to the women at the tomb, according to the Gospel of Luke.

"*Remember* how he told you, while he was still in Galilee, that the Son of Man must be handed over to sinners, and be crucified, and on the third day rise again."

Now you can't remember what you never heard in the first place.

The command to remember requires that there's something to remember.

And this is probably going to scotch all our old pictures of the disciples.

What do you usually think of when I say "disciples"? Twelve guys in bathrobes and sandals.

But if *we* remember Luke's story well enough, we remember that after Jesus sent out twelve, he sent out 72.

And some of those 72 must have been female.

Luke in fact tells us that a great many women followed Jesus; some of them were rich women, because they provided for him out of their own bank accounts.

The picture is not of a male-only handful, but a large mixed crowd, including an entire entourage of sisters and cousins and aunts who were themselves faithful disciples.

They were there to hear what he had to say.

They remembered his words.

And they were the first to pass along the news that what he said was true.

The men caught on eventually.

> Peter in his sermon in the Book of Acts says that God raised Jesus on the third day, and allowed him to appear, not to all the people, but to the ones chosen by God as witnesses, who ate and drank with him after he rose from the dead.

> "He commanded us to preach," Peter says, "and to testify that he is the one ordained by God as judge of the living and dead."

> And preach they did.

> Here we are.

> They passed it along over the years, across the centuries, until it reached us —

> Not simply as arcane, wondrous, and perhaps debatable claims about something that happened long ago —

> No. What they passed along was the secret of getting up out of bed in the morning, and living life seven days a week.

For Peter and the women and all the rest, resurrection was not just a claim about Jesus, it was a claim on their lives.

> It set the basic pattern for life.

> Paul makes it clear in his letter to the Colossians, using the image of dunking, baptism by immersion.

> You died with Christ, he says, when your head went under the water.

> When you came up into the light again sputtering, that's resurrection.

> "If you have been raised with Christ," then, "seek the things that are above."

> "Set you minds on things that are above, not on things that are on earth, for you have died, and your life is hidden with Christ in God."

> You see, it's not just that Christ was raised long ago and far away.

> And it's not even that he is still alive, and still with us today.

But it's also that when he died, we died. When he was raised,
we were raised.

"Seek the things above," Paul says, "where Christ is."

We can live new lives because of what he has done for us.

Death and resurrection are not the exception, but the rule, the
daily rule.

For every day when we get out of bed in the morning, God
offers us the chance to live the new life with Jesus.

I could give you a million examples of what it means to live the
resurrected life, but the one that strikes me this morning is
about how one community is living a new life today.

The Open Door Church in Minor, Alabama, held a sunrise
service in their parking lot this morning at 6:00 a.m.

Choirs sang *a cappella*, the preacher preached in open air.

Perhaps this would not be so remarkable, except that next to
that parking lot, where there was a church building a few
days ago, there stands only one hallway.

A tornado blew in Wednesday and took the church with it.

Sixty-eight people huddled in that hallway Wednesday, hiding
from the wind.

Children sang "Jesus loves me, this I know" over the noise
like a rushing train bearing down on them.

Sixty-eight people walked away from that choir practice alive.

They came out to see their cars blown off the parking lot.

Was it a tragedy? Yes. Was it a disaster? You bet. But so was
the cross.

On that same lot this morning, they celebrated their resurrection, the resurrection of Jesus.

We've never understood the resurrection of Jesus until we've seen
that it is our resurrection.

There are no raging winds, there is no high water, there is
nothing that we can go through that he has not already
been through, and come out on the other side.

219

He has been to hell and back, through the wind and the waters,
    but at the last, God has taken his hand and lifted him up.
Jesus steps out of the tomb and offers us *his* hand.
He wants to take his friends with him.
Untiring, that hand reaches out to us.

Up, Up, But Not Away

Ascension Day — Acts 1:1-11; Luke 24:49-52
May 25, 1995

This sermon was preached at Emmanuel Episcopal Church in Quakertown, Pennsylvania, at a joint Ascension Day service with the local Lutheran Church. The Episcopal Church, U.S.A. and the Evangelical Lutheran Church in America had for several years been exploring a mutual recognition of ministry, and this yearly joint service was one manifestation of that effort on a local level.

Preaching to strangers is always difficult, since you don't have any way of knowing your audience. Preaching to an ecumenical group is that much more perilous. Frankly, I take quite a chance with my opening — anyone who chooses not to listen to the end might conclude that, "Those Episcopalians are pretty skeptical." I thought the message worth the risk in this case.

Scripturally, this sermon builds on Luke's two versions of the Ascension. Rather than highlighting the differences (which perhaps would have been far too overwhelming for this crowd), I put both stories into a broader context, that of Luke's larger story.

One local and topical reference may be too obscure now, though it was publicized quite heavily in the Philadelphia area: a man named John Bennett, who ran an outfit called the Foundation for New Era Philanthropy, was accused of pocketing donations and stiffing a number of religious colleges and other institutions who had invested their money with him. It was quite the scandal at the time.

———

There is a story in the play *Mass Appeal* that I don't think made it
    into the Jack Lemmon movie version.
    Young Deacon Dolson tells of going to an Ascension Day
      service.
    They tied a crucifix to a Roman candle, lit the fuse, and sent
      the crucified, crowned Christ up, up, and away.
    The choir sang, "Leaving On A Jet Plane."

221

Which just highlights the ludicrousness of what we are doing here
  tonight.

  Episcopalians and Lutherans together, celebrating the feast of
    the Ascension.

  It is silly, inane, at worst.

  At best, wishful thinking, unrealistic hope.

  Marx said that religion is the opiate of the people, and the
    ancient Christian celebration of Ascension Day may be
    exactly the kind of thing he had in mind.

  A belief in an ascended Messiah could be seen as roughly the
    same as a modern-day UFO cult, the belief that there are
    friendly, benevolent aliens out there who take care of us,
    and the fortunate few who have had Close Encounters of
    the Third Kind are here to tell us the truth.

  It is the spiritual equivalent of a lottery ticket, or yet another
    entry into the Publishers Clearinghouse Sweepstakes, in
    the faint hope that this time Ed McMahon will announce
    our names on television.

    The difference being that we can compute the odds on the
      lottery or the sweepstakes.

But of course, the skeptic will say, it's all ludicrous.

  How is the Ascension different from any of the rest?

  Incarnation, miracles, healings, exorcism, water-to-wine and
    bread for the world, resurrection.

  The Ascension, the skeptic will say, is part and parcel of the
    whole package, none of it more likely than the rest.

  Just tales from the Flat-Earth Society, from a time when people
    thought the earth was a disk floating on a vast sea, and the
    sun, moon, and stars were fixed in an arch overhead.

  As the Russian cosmonaut said, there's no sign of God in outer
    space. Nor of an ascending Jesus.

  We Lutherans and Episcopalians here tonight have to admit
    that we have not a grain of scientific proof in our test tubes,

not an iota of evidence, no indication whatsoever that our beliefs are any more probable than, say, the so-called science of the scientific creationists who fight to keep the teaching of evolution out of their children's schools.

But unlike scientific creationists, we celebrate with fingers crossed behind our backs, not willing to sacrifice our sober exteriors, nor to lobby for new textbooks, nor to push our beliefs through the courts.

Just a friendly potluck dinner, thank you very much, and a nice quiet service, that's all.

And maybe that's our problem — the fingers crossed behind the back.

The skeptic would call us all hypocrites.

The skeptic sees us sitting smugly, listening to drivel that makes no difference to anything we really do.

Meanwhile the church dips into our pockets. Not the opiate of the people, but the snake oil.

For the skeptic, John Bennett and the Foundation for New Era Philanthropy sum it up for a gullible, naive, greedy, and hypocritical people willing to believe any huckster with an expensive suit and a good haircut.

Or maybe it is the skeptic who is spouting drivel.

Maybe, just maybe, the down-to-earth, sane, sober, realistic, common sense skeptic is wrong.

Maybe we Christians know something the skeptics have overlooked.

Luke wrote two versions of the Ascension story.

We read both versions tonight. The first is the ending of the Gospel of Luke; the second is the beginning of the Acts of the Apostles.

223

Both versions are part of Luke's larger story — a story about a prophet who in fulfillment of scripture came to visit the people, who was received with joy by some but rejected by others, who although he was handed over to torture and death was vindicated by God, and who carries on through his disciples as they spread his message to the ends of the earth.

Like the prophets before him — Moses, Elijah — he was taken by God, and his Spirit given to his followers.

Wait in Jerusalem, he told them, for the promise of the Father. "You will be clothed with power from on high." "You shall receive power when the Holy Spirit comes upon you, and you will be my witnesses in Jerusalem, in all Judea and Samaria, and to the end of the earth."

We Episcopalians and Lutherans in Quakertown follow in the steps of those first disciples.

Like them, we believe in the Holy Spirit.

Like them, we proclaim the coming of the Kingdom of God.

And like them, we see the Kingdom of God in the life and death of the prophet, and in the community he called together to remember his body and blood.

We have Jesus with us in the person of the Holy Spirit, which gives us power to live the life God has called us to live.

And we have the promise: an end, a goal, a point to it all. "This Jesus, who has been taken up from you into heaven, will come in the same way as you saw him go."

The answer to the skeptics is that their common-sense down-to-earth wisdom is really just fear and despair in disguise.

Because if there is nothing but dirt and water and sky on this globe which circles a giant flaming ball of hydrogen, then there is ultimately no point in getting up in the morning,

except the feeble ideologies that we humans wield like
clumsy broadswords to wound one another.

But if this globe has been visited by the One who made us,
and if that One is somehow still present among us, then it
is the skeptics who are the bitter fools.

Because the One who has ascended to heaven sees us all, and
sees us truly.

Let me put it in a parable.

I know a woman who was lost.

She was scheduled for a meeting somewhere out in the countryside, somewhere she had never been; she was late. She
had directions, but they just didn't seem to make sense.

She turned at the crossroads, then left at the next road, then
left again. But the sign she was looking for never appeared.
It was empty landscape — nothing there but a deserted
gas station and vacant greenery, no place to stop, no one
to ask for directions.

When she passed that big gnarly oak tree for the third time,
she knew she had been going in circles.

It was getting dark, it was vacant country, she was late, she
was lost.

That was when it happened.

The phone rang.

She had forgotten all about the cellular phone.

It was a wrong number, but that didn't make any difference.

Because now she knew that help had been there all along.

She just needed the reminder.

It may sometimes seem like the journey of the third planet from
the sun is a pointless, repetitive cycle, and the spinning of
the earth, a dizzying exercise in futility, our very lives going
around in circles.

But we are not lost.

225

The one who ascended into heaven sees us, is with us now, and will come again.
Only sometimes we do need the reminder.

Bulldozer Bible

Easter 6, Year C — Acts 14:8-18; John 14:23-29
May 17, 1998

This is an instance of a sermon that focuses on a single text, in this case from the Book of Acts, but uses another biblical text in an auxiliary fashion. The Gospel of John is introduced at the end of the sermon as an answer to the theological problem posed by the story in Acts. The Gospel is thus crucial to the movement of the sermon from sin and idolatry (as illustrated so clearly in Acts) to the good news and the power to have faith (as promised in John). While the actual use of John is brief and suggestive (I preferred to have people go home and think about it rather than spell it out at too great a length), it is essential to the message as a whole. Without it, the sermon is little more than a fuss; with it, there is a promise from God for help.

This sermon was preached at Christ Church, Avon, Connecticut.

Long ago and far away, in a place called Lystra, there was a man
    sitting.
    He was sitting because he could do no other — he could not
        stand or walk or run — he could not use his feet at all.
    Crippled from birth, his legs were useless withered stumps.
    But he had ears. He could listen. He listened to a man named
        Paul.
    And he caught the attention of Paul, who saw something more
        than disability.
    Paul saw "faith to be healed."
    So Paul yelled at him: "Get up," he cried.
    And the man sprang up and began for the first time to walk.

I don't know what it is about human nature, but we can only be
    happy for this man for a few minutes —

Just a few moments, before someone asks the question:
What about the rest?
What about all the other lame people in Lystra?
There were probably more sick people in that town than all
the people that Paul fixed in the pages of the Bible.
It doesn't seem fair.
Why don't they all get fixed?

The usual answer makes faith the scapegoat.
It requires faith to be healed, they say. You've got to have
enough faith.
I remember being at a prayer meeting in college, where a
woman "claimed her healing" from diabetes.
"Insulin is horrible stuff," she said, "it abuses your body."
She wasn't going to take it anymore.
She had faith to be healed.
I went home more than a little skeptical. I expected to
come back in a couple of weeks to find her dead.
My next-door neighbor was one of the ringleaders of this
prayer group. He told me a few days later that the
whole scene had been a mistake.
The woman's parents had not wanted her to go off insulin.
She had broken a commandment; she had been
disobedient.
Her faith had not healed her, because of a little chink in
the spiritual armor.
But I walked away thinking, What's wrong with this picture?
What kind of God is this that plays such games?
The problem seemed not so much a lack of faith, but a
poverty of imagination.
Rather than an abundant giver of good things, in the end
we can imagine only an accountant, a divine bean
counter, a petulant stickler for the rules, rules which
at best are slippery.

228

The crucial piece we've missed is how slippery the story was in the first place.

We think it's straightforward, but it's not; it's full of double meaning.

The words we translate, "he had faith to be healed," could just as easily mean "he had faith to be *saved*."

Paul didn't make any distinction between being healed and being saved.

And so the story about a crippled man being healed is just as much a story about a cracked soul made whole, a fractured life saved.

The crowds in Lystra certainly saw what was at stake here.

Barnabas they called Zeus; Paul became Hermes the messenger of Zeus, because he talked so much.

The priest of Zeus came from his temple outside the city, bringing oxen decked in garlands, determined to offer sacrifices to these two gods come down in human form.

The misplaced religious outpouring is almost comical — it was standard in Greek and Roman entertainment to laugh at dumb rustics who take mere mortals from the big city to be gods — it's like in *Star Trek,* where the primitive people mistake technology for magic. It's always good for a laugh.

It would be funny, were it not so serious, and so typical of human nature.

The Lystrans mistake creation for Creator. They offer their worship at the wrong altar.

It is the human tendency to squeeze God's grace to manageable, bite-sized chunks.

We take the ineffable and reduce it to human proportions.

I don't think we should laugh too hard at the Lystrans.

I don't think we should laugh, so much as ask *ourselves:*

Where will we offer our sacrifices?

What altar will take our oxen and garlands?

The altar of politics?

Money?

Love?

Religion itself?

Let's not kid ourselves. There is no created thing that we cannot turn into an idol.

But no created thing can satisfy; no creation can fill the hole
in our hearts. The hole is God-shaped, one-size only.

For Paul and Barnabas, idolatry was another opportunity to proclaim the good news.

They tore their garments, the traditional sign of blasphemy.

But they were not angry; they were almost amused that
anyone would try to worship such "worthless things" as
themselves.

God is gracious, they tell the people of Lystra, God has given
you a chance to turn from these worthless things to the
living God, who made heaven and earth and the sea and
all that is in them.

God is gracious, yes, but God now requires a choice.

There's a scene in the Robert Duvall movie, *The Apostle*:
The little country church is having a picnic, when
up roars Billy Bob Thornton and his buddies on a
bulldozer, determined to put an end to the integrated
congregation.

The Apostle Robert Duvall and his congregation stand between the bulldozer and the little church building.

Get out of the way, says Billy Bob, I'm going to bulldoze
you. This ain't our kind of religion.

No, you're not, says the Apostle, and he stands firm.

Then he stoops and carefully lays his Bible down on the
grass before the giant ram.

Talk about an icon, it's one of those big floppy preacher Bibles, leather bound — they don't call it the Bible Belt for nothing — belt leather.

One by one, Billy Bob's friends jump off the bulldozer. There are certain things you do not bulldoze in that part of the country.

Eventually Billy Bob himself jumps down and tries to move the Bible, but the Apostle holds on to him and says, I know you didn't come here to bulldoze this church. I know you came for something else. He holds on, he won't let go, he knows.

And finally Billy Bob breaks down and admits, that Yes, he came for God.

Idols are strong, even when they become occasions to preach the gospel.

Paul and Barnabas were just barely able to restrain the Lystrans from making their sacrifice.

But we shouldn't be too hard on these people — they're just human.

And besides, they knew salvation by faith when they saw it.

Will we?

Here Jesus himself leaves us with some assurance.

In the Gospel of John, he tells his disciples that "The Advocate, the Holy Spirit, whom the Father will send in my name, will remind you of all that I have said to you."

In the constant tug of war between idols and the true God, we are not alone. There is help.

The Spirit will teach you everything, he says.

In other words, we have something to look forward to.

The Harmony Of The Spirit

Pentecost Day — Acts 2:1-11;
1 Corinthians 12:4-13; John 20:19-23
May 18, 1997

Sometimes a modern conundrum can set up a focus for hearing several scriptures speak at once. In this case, the problem is set off by the two contrasting stories (once again, I break my rule against first-person stories!). Each scripture is allowed in turn to address the issue; I neither emphasize nor ignore the different perspectives of each scriptural passage, but try to allow them to speak for themselves. The final illustration provides the basis of the exhortation, and, I trust, a metaphor for how the different voices can speak together.

This sermon was preached at St. Luke's Episcopal Church, Katonah, New York.

It was a last minute call.

There was desperation in the Senior Warden's voice.

"Our priest is sick, we need someone on Sunday morning."

I didn't really want to go, but it was an emergency, so I went.

When I got there, I thought I had walked into the wrong church.

In place of choir pews, there was a drum set — not even real
drums, but those electronic pads.

There was no organ, but a keyboard with a microphone, like at
a nightclub.

And next to the altar was the overhead projector for putting
the words of the songs on the wall.

And then it hit me: I had heard that there was a charismatic
Episcopal church in this town, and I had just walked into
it.

For those of you who have never been, charismatic churches
put a high value on the spontaneous working of the Spirit,

232

and their worship tends to be less formal, with movement
and dancing and pop music.

I felt like the guy who showed up at the Grateful Dead concert
wearing a tuxedo; he thought he was going to the Three
Tenors.

My out-of-the-prayer-book contributions seemed just a little
stiff in the midst of the hand-raising and praise-chanting
and Yes-Lord-ing.

Now, don't get me wrong, I don't have anything against the
occasional folk mass, or even a rock mass. There are many
ways to worship God.

But I personally don't want the Grateful Dead in church every
week.

And after the service when they came up and told me about
going to Conference ABC or Program XYZ, I just had to
smile politely and not say what I really thought of ABC or
XYZ.

It was somewhat a matter of taste, somewhat of theology; I
just didn't feel quite comfortable there.

Now here's another picture entirely.

My wife and I went to a conference last week with James
Forbes. He's the pastor of Riverside Church in New York
City, and an inspirational speaker for preachers.

We had gotten up too early Thursday morning, and driven too
far to Long Island, having too many things hanging over
our heads back at the office, not to mention Sunday sermons — well, there we were sitting with fifty other pastors who were in the same boat.

And we waited for the lecture to begin.

But it didn't begin, or rather Forbes didn't begin with a lecture, but with a song.

He stood us up and made us sing, a song I didn't know but a
lot of them seemed to know, fifty preachers of all stripes,

all denominations, male, female, black, white, Asian, people from the islands of the Caribbean, all singing together, "Glorify your name, Glorify your name, Glorify your name in all the earth."

And somehow with that song it was no longer a burden to be there.

It was refreshing.

Dr. Forbes' topic for the day: The Holy Spirit.

These two contrasting images show the problem.

When Christians talk about the Holy Spirit, we tend to speak out of both sides of the mouth.

There is both threat and promise with the Spirit.

On the one hand, it is deeply unsettling to talk too much about it, to get too close to the Spirit.

The threat is that the Spirit may change our lives.

Are we going to have to give up our nice, comfortable, beautiful worship and end up at a church with a drum set, singing mindless chants over and over?

Or worse, if we pay attention to the Spirit, will God demand some really great sacrifice?

On the other hand, the promise is also that the Spirit will change our lives.

And it will be the change we really need and really want.

Life in the Spirit may refresh us.

In the story of Pentecost in Acts, there is both threat and promise.

The threat is obvious.

Here are these disciples, with all this weird stuff — the tongues of fire on their heads, the speaking in languages they didn't know:

"Divided tongues, as of fire, appeared among them, and they were filled with the Holy Spirit and began to speak in languages."

It's very odd stuff.

234

And worst of all, this preaching in public —

As some of you know, I was part of a very conservative campus group in college.

One of our members, named Wayne, decided one day that God was calling him to preach in front of the campus union.

Our leaders wanted us to stand up behind Wayne in support, just as the eleven apostles stood behind Peter as he gave that first Pentecost sermon.

But as my roommate put it, "Not on your life."

There was no way.

How much more so today for us stiff, traditional Anglicans.

And yet the promise is also palpable.

Think about the power here — these were the wimps who left Jesus to be brutalized.

They ran away, and denied even knowing him.

And yet here they are, a few weeks later, boldly speaking the good news of God.

And the promise is the growth of something even bigger.

The Book of Acts makes it clear that there weren't just twelve apostles there that day, but over 120 disciples.

A whole community was empowered; there were no laggards.

They all spoke to this crowd of Jews from every land, Parthians and Medes and Elamites and all the rest.

We later learn that over 3,000 people joined them that day.

Now I'm not saying that we could be so lucky — that we could even get half as many, or even ten percent.

But what if we drew in just one percent of the crowd that Peter and the others drew that day?

Who wouldn't want to see this place full, to look around and see Parthians and Medes and people from the ends of the earth?

235

The Gospel of John, too, offers threat and promise when it talks about the Spirit.

It is oh so weird, with Jesus huffing and puffing in their faces.

"He breathed on them and said to them, 'Receive the Holy Spirit.' "

As if the answer really were blowing in the wind.

And then in effect he hands them the keys: they can say who's in and who's out, who's forgiven and who's not.

"If you forgive the sins of any," he says, "they are forgiven; if you retain the sins of any, they are retained."

I ask you, who wants to be responsible for anyone else's forgiveness?

And yet forgiveness is also the promise.

As in Acts, the audience is more than just twelve apostles.

Jesus is talking to the whole community here.

The forgiveness he's talking about is not in the hands of just the apostles or the clergy or the leaders, but everyone.

Jesus offers them the opportunity to become a community defined by forgiveness —

People who know they are forgiven by God, and live out that forgiveness.

Of course, I don't know what we would do without the pettiness, without the gossip, the backbiting, the little foibles of human nature that would be transformed by the Spirit of God.

What would the church do without the personality conflicts and the sniping?

One of my friends likes to say that the church is a place where if you put your foot down, somebody fifty feet away claims you stepped on it.

I always say that the reason church fights are so fierce is that there's so little at stake.

236

The promise of the Holy Spirit is to lift us above the petty bickering, to live like people who are forgiven.

Jesus literally blew those first disciples into a community of forgiveness.

And we are called to follow — or shall I say, float — where that wind blows.

There is one more vision of life in the Spirit to consider.

Paul in his first letter to the Corinthians used the metaphor of the body.

The promise again is obvious.

"In the one Spirit we were all baptized into one body."

And with one body, there is one accord, a unity of action, and that's attractive.

One of my friends went to a church in Atlanta, a conservative Presbyterian church. The place was packed, and the pastor was being coy.

"Don't you tell the church board, but at our meeting Thursday night, I'm going to ask them to raise $500,000, half a million, and we're going to add an educational wing to this church, and we're going to start a day school."

"Now don't you tell them, but that's what I'm going to do." And the congregation was nodding and smiling.

My friend said that theologically, the church held no appeal for him, but he otherwise could understand the attraction of this group moving with vision in one accord.

But the threat is also clear.

There can be a stifling uniformity in that kind of unity.

There's something called the "church growth movement," that says the churches grow when the congregation is homogeneous — everyone alike, with the same interests, the same concerns, the same backgrounds and culture and politics and social and economic status.

237

It almost seems like an ecclesiastical rationale for separate but equal.

It's disturbing, especially considering that even today the old saying is true: the most segregated hour in America is 10:00 Sunday morning.

It does raise the question, though, of how a diverse group can be a unity.

Is Paul just being optimistic when he compares the church to a body with many members?

I look at it this way:

When I was in college and majoring in music, I was required to sing in the University Chorus.

One semester we started to rehearse a certain piece, and we went off separately for sectional rehearsals: soprano, alto, tenor, bass.

I sang with the basses, and we were just flabbergasted and drained, we didn't know how we could sing this — it had jumps and leaps and strange moves; it was very difficult to sing.

When we joined with the tenors, it seemed even worse, with these strange juxtapositions of notes, dissonances.

The joke started going around that the composer was deaf when he wrote it.

It wasn't until we were added to altos and sopranos, and later flutes, clarinets, horns, strings, timpani — only then did it start to make sense, to turn into music, and when we sang we felt not drained but revived.

The piece was Beethoven's Ninth Symphony.

And Beethoven was stone deaf when he wrote it, and as the story goes, he had his back to the audience at the first performance, and they had to take him by the arm and turn him around to see the crowd on their feet cheering, and tears streamed down his cheeks.

Much like the tears that must flow on the face of God when the church, working diverse gifts, together sings in the harmony of the Spirit.

There remains only the question.
How do we do it?
How to speak the good news in the power of the Spirit?
How do we live as a community of forgiveness?
How do we create one body by the working of many gifts?
My answer is one word:
Rehearse.

A Long, Cold Drink

Pentecost Sunday — Acts 2:1-11;
1 Corinthians 12:4-13; John 20:19-23
May 31, 1998

Here is another take on the Pentecost scriptures, again incorporating the entire lectionary (apart from the Psalm). Here the stories of scripture are set in contrast to a modern-life story (culled from public radio). Again, the goal is to allow the different stories to speak for themselves, yet as one work of God.

This sermon was preached at Christ Church, Avon, Connecticut. As is perhaps obvious from the text, the country was still reeling from a spree of graphic gun violence inflicted on our schools, not to mention escalating violence in the Middle East, and open nuclear weapons testing in India and Pakistan. The world had once again become a dangerous place.

―――――――――

Kaoka Chambers was on a mission.

Seven years ago, she was sent from Chicago to Omaha to kill.

She was a member of a gang, the Vicelords, and there was a girl in Omaha who was running off at the mouth, and the orders were to "beat her down until she don't get up."

I heard Kaoka talking on the radio the other day, and she described herself in those days as someone who "didn't have no feelin's. I didn't care what happens," she said, "it just happens."

Then she drove by Grace Apostolic Church, a converted theater in the heart of Omaha's gang territory. Something made her stop and go in the church.

In Kaoka Chambers' own words, "Something grabbed me by the shoulders, and I fell, and I'm like dang, it's something you can't explain" — and the next thing she knew, she was getting baptized and filled with the Holy Spirit.

240

Some people, I suppose, are put off by that kind of religion.

But I think the proof is in the pudding, or to mix the cliche, you shall know them by their fruits.

Kaoka Chambers now works full-time as a school bus driver, the first job she's had besides slinging dope and breaking legs.

But her real job is head of youth outreach at Grace Apostolic Church; you don't have to quit the gang to join the church, you can wear your gang colors to church. Kaoka Chambers brings these kids into the church because she speaks their language: "I kick it straight with them," she says, "I don't come with no alleluias — that's church stuff, that's gonna come. You got to catch a fish to clean a fish, and once you clean a fish, it takes a process, the fish'll be clean."

As for Kaoka herself, "I'm free," she says. "I get to crying when I think about that. God knew I was the person to do the work. All I was looking for was love."

Some people will say it's strange, this story of Kaoka Chambers grabbed by the Spirit and dragged out of the Vicelords into the baptismal trough.

But is it any stranger than the story the Book of Acts tells?

One-hundred-twenty disciples crammed in an upper room — the day of Pentecost, that great pilgrimage feast, when all the Jews gathered in Jerusalem to celebrate the wheat harvest, and the giving of the Law to Moses.

Suddenly the sound of a twister from heaven, the roar filling the whole house.

One-hundred-twenty tongues of fire resting on their heads.

And they begin to speak in other languages, as the Spirit gives them ability.

Devout Jews from every nation hear them speaking about God's deeds of power in their own native tongues. Partians, Medes, Elamites, the whole long mouthful.

241

The universal mission has begun. "You shall be my witnesses,"
Jesus has told them, "when the Holy Spirit has come upon
you." And here they are, witnessing.
So what do you think? Do you buy it?

Or how about the story that John tells?
It's a slightly different version of the coming of the Spirit, but
it's no less strange.
Here the disciples are, Easter Day, Resurrection Day, locked
in a room out of fear.
Jesus appears among them despite the locks, bringing his peace.
"Peace be with you," he says not once but twice.
Then he does something really odd. He breathes on them.
Puff, with commentary: "Receive the Holy Spirit."
It's a new creation by the breath of God.
The purpose: "As the Father has sent me, so I send you."
"If you forgive the sins of any, they are forgiven; if you retain
the sins of any, they are retained."
In other words, the disciples are to do what Jesus has been
doing all along.
And Jesus has given them his breath, his Spirit, so that he will
be with them all along.

I don't know if you buy that one either.
It's all very strange, this business about wind and fire and
tongues and the breath of Jesus, forgiving sins.
But it has dawned on me that maybe it's supposed to be strange.
It's supposed to seem odd — I think that is what Paul was
trying to tell the Corinthians.
"There are varieties of gifts," Paul says, "but the same Spirit.
Varieties of services, but the same Lord. Varieties of ac-
tivities, but one God."
And then he lists his list of gifts, and they are strange: word of
wisdom, word of knowledge, faith, healing, miracles,
prophecy, discernment, tongues, interpretation.

242

If I asked you to make a list of the gifts of God, I doubt that this is the list you would come up with. Most people would say things like, talent and ability, skills, friendliness and hospitality, virtue or wealth or education, our families.

Our list would not be the same as Paul's. Outside of certain circles, most people would find Paul's list odd.

But the difference is the point.

One Spirit. Many gifts. God's choice.

The world wants to kill the difference.

The mission is: beat the difference down until she don't get up.

This is why India and Pakistan are setting off bombs. This is why Israel and Arabs argue over slivers of land, the way teenage gangs fight over turf.

You back down, you're dead. You can't survive difference in this world.

We moan and cry about schoolkids with guns, but they're just doing what they see their parents do — it's all over television, movies, books, the courts. We've told them that violence is a solution, we've put guns in their hands, and then we're surprised when they pull the trigger themselves.

The world kills difference.

God says, Difference is gift. My gift.

Paul tells the Corinthians, "All these gifts are activated by one and the same Spirit, as the Spirit chooses."

"For just as the body is one and has many members, and all the members, though many, are one body, so it is with Christ."

Even the metaphor that Paul uses for the Spirit is different. John and Acts picture the Spirit as breath or wind. Paul talks about the Spirit as water.

Even then, he can't decide if the Spirit is a dip in the river, or a long, cold drink. "For in the one Spirit," he says, "we

243

were all baptized into one body — Jews or Greeks, slaves or free — and we were all made to drink of one Spirit."
Dunking or drinking, what's the difference?
Whatever it is, we need the water.
It's a desert out there.

The pastor of Grace Apostolic Church in Omaha, where Kaoka Chambers was grabbed by the Spirit — her pastor is a man named Bishop William T. Barlow.
William Barlow has this to say:
"I am a blessed man," he says, "but it is important to me not to bathe in my blessing. I have to get out and dry off, and go help someone else. I have to introduce them to the tub. You can jump in," says William Barlow. "You can jump in, too. There's enough water for all of us."

Cats And Sheep

Easter 4, Year A — Acts 6:1-9, 7:2a, 51-60;
1 Peter 2:19-25; John 10:1-10
April 25, 1999

This is a sermon that focuses on the Gospel of John, using the other lectionary texts in an illustrative and supportive role. Here the biblical texts from Acts and 1 Peter play much the same role as the contemporary stories about the comic book and the cat. Scripture has great potential as illustrative material — it is readily at hand, easy to adapt, and will go a long way toward reducing the oft-lamented "biblical illiteracy" of our congregations — illiteracy which too often can be laid at the feet of preachers who make use of scripture only tangentially.

This sermon was preached at Christ Episcopal Church, Avon, Connecticut.

My friend was disturbed by something she had read.

It was a comic book. Not a comic comic book, not Archie and Jughead or Peanuts.

She had gotten it at the local Christian bookstore, where yes, believe it or not, you can buy Christian comic books.

But as I said, there was nothing comic here.

It was the vilest piece of slander I had ever seen, all about how a particular brand of Christians — and I'm not even going to dignify the slander by saying which brand — was actually a tool of Satan, determined to destroy "real" Christianity by a system of secret agents and sabotage. It ended with an invitation to join the secret battle.

I would have laughed if it weren't so sad.

I told my friend not to buy any more comic books.

But she was still upset. She thought everything you could get at the Christian bookstore would be "safe."

"Why would they say such things," she said, "if they weren't true?"

"My sheep hear my voice," said Jesus.
    But it's obviously not automatic.
    The thief and the bandit and the stranger have been known to do awfully good impressions.

And disputes between different brands of Christians are nothing new.
    We read about the first one in the Book of Acts.
        Some of the Greek-speaking Christians in Jerusalem complained against the Hebrew- or Aramaic-speaking ones because the Greek widows were getting short shrift at the daily soup kitchen.
        You will recall that one of the prime commandments of the Old Testament was to care for the widow, who in most ancient societies would be left destitute when her husband died.
        Imagine what it would have been like — all those women scrapping for whatever food there was, barely able to speak to one another —
        Sarah fighting in gibberish with Phoebe over the size of their bagels; Esther pantomiming the division of a sandwich with Zoe.
        Hebrew women elbowing their way to the front, while the Greek women at the end of the line go hungry.
        Talk about ethnic strife.
    The solution suggested by the Twelve was the obvious one, though it seems to be the last resort these days.
        It required no troops, no missiles, no pipe bombs, propane tanks, or automatic pistols.
        Force was not an option.
        Instead, they held an election.

Stephen, Phillip, Prochorus, Nicanor, Timon, Parmenas, and Nicolaus were chosen to wait on tables.

You'll notice that they're all Greek names.

But the qualifications for appointment were not ethnic or linguistic —

"Friends," said the apostles, "select from among yourselves seven men of good standing, full of the Spirit and of wisdom."

In other words, they were looking for people who in the middle of a thorny and possibly explosive situation could exercise some discernment.

The qualification for running the first Christian soup kitchen was to be one of the sheep best able to hear the shepherd's voice.

Or to shift the image, it's a matter of knowing your own front door.

Jesus was not above mixing his metaphors, and when he saw the puzzled looks on their faces, he shifted gears, and started talking about doors.

"I am the door to the sheepfold," he said, "I am the gate for the sheep."

"Whoever enters by me will be saved."

Think of it as an elaborate game of "Let's Make a Deal."

Monty Hall is offering you Door Number One, Door Number Two, or Door Number Three.

Behind two Doors are thieves, bandits, and strangers.

Behind one of those Doors is eternal life.

Which Door do you choose, as the crazy costumed crowd screams your name?

What keeps this from being a guessing game is that we can know what kind of Door we're looking for.

Not all the Doors look the same on close examination.

We can usually spot the Door that is Jesus by its familiar texture and pattern.

I've always found it interesting that when Stephen and Phillip and the rest are elected to wait on tables, they immediately go out and start preaching the word.

There is little that separates the eloquence of giving from the eloquence of speech — what you do with what you have says as much or more about you as whatever it is that comes out of your mouth.

Your wallet is as much an evangelist as your words.

We did not get to hear most of Stephen's speech today — it's a whole chapter long.

The thing that really got them mad was the way he recounted the whole history of Israel as if it were really about Jesus:

How Jesus was a prophet like Moses, sent by God once to the people, rejected, but now sent back in the guise of his disciples, to offer one last chance for repentance.

Stephen's audience, of course, responded in what is still today the most popular solution.

You don't like what you hear, pick up a rock. Plan an assault.

Rocks, knives, guns, bombs, attack helicopters, cruise missiles, what's the difference?

If you don't want to hear the voice of the shepherd, there are plenty of thieves, bandits, and strangers out there who will sell you a quicker solution.

What's remarkable is how much like Jesus Stephen is in the end.

"Lord Jesus, receive my spirit," he says.

"Do not hold this against them" —

Words echoing Jesus on the cross.

Plus the promise of a future, when he sees the heavens opened and the Son of Man standing at the right hand of God.

Stephen follows the pattern of Jesus to the end.

It's a theme repeated again and again through the Book of Acts, throughout the New Testament.

We read today from the First Letter of Peter advice for Christian slaves mistreated by pagan masters.

If you suffer for being a Christian, for doing what is right, endure it.

"For to this you have been called, because Christ also suffered for you, leaving you an example, so that you should follow in his steps."

"When he was abused, he did not return abuse; when he suffered, he did not threaten."

In short, he did everything the opposite of the way the turn-of-the-millennium world seems to have chosen.

Yet what Jesus did allowed us to choose another way:

"He himself bore our sins in his body on the cross, so that free from sins, we might live for righteousness."

"For you were going astray like sheep, but now you have returned to the shepherd and guardian of your souls."

Now that we've come full circle with our metaphors, let me mix in a new one.

Let's not be like sheep. Let's be cats.

Sheep have the reputation of being the dumbest animals alive.

They also are rumored to be quite dependent.

It seems to me that if we are going to discern the pattern of Jesus in a hostile environment, we don't need to be stupid or naive. We don't need to be conformists in a society that is going astray.

Cats on the other hand are known to be smart and independent.

Believe me, I've got a lot of experience with cats.

No cat is going to come just because you call.

If a cat comes running at the sound of your voice, it's because the cat knows from long experience that what you've got is worth running for.

My wife will tell you about her mother's cat John, who liked to climb up inside the fender of their old Studebaker and sleep all night.

One morning her father drove off to work at the repair shop earlier than usual.

Her mother poked her head out the front door a little later, calling John to his fried egg and saucer of milk breakfast. (I just tell the story; I don't vouch for the details.)

When no John appeared, a search party was organized. The neighborhood was scoured block by block.

Meanwhile, down at the shop, a farmer came in to pick up his machinery. "There's an old yeller cat out in the parking lot," he said. "Look like a good mouser. Mind if I take him home?"

It wasn't until Father came home to a frantic wife and children that he realized what had happened.

It was almost dark when they pulled up at the farmer's house.

But as soon as Mother let out with his name, they could see the ball of yellow bouncing toward them out of the barn an acre away.

Here was a cat who knew that he had missed his fried egg.

"They hear my voice," said Jesus, "and they follow me."

What he doesn't say is how much practice they have put into it, through years of worship, study, and service, trying to discern the pattern he set for them.

What he doesn't say is how long they have been listening, their feet ready to spring, their ears perked up, waiting, trusting, hoping, for his call.

250

Bibliographic Note

Those who are interested in reading further about the resurrection texts of the New Testament may benefit from the following books, which have been influential in my own interpretation. Except for a few fat commentaries, these are works that may be challenging but will not be inaccessible to non-specialists.

Those who are familiar with biblical scholarship will have already noticed my deep debt to my teacher Luke Johnson. His views are foundational for my own work, and are found conveniently in *The Writings of the New Testament*, rev. ed. (Minneapolis: Fortress Press, 1999).

On reading the Bible in community, see Sandra M. Schneiders, *The Revelatory Text: Interpreting the New Testament as Sacred Scripture* (San Francisco: HarperSanFrancisco, 1991), and Luke Timothy Johnson, *Scripture and Discernment: Decision Making in the Church* (Nashville: Abingdon Press, 1996). My own book, *No Deed Greater Than A Word: A New Approach To Biblical Preaching* (Lima, Ohio: CSS Publishing Company, 1998), deals with preaching as a kind of communal reading.

On Matthew, my favorite commentary is Daniel J. Harrington, *The Gospel of Matthew*, Sacra Pagina Series, v. 1 (Collegeville, Minnesota: Liturgical Press, 1991), which does a good job of explaining the Old Testament/Jewish undercurrents, while remaining pulpit-friendly. A comprehensive treatment of the Greek text is Dale C. Allison and W. D. Davies, *A Critical and Exegetical Commentary on the Gospel According to Saint Matthew*, International Critical Commentary, 3 vols. (Edinburgh: T & T Clark, 1997). A handy and practical guide to Matthew's thought is Mark Allan

Powell, *God with Us: A Pastoral Theology of Matthew's Gospel* (Minneapolis: Fortress Press, 1995).

On Mark, Joel Marcus has begun a commentary which when finished will be the thorough, high-quality scholarly reference that Mark has lacked for some time; the first installment is *Mark 1-8: A New Translation with Introduction and Commentary*, Anchor Bible (New York: Doubleday, 2000). Short but insightful is the old commentary by D. E. Nineham, *The Gospel of Mark*, Pelican Gospel Commentaries (Baltimore: Penguin Books, 1963); it's worth looking for a used copy of this prescient interpretation (I got mine for 65 cents!). My reading of Mark is influenced by Robert M. Fowler, *Let the Reader Understand: Reader-Response Criticism and the Gospel of Mark* (Minneapolis: Fortress Press, 1991), and Donald H. Juel, *A Master of Surprise: Mark Interpreted* (Minneapolis: Fortress Press, 1994).

On Luke-Acts, my pick for both volumes is definitely Johnson, whose work forms the basis of my own (Luke Timothy Johnson, *The Gospel of Luke*, Sacra Pagina Series [Collegeville, Minnesota: The Liturgical Press, 1991], and *The Acts of the Apostles*, Sacra Pagina Series [Collegeville, Minnesota: The Liturgical Press, 1992]). Excellent for preachers is Fred B. Craddock, *Luke*, Interpretation (Louisville: John Knox Press, 1990). For broad and deep coverage, especially of the Gospel, see Joseph A. Fitzmyer, *The Gospel According to Luke*, Anchor Bible, 2 vols. (Garden City: Doubleday & Co., Inc., 1981-1985), and *The Acts of the Apostles: A New Translation with Introduction and Commentary*, Anchor Bible (New York: Doubleday, 1998). For depth on the Greek text of Acts, see C. K. Barrett, *A Critical and Exegetical Commentary on the Acts of the Apostles*, International Critical Commentary, 2 vols. (Edinburgh: T&T Clark, 1994-98).

On John, I am especially indebted to the fine commentary by Gail R. O'Day, in *The New Interpreter's Bible*, vol. 9 (Nashville: Abingdon Press, 1995), 491-865; no preacher should be without this volume. For depth of coverage, nothing beats Raymond E. Brown, *The Gospel According to John*, Anchor Bible, 2 vols. (Garden City: Doubleday & Co., Inc., 1966-1970). A helpful guide is

Sandra M. Schneiders, *Written That You May Believe: Encountering Jesus in the Fourth Gospel* (New York: Crossroad, 1999).

On Paul in general, I owe much to the work of Abraham Malherbe; see his *Paul and the Thessalonians: The Philosophic Tradition of Pastoral Care* (Philadelphia: Fortress Press, 1987). My favorite of many good guides to Romans is again Luke Timothy Johnson, *Reading Romans: A Literary and Theological Commentary* (New York: Crossroad, 1997). On 1 Corinthians, a good commentary geared to the preacher is Richard B. Hays, *First Corinthians*, Interpretation: A Commentary for Teaching and Preaching (Louisville: Westminster John Knox, 1997).